PHYLLIS COATES
Not Just Lois Lane

By Bill Cassara

PHYLLIS COATES – NOT JUST LOIS LANE
By Bill Cassara
Copyright © 2024 Bill Cassara
All Rights Reserved. No part of this book may be used, transmitted, stored, distributed, or reproduced in any manner whatsoever without the writer's written permission, except very short excerpts for reviews. The scanning, uploading, and distribution of this book via the Internet or by any other means without the publisher's/author's express permission is illegal and punishable by law.

Published in the USA by:
BearManor Media
1317 Edgewater Dr #110
Orlando, FL 32804
www.bearmanormedia.com

Perfect ISBN 979-8-88771-544-5
Case ISBN 979-8-88771-545-2
BearManor Media, Orlando, Florida
Printed in the United States of America
Book design by Robbie Adkins, www.adkinsconsult.com
Back Cover Image: *Leo Gorcey carrying young Phyllis Coates in a scene*

"Who knew we would still be discussing Superman 50 years later?"

– Phyllis Coates (2000)

Table of Contents

Acknowledgements vii

Foreword   By Tyler St. Mark. x

Prologue   Setting the Stage .xiii

Introduction   Boyhood Memories of Superman xvi

Chapter One   A Fresh Flower Rises 1

Chapter Two   Gypsie Ann Stell 7
Parents/High School/Moving West/Ken Murray/
Earl Carroll's Vanities/USO/Nuremberg/*Girl Crazy*

Chapter Three   Richard Bare Enters Phyllis' Life 23
Marriage to Director Bare/Harpo
Meets Phyllis/Starlet to
Odessa/Photographer's Model/*Joe McDoakes Comedies*/
Divorce/New Marriage/Birth of Daughter-Christopher
Ann Nelms/Early Television/*Blues Busters*

Chapter Four   Superman. 47
George Reeves/*Superman and the Mole Men*/
Adventures of Superman

Chapter Five   Life Gets in the Way 60
Westerns/Marriage Trouble/*The Lone Ranger*/*Jungle Drums of Africa*/*Myrt and Marge*/*Perils of the Jungle*/
Gunfighters of the Northwest/*Leave it to Beaver*/
Lassie/Marriage to Norman Tokar

Chapter Six   Panther Girl of the Kongo. 78
Son David Tokar Born/*I Was a Teenage Frankenstein*/
Marriage Trouble/Stage Work/George Reeves Dies

Chapter Seven   A Doctor's Wife 98
Marriage to Dr. Press/Birth of daughter Laura/Move
to Big Sur/*Never Too Late*/Bart Williams/Divorce

Chapter Eight	Meeting Phyllis Coates .... 109 Sons of the Desert/Clint Eastwood/David Tokar/ Conventions/*Kiss Shot*/KGO Radio/*Love Letters*	
Photo Gallery	 130	
Chapter Nine	A Return to Lois Lane .... 152 Plays Mom in *Lois and Clark*/ Superman Festival in Metropolis/Edgar Kennedy Celebration in Monterey/Raymond Daum	
Chapter Ten	Move to Sonoma .... 162 *Hollywoodland*/David Tokar Dies/New York City Collectors Show	
Chapter Eleven	Cinecon Interview w/ Phyllis and Dick Bare 169 Screening of *So You Want to be Pretty*/*So You Want to Wear the Pants*/Testimonial Dinner	
Chapter Twelve	The Final Curtain.................. 179 Moving to the Motion Picture Home/Death/Epilogue	
Chapter Thirteen	What People Say About Phyllis Coates.. 182 Author's Top Ten Phyllis Film/TV Roles	
Chapter Fourteen	Film, Television, and Theater Credits.... 198 Phyllis Coates in Documentaries	
Chapter Fifteen	Bibliography....................... 244 Books/Magazines and Newspaper Credits	
Appendix	Letter to Author from Bart Williams ... 248	
Index	 250	
About the Author	 256	

Acknowledgements

Robbie Adkins, Dave Allard, Anthony Balducci, Nancy Bainter, Lloyd Beardsley, Kimm Benton, David Bressler, Rosylynn Carter, Tori Chesebrough-Buckles, Douglas Cassara, Zoe Christopher, Gary Cohen, Bruce Dettman, John DiCarlo, Bill Dillane, Diana Dohnert, Andy Edmonds, Brad Farrel, Bevis Faversham, The late John Field, Ronald J. Fields, Richard Finegan, Superman expert-Chuck Harter, Gary Hascall, Rick Greene, Gary Grossman, Colin Hilton, Becky Kane, Glenn and Mark Kennedy, Leonard Maltin, Jim Maley, Kerry Manderbach, Ted Meece, Jim Neibaur, Ben Ohmart, Laura P. Olson, Marcia Opal, Kit Parker, David B. Pearson, Anthony Petkovich, Jack Roth, Steve Rydzewski, Randy Sadewater, Bob Satterfield, Randy Skretvedt, Paul G. Smart, Tyler St. Mark, Stan Taffel, Steve Thomson, Irene Valesquez, Jeff Vilencia, Stone Wallace, Tom Weaver, Jeffrey Weissman, the late Bart Williams, Nan Zane, Bob and Duon Zeroun.

I also owe a debt of gratitude to the Margaret Herrick Library and to Ben Ohmart who as publisher for BearManor Media, always gives me "the green light." Special thanks go to Nancy Bainter my friend of over forty-five years, who took an interest in my projects. A hearty thanks to the two Superman Facebook pages: "The Adventures of Superman Starring George Reeves," and "George Reeves as Superman." And a sincere thank you to all who unselfishly participated in the "What Do You Think About Phyllis Coates" section of this book.

A special thank you goes to Tyler St. Mark who wrote the foreword for this book. He is an author, an actor and was a close friend of Phyllis Coates. He was always there for encouragement to see this project through. Thank you to Marcia Opal, the official photographer for Sons' events for many years. She shared some terrific photos of Phyllis Coates while at the Edgar Kennedy Celebration in 1997 and at the 2010 Sons of the Desert convention in Sacramento. Thanks also to Mark Petkovich, a writer who interviewed Phyllis at her home in 2009. Phyllis loaned him her baby pictures, and Mark shared them for this publication.

This book is dedicated to my wife, and muse,
Michelle Benton Cassara

Foreword

When my good friend and theatre colleague, Phyllis Coates, passed away on October 12, 2023, I cannot say I was surprised or too profoundly distraught. "Gypsie" as she was known to her intimates, had been in steady decline both physically and mentally for nearly a decade.

Those of us privileged to have her regard and confidence through these last and difficult years worried not just about her personal welfare but whether her unique legacy would endure beyond her lifetime and be celebrated in the years to come.

We need not have worried; Bill Cassara's book is a formidable and worthy tribute to Gypsie's artistic legacy as well as offering keen insights into what made her the extraordinary and eccentric artist she was, so I will not risk "gilding the lily" here.

Instead, I will simply reflect upon a fact rarely touched upon or much celebrated by her many fans and admirers; Phyllis Coates was one of the finest stage actresses of her generation, period.

I can say this as someone in the industry who met and studied some of the greatest thespians of the 20th century; the likes of John Gielgud, Ralph Richardson, Michael Redgrave, Alec Guinness, Judith Anderson, Edith Evans, and even the actor's actor, Laurence Olivier.

In my opinion, scene for scene, line for line, Phyllis could hold her own with any of these greats and it is tragic, I think, that due perhaps to her iconic role as the first Lois Lane on TV, those opportunities to fully demonstrate her acting chops on the professional stage were too few and far between.

One evening when she was still the charming, gracious, and able-minded lady that I had come to know and adore since our first encounter, we found ourselves alone discussing the Theater and I casually mentioned having briefly attended the Royal Academy in London. Phyllis abruptly burst out in William Shakespeare's famous "2-2-Two" (Act 2/Scene 2/Two Lovers), or Garden Scene from "Romeo & Juliet."

Suddenly, my venerable and aging friend became that innocent Capulet maiden who is passionate and headstrong. Phyllis suddenly was the young and idealistic girl-child and, taking her cue, I fell equally into the naive and impetuous boy-man of the Montague household who sets his stars and, most fatefully, his life upon her.

Gypsie and I sat together savoring the poetic lines we were both far too old now to perform with any credibility and, for a brief and shining moment, this remarkable lady personified Juliet and I was very much her Romeo, while her modest living room was transformed into Capulet's Garden and the cluttered dining table became an ivy-covered balcony!

In that magic twinkling, Phyllis was utterly flawless in her performance and every inch the impeccable and commanding thespian I knew she was; the actress who brought to every role she ever performed in film and on television, a particularly rare quality of artistry that always lifted her characters above and beyond the call of artistic duty. Phyllis consistently elevated her work to another level altogether, along with those fortunate actors who were so privileged to perform with her.

When we had finished our spontaneous rendition of that definitive garden scene, we sat quietly at the table reflecting on all the parts and projects that might have occurred had we been in the right place at the right time with the right people or had other prospects not more easily prevailed. Our mutually wicked sense of humor disguised any hint of sorrow or regret we might have felt for what was lost.

Regardless, there was a special "connect" between us two "reckless teenagers" for a while after that but, eventually, I moved far away from the city and dear Gypsie found others better suited to become her sturdy bridge over troubled waters.

Of course, I planned habitually over the years to stop in to visit her if I was ever back in town but, as they say, life is what happens while you're making plans.

I am sorry but not so regretful that we gradually lost touch after dear Phyllis was admitted to the Motion Picture Home. Our phone chats became fewer and more detached over the months then years and it became progressively more futile to contact her as her personality and memories drifted further and further away until she was no longer allowed to answer her phone.

I'm grateful now that my memories of Phyllis Coates are as she was that night in Capulet's Garden; fair Juliet to my Romeo, the moon full and shining on her young and passionate face, her eyes ageless and sparkling with loving innocence and deep romantic yearning; for an instant and a moment, we were those star-crossed lovers.

"Sleep dwell upon thine eyes, peace in thy breast. Would I were sleep and peace so sweet to rest."

– Tyler St. Mark

Prologue

PHYLLIS COATES' BIRTH NAME was Gypsie Ann Stell, she was born in 1927. There are other notable people born that same year: Edie Adams/Harry Belafonte/Rosalyn Carter/Peter Falk/Dickie Jones/Harvey Korman/Janet Leigh/Gina Lollobrigida/Roger Moore/Patty Page/Barbara Payton/Sidney Poitier/Neil Simon/ Vin Scully/George C. Scott/Carl 'Alfalfa' Switzer, and Andy Williams. It was a good group of talent especially considering almost three million babies were born in America that year. What were the chances of little Gypsie becoming a cultural icon later in life? The numbers are so statistically infinitesimal that it renders the question moot, especially taking into consideration what her family situation was at birth. It was a hard road ahead.

In preparation for this book, I tried to view every Phyllis Coates' film, TV appearance, and readings to have a better sense of the person and career of this gifted and talented actress. Public documents and archival newspaper accounts were imparative to help tell the story. Those resources mentioned were simply not available in the year 2006 when this project was first discussed as a possibility. Phyllis, too, was a bit reluctant to dive headlong into her past, mostly because she did not remember everything she did or experienced. There were no scrapbooks or photos to pour over to inspire her memory. Most of the photographs contained in this book are professional ones I obtained over the years, including a rare original artist's contract for Phyllis' services from 1953. I am thankful to Marcia Opal who took pictures of Phyllis during the Edgar Kennedy Celebration in Monterey in 1997 and the Sons of the Desert Convention in Sacramento in 2010. They help to tell the story.

An important note regarding Phyllis' television and film listings; I have diligently tried to corroborate all the listed credits on the Internet Movie Database (IMDb). It has a deserved reputation for unreliable information put forth by well-meaning fans. For instance, there is an IMDb listing of an "Ann Stell" for an early local TV program in 1946 called, *Faraway Hill*. Ann Stell is the name the nuns used to call Phyllis when she was in the convent, so it seemed entirely possible she was using this name in the early days of TV. Since there are no film, photographs, newspaper listings to confirm details of this program, I cannot put it into her television credits. During this period of Phyllis' life, she used the name Gypsie, so it is doubtful the "Ann Stell" in *Faraway Hill* is the same person. In addition, Phyllis was in Europe from June 1946 to Christmas day. The *Faraway Hill* program by Dupont was a soap opera on early television, shot between October 2nd and

December 2, 1946. The broadcasts were live, so it is impossible for Phyllis to be the same Ann Stell as the actress in the credits.

For clarification, Phyllis' first-born daughter was named Christopher, sometimes spelled as Christop, and her nickname was "Crinker." When she grew up, she changed her name to Zoe Christopher. References to her in this book pertains to the time intervals to which she is referenced.

Introduction

I was a child of the 1950s when our new Admiral TV was delivered to our home in San Jose. To my parents this new contraption was "radio with pictures." To me and my siblings, it was a life-line of entertainment that captured our imagination.

The Saturday morning and afternoon programs were filled with westerns, cartoons and comedies. Monday nights featured *Adventures of Superman*. The lead-in was a visual and audible extravaganza of close-ups of a gun firing, a powerful locomotive and men in their fedoras looking up and pointing. The spirited theme music of an orchestra highlighted by a harp, bass-drum and narration gave way to Superman in flight. This culminated in capturing the fantasy of flying. We could *hear* the sound of the wind whistling as he pierced the sky.

Every kid in the neighborhood knew the opening lines to the show. We had a new idol, George "Superman" Reeves, he of the kind face and heroic deeds. Here was a trusted adult that we could all count on. We even saw him in commercials eating cereal in the mornings and winking at us. We were in on the classified information that included Superman's secret identity of Clark Kent. Apparently, the adults couldn't catch on to that *fact* if and when they did watch the program.

What allowed Superman to fly? We were too young to comprehend his other worldly beginnings of powers and abilities far beyond those of mortal men. Superman wore tights and a magnificent red cape that helped guide him into the night to save people and to prevent disasters. The bright red "S" on his chest announced who he was to all evildoers. Bullets bounced off it.

Kids emulated their hero by wearing a tucked-in towel down the back of a T-shirt. Superman seemed to need a running start or a launch. Mine was the front porch of our house. We quickly learned the laws of gravity while we crashed to the ground. Somewhere Isaac Newton must have been chuckling.

Then there was that day in 1959 that my father informed me that the actor who played "Superman" died. "He jumped out the window and thought he could fly." I was horrified at the news and at my father's calloused announcement. My attention diverted to watching Walt Disney's *Zorro* as my new hero.

While *Adventures of Superman* disappeared from prime-time, episodes showed up in repeats on Saturday afternoon. This time, I was a little more aware and appreciative of the actors in the program. There was "The Chief," who yelled out the assignments on behalf of a great metropolitan newspaper. Jimmy Olsen was the "cub" reporter, who irritated the Chief by his mere presence. It was comical interaction. Reporter Clark Kent, the unassuming member of this press pool, was described as "mild mannered;" he was anything but. Harry Langdon was mild mannered; Clark Kent was a diplomatic, forthcoming journalist. The cast included a dynamic female by the name of Lois Lane, a focused and specialized expert who very competitively tried to out-scoop her male peers.

With repeated watching, I was now able to read the credits identifying the actors. I was interested in who they were. The Chief was played by John Hamilton. Jimmy Olsen was performed by Jack Larson. We all knew that George Reeves played both Superman and Clark Kent, but there seemed to be two Lois Lanes. One was played by Noel Neill; the other was identified in bold lettering under George Reeves' title as Phyllis Coates.

The Phyllis Coates version of Lois Lane was feisty, aggressive and didn't let anyone stand in her way. She was the consummate professional who had everyone's respect. She was not averse to socking her way out of danger. Noel Neill's portrayal of Lois Lane was toned down somewhat and became more of a "damsel in distress" to be rescued by Superman as needed. Both actresses playing Lois were attractive and successful in their own way. It seemed that they, with the help of Superman, solved all the crimes and dutifully dropped the culprits off for Inspector Henderson to book.

As a young boy I noticed that the actress who played Lois Lane during the first season had multiple roles in other performances on television. I could always identify her by her *voice,* a distinct low tone that resonated like a finely-tuned cello, with great vocal range reaching the highest octave with her legendary shrieks. Indeed, she became known as one of the best "Scream Queens" in the business.

I may not have noticed Phyllis Coates as a rancher in an episode of *The Lone Ranger*, but I sure recognized her voice in the episode: *The Woman in the White Mask.* The character had to resort to robbing stagecoaches to pay for her many family expenses. She needn't have bothered to disguise herself in a wig and white mask, because her voice gave her away.

Some actors need voice training to put their character over, whether it be a high or low pitch. Phyllis naturally spoke in the way she always had. Even during casual contacts with people, her voice could precede her presence. She was often recognized as "Lois Lane" by her vocal patterns even years later. She would have been great during the Golden Age of Radio, but she excelled visually even more so.

As the years went by, I became quite knowledgeable of the old Hollywood actors and delighted in the fact that I spotted Phyllis Coates sharing the television screen with: Herbert Anderson, Duncan Renaldo, Leo Carillo, Clayton Moore, John Hart, Buddy Ebsen, Jock Mahoney, Donald Woods, Jack Carson, Allen Jenkins, Leo G. Carroll, Jerry Mathers, David Janssen, James Arness, Raymond Burr, Jackie Cooper, Robert Stack, Patty Duke, Bert Lahr, Loni Anderson, Whoopi Goldberg, Imogene Coca, Jane Seymour, and Terri Hatcher just to name a few.

Life took me in different directions growing up and I took the path of law enforcement as a career. My beat took in the whole Monterey peninsula, including the coastal communities in the historic and beautiful area in central California, including parts of Carmel, Big Sur, Pebble Beach, and Carmel Valley. Along with Salinas, this was an area so revered by local author John Steinbeck that many of his most famous books had references to this famous spot in the world.

In 1987, I was introduced to Phyllis Coates by a mutual friend, Lois Laurel Hawes, who happened to be the daughter of Stan Laurel. Both of them were in the same Bliss-Hayden acting school in Hollywood 1947-1948 and kept in touch over the years. Phyllis was living in Carmel during this time and had previously been living in Big Sur with her husband and family. We became friends and I got to know the actress who made her film and TV characters come to life.

Phyllis Coates never became a huge movie star. It wasn't because she lacked talent, great looks, or charisma. It might be partially because the studio system of Hollywood's heydays was drawing to a close, there was no studio in the 50's and 60's to envelope her and shape a career. It was the birth of commercial television that

Phyllis became prominently known. She freelanced and became a working actor without any pretentious notions; she was admired for it in the industry.

Phyllis loved acting and performed in as many varied roles as she could find. She became famous because of her "Lois Lane" role, but that was a long time ago. She never got any residuals, so it was hard to wrap herself around a character that Noel Neill capably took care of. In her later years, she did start to embrace it, especially because of her fans. However, it was the juicy roles that she preferred best. Her daughter, Zoe Christopher, confirmed this. She said her mom really enjoyed being the "villainess" in performances. Some of them are discussed here. Directors certainly knew of her talents, I can imagine a call going out for her: "GET ME PHYLLIS COATES!"

– Bill Cassara 2024

Chapter One
A Fresh Flower Rises

PHYLLIS COATES IS MOSTLY known today for her epic role as "Lois Lane" during the first year of *Adventures of Superman* (1952-1953) on television, starring George Reeves. She has become an iconic symbol of the modern woman ever since. Phyllis was in some one hundred forty-five movie and television roles dating as far back as 1948. Even before Superman burst from our television screen, Phyllis was the leading lady for many westerns including some of the episodes of *The Cisco Kid*. The early color film enhanced her looks, but there were not many televisions that had color-receiving capabilities in the early years.

Phyllis was one of those Hollywood pretties that came to town at the age of sixteen and carved out a long career for herself. This Texas beauty was born Gypsie Ann Evarts Stell on January 15, 1927, in Wichita Falls, and her first name says something about her rather complex beginnings. Her life was not destined to be a storybook fairytale.

Her parents, Jackie and William Robert "Rush" Stell, knew that they would be on the go and would not have a steady home life for their child. The country was still in the throes of the Volstead Act that established the prohibition of alcohol. Phyllis' parents were notorious; she confided in me some of the details that she never would have shared before.

Gypsie was signed to a movie contract in 1948 for Warner Bros. Studios; it was here that they changed her name to Phyllis Coates. They also invented her background. They had to for her to have a chance at stardom.

"Bull Session Gets Texas Girl in Movies."[1] The story goes that young Phyllis came to Hollywood with the intention of enrolling at UCLA for a career in journalism. Another account had her finishing up her units at the Los Angeles City College. While a student there, she and her girlfriends participated in a "gab-fest" and decided that they were just as pretty and talented as other movie actresses. They all decided to "try out" and in the competition, Phyllis won. She was handed a seven-year contract and had a bright future in the business. It wasn't that simple, nor was it true.

As Gypsie Ann Stell, she was "discovered" by comic Ken Murray who spotted her in a local restaurant. She was only sixteen when this old vaudeville comedian offered her a job for his show in Hollywood. Gypsie performed as a chorus girl in the review and was even elevated to share quips with the cigar-chomping impresario.

---

1 *The Austin American* (Austin Texas) October 6, 1944)

Phyllis was paying her dues in show business taking advantage of her natural beauty. She was in various shows and even performed overseas. When she became a contract player for Warner Brothers, director Richard L. Bare found his next leading lady …and bride! Bare was climbing the ladder of success at Warners for his early short film comedy series called the *Behind the Eight Ball*, starring George O'Hanlon as Joe McDoakes. Phyllis co-starred as his wife in about half of them over the next seven years. Phyllis and Richard Bare had an amicable working relationship, but their marriage fell apart in less than one year's time.

Phyllis was married four different times and had three children from three different husbands. She had a full active life but had regrets over her family; she lost a son to drug addiction and one of her daughters was estranged to her. Though Phyllis was living in Carmel during the time I met her, she had just gone through a divorce and shared an apartment with two of her youngest off-spring.

Phyllis was fifty-nine years old then, but looked terrific. She had been out of the public eye for many years, but she resurfaced on "The Perfect 36," a local San Jose independent television station to introduce a special marathon, *Adventures of Superman*, over the Labor Day weekend. Phyllis was THE choice to host the series since she was available, and lived only seventy miles away from the station.

It was during the mid-80s when VCRs became a household item. And unless one was a film collector, taping them on the air was the only way anyone could see the 104 *Superman* episodes in a marathon program in chronological order. This was way before anyone had released the series on tape or DVD.

In 1986 Lois Laurel Hawes was in town with her husband as special guests for our banquet celebrating the second anniversary of our Laurel and Hardy appreciation society, better known as *The Sons of the Desert*. We were one of hundreds of chapters around the world and identified ourselves as "Tents." Our chapter was known as the *Midnight Patrol* named after a Laurel and Hardy comedy that portrayed their characters as bumbling cops. Three of our founding officers were sworn deputy sheriffs for Monterey County. I was hired by Sheriff Cook in 1981.

It was a proud moment to introduce our special guests at our banquets. I had the chance to pre-edit highlights on videotape of some of Phyllis' best *Superman* moments and showed them on the big screen. The crowd especially enjoyed her patented screams, and Phyllis got a kick out of the audience reactions. She had always been keen for participating in stage plays, specifically so she could see and hear the response.

Meanwhile, I was busy with my work and family. Besides all that, I shared company with Phyllis whenever I could, she was delightful. In the course of my deputy sheriff duties, I considered myself an ambassador for our department; it was inevitable that I would cross paths with many famous people in our corner of the world. Over the years I had professional dealings with Doris Day, Terry Melcher, and Joan Fontaine, we eventually became buddies. I even got married at Joan's house.

One thing I learned over the years is friendship is acquired, not obtained. Though I would have loved to have interviewed those ladies, I was not a journalist and I was cognizant of their privacy. We always stuck to conversations of mutual interests, otherwise, it might have infringed on our friendship. The same went for Phyllis--who *interviews* their friends? This is not to say that occasionally things would pop up as part of a discussion. Sometimes she answered questions in one-word responses. For example, after viewing Phyllis in the film *I Was a Teenage Frankenstein* I asked Phyllis, "What was [mad scientist] Whit Bissell really like?" She answered, "What you see is what you get." Another time Phyllis and I were watching an old *Death Valley Days* episode in which she played a saloon girl. Phyllis volunteered: "A whore with a heart? Those are the *best* kind of roles."

It is interesting to know that Phyllis was never interested in comic books growing up. For a time, she did follow the comic pages of the local newspapers of *Little Orphan Annie*, until she realized the character never grew up. Her role model in the movies was "Torchy Blane" the fictional female journalist, at times played by Glenda Farrell, Lola Lane, and Jane Wyman in the late 1930s. Not surprisingly, it was Glenda Farrell that impressed Phyllis most.

It has been said that the creators of the *Superman* comics, Joe Shuster and Jerry Siegel, were inspired by Farrell's interpretation of a female reporter to generate the character of "Lois Lane." There are parallels; for instance, Torchy Blane was in a competitive "man's world" fighting for news stories, often obtained in an unorthodox manner.

Over the years, Phyllis retained her legal name of Gypsie Ann Stell. Her family and close friends called her "Gypsie." For the sake of brevity and consistency for this book, she will be referred to as Phyllis Coates with a few exceptions.

It should also be mentioned that Phyllis was very hesitant to discuss the "George Reeves Case." His death was very personal to her, but it was very surprising how complete strangers would walk up to her and ask her *opinion* about his death. It was a great loss, and she said she had never "accepted it." It was a shock to everyone who knew George Reeves, but everyone is vulnerable under certain circumstances.

One of the reasons I did not initially want to write this book was because I knew a little too much about the case being a career law enforcement professional. I didn't want to be boxed in to prove or disprove the circumstances surrounding his demise. And besides, readers have a certain protectiveness about Reeves. He was a hero to many. I was reluctant to be the bearer of bad news, something I did not enjoy during my career.

The scope of this book is about Phyllis Coates, not George Reeves, though the two are intertwined forever in our consciousness. Despite encouragement from her confidant and friend, Bart Williams (*see letter to author in the Appendix*), Phyllis did not want to write a tell-all book. Quite honestly, her memories were supressed over the years. The project was put on hold indefinitely while I researched and wrote five other Hollywood biographies.

Phyllis was pretty much incapacitated since 2015 when she entered the Motion Picture and Television Home in Woodland Hills, California. She passed away quietly there on October 11, 2023. With Phyllis' passing, I sought to put together a tribute book with as much biographical details as I could accumulate to help celebrate her life. It is hoped that this book helps to spotlight her legacy and to entertain her legions of fans that she cared so much for.

Chapter Two
Gypsie Ann Stell

"Doesn't Gypsie Ann Stell sound like a striptease artist in Burlesque?"
– Phyllis to author

As WITH ANY biography of a book subject, the parents are imperative to the story; it all started there. Phyllis' mother and father were married at the Wichita County Courthouse, Texas, on March 21, 1926. Her dad, William Robert "Rush" Stell, hailed from Pecos, Texas, and was born there in 1906. He had four siblings. In the city directory of 1926, he and his bride were living under the roof of his father's place on 208 Bluff Street in Wichita Falls, so

With Ken Murray (1944).

named for a river and five-foot waterfall going through the city. It had a population of approximately 50,000 people nestled in the greater Wichita County, mostly known for cattle and oil wells. It is about eighteen miles from the Oklahoma state line. At one time this Northern Texas area was inhabited by nomadic Native American tribes, mostly the Kiowa and Comanche. In later years the railroad emanating from Ft. Worth and Denver extended to the town and became a rail center for the whole area.

Phyllis' mother was Jackie Lorraine [Luzzie] Teel, born in Oklahoma on May 30, 1910. It was said she was born in Indian country. In 1926, when the new couple was married, Jackie was only fifteen years old. Rush was twenty and was working as a laundry presser at the City Laundry in Wichita Falls.

Rush Stell was in trouble with the law long before he married. In 1925, he was arrested with two others for a series of armed robberies. The ringleader implicated Rush in a confession, but since a victim couldn't identify the co-conspirators, the district attorney dropped the charges.

When Rush married the former Jackie Teel, he must have thought he was turning over a new leaf in his life. Gypsie Ann Evarts Stell, was born on January 15, 1927. In later years, Phyllis explained her mother had seen the name on a *True Confession* magazine, a short story about a horse named Gypsie.[2] It may also have been true that "Gypsie" was an apt name for someone who would be moved all over Texas in her young life. It was a blessed event when the couple's young daughter was born.

Rush soon went back to what he knew best, making money the easy way. Just before November of 1927, he was promptly arrested in Knox County, Texas, on several charges of robbery, assault, and burglary after a spectacular raid. Several places were burglarized after a night watchman had been captured and tied to a wagon."[3] Rush was sentenced to Clemens State Prison Farm for a twenty-year sentence in the Gulf region of Texas. He received his mail keeping him informed on his new baby girl, and then he got "rabbit in his blood."

Phyllis was only eleven months old when her father escaped from the work farm along with eleven other prisoners. On November 6, 1928 a manhunt ensued and the local newspaper screamed:

---

2 *Phyllis Coates Reporting on a Career-Ladies of the Western.* Fitzgerald, Michael & Magers, Boys. McFarland & Co., Inc. Publishers Jefferson, North Carolina, and London 1999

3 *Bryan Daily Eagle* November 20, 1928

"Three Wichitans-Claude Reeves, Rush Stell and Willie Webb are Hunted."[4]

On November 17, 1928 Rush Stell was captured outside of Wichita Falls. He had travelled almost 375 miles and, according to the *Bryan Daily Eagle*, Rush "returned to see his wife and child where he spent several hours, then surrendered to authorities."[5] The story even made the *Associate Press* newsfeed. This time, Stell was removed to the infamous Huntsville state prison, a high security lock-up facility.

Jackie Stell had to survive as best she could with her newborn daughter. When one is desperate, one might do desperate things. In 1930 Jackie and her three-year-old daughter moved to Shawnee, Oklahoma. During the height of prohibition Phyllis' mom helped to move bootleg liquor. As far back as Phyllis could remember, she recalled the warning: "douse the lights, it's the law."[6]

In a latter-day interview, Phyllis recounted: "I came from a broken family and grew up in convents and Catholic schools all over the state; we were a very dysfunctional family." Phyllis and her mom moved to Pampa, Texas by 1934; it was some 200 miles away from Wichita Falls. She grew up into a very beautiful child with an infectious personality. It was decided that Phyllis might be suited for the stage. Her first known show business exposure was to impersonate child star Shirley Temple at the La Nora Theater in Pampa, Texas. Phyllis was only seven years old at the time and shared the evening's entertainment with a gaggle of youngsters also doing impersonations of Hollywood stars.[7] It so happened that a Shirley Temple film, *Little Miss Marker*, was on the bill that evening.

With the success of her stage appearance, Phyllis' mother enrolled her daughter as a child model and she was hired by Montgomery Ward Co.[8] Phyllis was being indoctrinated early as a photographer's model.

---

4 *Wichita Falls*, Texas Times November 6, 1928
5 *Bryan Daily Eagle November 29, 1928*
6 Bart Williams email to author 2006
7 *Pampa Daily News* Sept 9, 1934
8 *Pampa Daily News* Sept. 16, 1934

By 1935, Phyllis and her mother were listed as still residing in Wichita County, but by 1940, mother and daughter moved in with the grandmother, Anna Davis. They lived in Gaines, Texas, in the Malone Addition North Seminole near the New Mexico border. This was Comanche territory until 1875 when the U.S. Army campaigns took the land. Phyllis went to a Catholic school there for her education. At one time during those years, Phyllis told me that she wanted to be a nun.

Phyllis was twelve in 1939 and was enrolled in the St. Joseph Academy in Abilene, Texas. In later years she referred to this institution of higher learning as a "convent," in actuality, it was a Catholic school for girls. Phyllis said the nuns never called her "Gypsie," instead referring to her as "Ann Stell." Phyllis remembered, "I got into trouble in the convent for smoking dried bark off the trees."[9]

Mentioned in the Abilene newspaper as "Gypsy Ann Stell," Phyllis was a member of "The Merry Makers Club," a student organization of St. Joseph Academy. In the late fall of October, 1939, a little news article declared that there was to be a dance at Blue Room of the Hilton Hotel. It cited the students attending to include Phyllis.[10] Her duties extended to the end of the school year to include the graduation ceremonies for the seniors.

December 7, 1941 Attack on Pearl Harbor

As with every American on the above date, the attack and ultimate entry of the U.S. into the world war impacted everyone. Patriotism was at the highest point and now fourteen years old, Phyllis poured herself into school activities.

In 1941, Phyllis was enrolled into a public school in Pecos, Texas. She was one in four new members of the Pecos High School band who were outfitted with new uniforms.[11] Phyllis made the local paper again four months later when she was in the running for "The Sweetheart" of the band. She lost out as did twelve other

---

9 *The Californian* April 30, 1990
10 *Abilene Reporter News* October 29, 1939
11 *San Angelo Standard-Times* December 12, 1941

candidates; that must have been very disappointing to the fledging young ladies.

For whatever reason, possibly due to her mother's job or the war effort, Phyllis was moved again. This time she wound up in Odessa, Texas, enrolled at their high school. Unfortunately, because of the war, the school did not produce yearbooks for 1942 and 1943. They would have revealed what was going on in her life during those formative years.

On November 22, of 1942, Gypsie Ann Stell became a pledge, specifically a debutante. An article was written with heart about it by Marcy Townsley:

> One of the most outstanding social events of the season took place at the Country Club Friday night when the Sub Deb Sorority gave their presentation dance and introduced their pledges. More than 150 of the young set registered and the beautiful party went off like clockwork.
>
> Some of the beauties of the West Texas night were taken right into the club room with the sorority's colors of silver and blue being carried out in stars and a large half-moon, which was six feet in diameter and served as an entrance for the pledges as they were presented.
>
> At 10:30 o'clock Mr. Wesley May, high school band director, introduced the pledges who were Misses Pat Fisher, Dortha Polson, LaJuana Jones, Patty Smood, and Gypsie Ann Stell.[12]

By February 5th of the following year, plans were made for a dance to honor their new members of which Gypsie Stell was one.[13] Phyllis was maturing nicely and becoming quite a young lady. Phyllis made the news again two weeks later, this time the lead into the story was: **"Gypsie Stell Hostess to Sub Debs in Home of Aline Norcross"**

> The Odessa Sub-Deb Club held their weekly meeting Wednesday evening in the home of Aline Norcross. Gyp-

---

12 *The Odessa American* November 22, 1942
13 *The Odessa American* February 5, 1943

sie Stell was the hostess. A business meeting was held and plans were made for each girl to buy defense stamps at school each week."[14]

At the end of the school year in June of 1943, Phyllis would be a sophomore or junior if she were advancing in the normal progression of academics. Something happened over the summer that would alter the course of her life.

According to the late Bart Williams, she along with her mother and grandmother decided to leave all behind and relocate to California. Bart explained in an email: "Phyllis slugged a nun in the chops for saying 'she would never amount to anything,' and that was her exit from high school."[15]

Looking at the dates, Phyllis was enrolled in a Catholic school (1939-1940). It appears that Bart was inaccurate in the timeline as it is clear that she continued her public-school education in Odessa, Texas until the end of the school year of 1943.

Phyllis did tell later day interviewers that she had intentions to continue her education at Los Angeles City College. In other articles it was always mentioned that Phyllis planned to go to UCLA to study journalism; the truth is something less than that.

The reality was that Phyllis needed a job and things in Texas didn't seem promising.

> *I grew up in convents and Catholic schools all over the state. We were a very dysfunctional family, and Texas with all its oil fields and honkytonks was very depressing. Texas is a good place to be from, I couldn't wait to get out of there.*
> – Phyllis Coates to author

Apparently, Phyllis along with her mom and grandmother took the bus to California and wound up in Los Angeles. In Bart Williams' email, he described the mother as "crazy," and the grand-

---

14 *The Odessa American* February 19, 1943
15 Email from Bart Williams to author June 13, 2006

mother as an alcoholic.[16] Even Phyllis described her mother as "Crazy as a loon."[17] All three of them made the long trip to California, if for nothing else, to see its beauty. The journey was 1,254 miles, and they took minimal material goods. It was a fresh start for all.

The fractured family settled in Los Angeles where there were jobs, and Phyllis could allegedly continue her education. Except she didn't. It was now the summer of 1943, and with the war going on, there was a need for females to roll up their sleeves and contribute to the war effort. It was the age of "Rosie the Riveter," and there were plenty of employment opportunities in Los Angeles with the men off to fight the war.

Jackie immediately got a job as a waitress at the Melody Lane Restaurant in Hollywood at the hot spot corner of Hollywood and Vine. The place oozed with foot traffic, hopefuls and celebrities. One story is that Phyllis was at the restaurant visiting her mom and having lunch when big star, Ken Murray, came in and was taken with Phyllis' beauty. He said to her, "Hey, if you ever need a job come on up and see me." He left his card and Phyllis' imagination wandered. Jackie certainly encouraged her daughter to follow up; Ken Murray was a household name in those days thanks to his vaudeville and radio successes. He was headlining a show down the street at the El Capitan Theater called *Ken Murray's Blackouts*. It was a revival of the old vaudeville shows that were so popular before "talking pictures" took the country by storm.

Ken Murray (1903-1988)

This old-time vaudevillian was still a headliner name when Phyllis met him. She claimed she never heard of him, but the rest of America enjoyed his "Ken Murray Radio Shows" throughout the 1930s for NBC and CBS. The cigar-chomping comedian built a whole show with a variety/vaudevillian theme and spiced it up for the modern crowd.

---

16 *Ibid*
17 Fitzgerald, Michael, & Magers, Boyd. Ladies of the Western. McFarland & Co. Inc. Publisher's, Jefferson, North Carolina, and London

Phyllis' mom escorted her to Murray's office on her next day off. Jackie told her, "Make sure you introduce me as your sister." Once at his studio overlooking the theater, Murray immediately beckoned Phyllis to lift up her skirt to see her legs. That never happened to her before, but before she could recover, he squeezed her breasts. Murray asked, "Are these real?" Apparently, some new prospects came to him with tissue-laden *upholstery* and the boss didn't want to be fooled. Such was Hollywood in the "golden age."

Once the five-foot-four-inch young Phyllis was signed and broken-in on the show, her home town newspaper trumpeted the news:

> **Gypsie Ann Stell Stars**
> Former Odessa High school student, Gypsy Ann Stell, is appearing in Ken Murray's "Blackouts of 1943," now showing at the El Capitan Theater of Hollywood, Calif. The *American* was notified today. Miss Stell attended the Odessa, Pecos, Seminole and Abilene schools while living in West Texas.[18]

Sixteen-year-old Phyllis got the job as a chorus girl and they outfitted her with a skimpy chorus girl costume. She made her debut dancing in sync with the other scantily-clad girls as they bounced around to introduce the star to the audience.

Phyllis said that the place was packed with service men on leave. They hooted and yelled when Ken Murray would banter with his star performer, Marie Wilson. There were "boob" jokes galore.

Also on the bill was an old-time vaudeville musical artist by the name of Fred Sanborn. He was famous for his eccentric xylophone playing and his mute character. He had originally been one of Ted Healy's Stooges on Broadway along with Larry Fine, Shemp and Moe Howard in the film, *Soup to Nuts*. "Daisy the Wonder Dog, was also on Ken Murray's bill with nine others to include "The Glamour Lovelies." Gypsie Ann Stell was included in the program and was promoted to receive lines from her boss that generated comebacks designed to "humiliate" Ken Murray. The laugh-starved military men howled at the interactions. As Phyllis got

---

18 *The Odessa American* December 20, 1943

more comfortable with her role in the spectacle, she got to do more singing, dancing and tradeoffs with the star.

It is with complete conjecture that Phyllis had many proposals of marriage during her almost year with the show. As it was, Phyllis had been dating a young local by the name of Jerry Warren. He had an interest in producing movies in the future. He and Phyllis never lost touch and the young couple met again in 1959 (*See Chapter Six*).

> *"Ken Murray's Show changed my Life, I wanted to go into comedy"* – Phyllis to author

20th Century-Fox

Only seventeen years old, Phyllis was signed by a major studio, 20th Century-Fox. There was no press release but her hometown newspaper announced it to their readers:

> **Odessa Girl Wins a Movie Contract**
> Gypsie Ann Stell, former student of Odessa High school, began her work with Twentieth Century-Fox Thursday July 13th serving a seven-year contract with an option. Miss Stell was also a prominent member of the high school band and the Sub-Deb sorority. In June of 1943, Miss Stell moved with her mother, Mrs. Jack Stell. Where she was employed as a dancer for ten and one-half months.[19]

Being hired by 20th Century-Fox meant Phyllis was part of the studio system. That meant days of being taught the finer points of acting, speaking and poise. Phyllis also added the all-needed physical beauty, or as some may call it: "window dressing" to movies being produced.

Phyllis' first film (though uncredited) was released in May 1945, *Where Do We Go from Here?* It starred Fred MacMurray as an all-American boy who wanted to enlist in the army, but was instead labeled 4-F. According to the newspaper back home, Phyllis was "signed up for secondary leads with June Haver and other top

---

19 *The Odessa American* July 13, 1944

stars."[20] Not much happened for Phyllis after the film was released in 1945; it is likely that the studio dropped her option. That opened the door for Phyllis to pursue other avenues for her career.

In February of the same year, Phyllis was photographed in a group for a little news item. The world war was still firing on all cylinders and the neon lights of Hollywood dimmed at night. Phyllis (identified as dancer Gypsie Stell) was shown ringing in a ceremonial bell in a caption that read: "**Midnight Closing-Shown abiding by curfew regulations**."[21] There were five others identified at the table, but the most important was club owner Frank Bruni.

Frank Bruni was the entrepreneur of the Florentine Gardens on Hollywood Blvd. Built in 1938, it served as a nightclub and is still in use. There was a new review announced in the papers on May 2, 1945:

> **Swinging in Victory** is the title chosen by Producer Frank R. Bruni for his new review. Bruni is rounding up some of the top names in the show world for the new review, and Dave Gould is rehearsing lavish production numbers which he will stage with the Florentine glamor girls. Gypsie Ann Stell personifies glamor as one of the showgirls.

There was a quarter-page close-up of Phyllis' face adorning page twenty-six. It was also announced that the Mills Brothers would grace the stage along with a requisite comedian/emcee, Herman Hyde (the trick musician). There was also a dog named "Dimples" and, of course, swing music.

This time, Phyllis wasn't just a chorus girl; she performed in a featured spot. She was certainly being seen by the patrons around town; her picture was also presented in the pages of the *Los Angeles Daily News*[22] and the *Los Angeles Times*.[23]

---

20 *Wichita Falls Times* April 22, 1948
21 *Los Angeles Evening* News May 2, 1945
22 *Los Angeles Daily News* July 16, 1945
23 *Los Angeles Times* August 19, 1945

Earl Carroll's Vanities

This showman/producer established himself on Broadway as far back as 1923. Carroll would get the biggest stage stars with the most talent, and showcase them in a musical review. Busby Berkeley, the genius choreographer, was associated with Earl Carroll until the movies called him during the early talking days.

Earl Carroll's Vanities enjoyed new shows for every theatrical season. With the war's end in 1945, the man decided to put together a new cast and take them across America to entertain the troops. It was now September 30, 1945, and Gypsie Stell recently appeared in *Earl Carroll's Vanities* at the Midland Army Air Base.[24] It was a military airfield located outside of Midland, Texas. Phyllis had the opportunity to be a pretty "straight-woman" to the stand-up comedian whose name has been lost to time.

The Odessa paper picked up on the tour and clarified that "Miss Stell is on a nine-month tour which will cover the major portion of most of the United States and will continue the tour in Europe in May."[25] The paper also pointed out, "Gypsie Stell appeared in several motion pictures, one of which was *Men in Her Diary* starring Jon Hall."[26] The film was released earlier in the month and Phyllis/Gypsy was uncredited again. Apparently, she was on loan to Universal Studios for that one.

United Service Organization [USO]

It was also in 1945 that Phyllis signed up as a photographer's model in Chicago with the Al Seamon Agency.[27] The *Los Angeles Daily Times* reported in April 13, 1946 with a photograph lead-in: **"Flying Mule On Way to Greece."**

> Arriving from Detroit on American Airlines plane, 'Joe' the mule finds reception committee waiting. Happily greeting him are Greek war relief officials and Sherman Hotel models Candy Toxton and Gypsie Stell. The mule

---

24 *The Odessa American* September 30, 1945.
25 *Ibid*
26 *Ibid*
27 *Wichita Falls Times* April 22, 1948

will be shipped to Greece, to help relieve transportation shortages."[28]

It is seriously doubtful that "Joe the Mule" was shipped to Greece at all. It looks like it was simply an opportunity to publicize the Sherman Hotel of Chicago along with the two models sitting on Joe's back.

There were updates on Phyllis provided by her hometown newspaper, and what updates they were. It reported that Gypsy Ann Stell was rehearsing in New York for the USO production of *Anything Goes*[29] and was scheduled to go to Europe to entertain the occupation troops. A follow-up to the story let the readers know that the stage spectacle was in progress and touring the European Theater under the auspices of Theater Special Services.

Phyllis arrived June 22, 1946 and was cast as a dancer. The paper also proudly reported, "Gypsie had also modelled for well-known commercial photographers."[30]

Those lonely, love-starved, homesick boys in service must have cheered wildly to be entertained with good old American songs. *Anything Goes* was a famous Broadway play of the mid-1930s in two acts. The musical/comedy featured a romance on an ocean liner, but the real stars were the songs of Cole Porter. The stage play brought those familiar numbers to the front. The songs:

I Get a Kick out of You
Let's Misbehave
You're the Top
Anything Goes
Friendship

The *Odessa American* newspaper reported that Gypsie Stell was commended along with other USO artists by Major General A.R. Bolling, Chief of Special Services for the European Theater. It was also announced that, "USO Camp Shows will continue to play for veterans hospitalized in the States and to entertain the troops in the Pacific Theater."[31]

---

28 *Los Angeles Daily News* April 3, 1946
29 *The Odessa American* May 23, 1946
30 *The Odessa American* September 15, 1946
31 *The Odessa American* February 2, 1947

Nuremberg Trials

The Nuremberg hearings were world news as it was happening and history in the making. The gut-wrenching trials were to hold to answer the German leadership of the Nazi dictatorship during the reign of Adolph Hitler. Of the 177 defendants, 24 were sentenced to death.[32]

Many years later, Phyllis confided in me a story she had experienced during those days in Europe. The Nuremberg trials were in progress in Germany and her troupe was stationed nearby. She already had a USO uniform at her disposal, and cut through a considerable amount of red tape to attend some of the court proceedings. She said those trials and seeing war-torn Europe "Impacted me the rest of my life."

Marriage and Annulment

Another life-turning event occurred when Phyllis was in Spain during her USO tour; she fell madly in love with a Spanish bullfighter. She was young and beautiful and he was oh so dashing and daring. According to family lore, they married immediately. However, they annulled the marriage within two weeks, courtesy of the Catholic Church. After all, there was a boat to catch to come back home. Much later in life, Phyllis confirmed this fact to her youngest daughter, Laura. She chuckled about it when recounting it to me.

Phyllis was in Europe from June 1, 1946 to Christmas Day. They were scheduled for departure at Bremerhaven, Germany December 26th and to arrive in New York in January of the new year.

Bremerhaven is a seaport in Northwest Germany at the mouth of the Weser River. It was heavily bombed during the war. The troupe was transferred by the USS Henry Gibbins that was used during the conflict. It was no Queen Mary, but for this occasion, the vessel was refitted as a "war brides ship" with three decks of cabins, lounges, two formal staircases, and a formal dining room.

The experience of performing before thousands within the backdrop of world events might have left Phyllis sadder, wiser and dizzier, but probably the opposite was true. She was the epitome

---

32 The National WWII Museum

of youthful vigor, optimism, and boundless energy. Upon arrival stateside, she posed for a picture wearing her chorus girl gown for a Pennsylvania newspaper. The caption read:

> A little ahead of time, but still welcome is attractive Gypsy [sic] Ann Stell who asks you to be her valentine. Gypsy [sic] just got back from a USO camp show tour, and posed in the fetching costume as she reached New York.[33]

When the above article was published, Phyllis was just days away from her 20th birthday. At this point in her life, she would have no idea what was in store for her. The expression "the world was her oyster and she was the pearl" seems very apt here.

Girl Crazy

It was now well into 1947, and Phyllis continued with her USO commitments entertaining now in military hospitals and camp shows. There was a series of photos for the *Daily Item* of Phyllis for *Girl Crazy* at the Naval Hospital at Millington, Tennessee.[34] The pictures showed the pretty girls dancing up a storm, not on stages, but inside the hospital dorms themselves. Patients in wheelchairs and beds celebrated their efforts wildly. Some in pajamas and robes jumped to their feet in dance, and broke their collective *mental* crutches in half. The performances continued in the days following at the Kennedy Veterans hospital in Memphis and the Veterans Hospital in Lamar, Tennessee.

The hometown newspaper updated their readers:

> **Odessa Dancer, Gypsie Stell, plays in USO Show-**The cast of George Gershwin's show, *Girl Crazy* now playing as a USO camp show in Texas includes an Odessa singer and dancer, Gypsie Ann Stell, who has been on the stage and in films since her graduation from Odessa High School three years ago. [sic] Miss Stell takes over the role

---

33 *The Daily Item* January 22, 1947 *Sunbury*, Pennsylvania
34 *The Commercial Appeal* August 1, 1947

of Bessie in the four scene, one act comedy about adventures at a dude ranch.[35]

Vets at Papago to See Musical
Patients at the Papago Park Veterans Administration hospital will see *Girl Crazy*, the 90-minute George Gershwin production, Thursday, September 25. The show was produced especially for the United Service Organization Camp Shows for hospital circuits and includes a cast of twenty-one.

A double-feature program is planned. During the afternoon, two groups will tour the wards and present a series of vaudeville acts to bedfast patients, after dinner the entire troupe will present the show. Songs by Gershwin, dancing and comedy will feature the show. The comedy will be presented by Arthur and Morton Havel and specialty dancing will be by girls in the cast.

Besides the Havel's, the cast includes Dan Harden, Buddy Boylan, Lew Eckels, Muriel King, Jean Sheri, Martha Drew, Flo Baron and Gypsie Ann Stell.[36]

At the end of 1947 and free from her USO commitments, Phyllis enrolled into the Bliss-Hayden School of Acting. Harry Hayden and Lela Bliss both had film and stage credits to their name and pulled their resources together. In addition to their school, they also built the Bliss-Hayden Theater at 244 S. Robertson, Beverly Hills. One of Phyllis' classmates was Lois Laurel, Stan Laurel's daughter.

Lois had been married to Don Falconer in Santa Cruz in northern California, but separated from him on September 1, 1947. She moved to Southern California for a fresh start and possible career. Her divorce came through the next year.

---

35 *The Odessa American* September 14, 1947
36 Arizona Republic September 16, 1947

Marilyn Monroe

Another classmate of Phyllis' was a young Marilyn Monroe! Part of the acting class included the students to perform on the theatrical stage in Beverly Hills. Marilyn was a standout in a part in the play *Glamour Preferred*; it ran three weeks October 12, to November 2, 1947.

The only thing Phyllis remembered from this production was, "Marilyn *knew* what she was doing."[37] Once Marilyn got famous, she and Phyllis lost touch. However, Lois Laurel and Phyllis remained friends through their lives. During the 1950's Lois was married to cowboy actor Rand Brooks. He and Phyllis appeared in two motion pictures together. In a fantastic coincidence, Marilyn Monroe's character in the film *Monkey Business* (1952) is named, "Lois Laurel."

---

37 Casual conversation with author

Chapter Three
Richard Bare Enters Phyllis' Life

With Harpo Marx (1948).

RICHARD BARE, THE FUTURE husband of Phyllis Coates (Bare's second wife) was born Aug 12, 1913, in Turlock, California. Located in the San Joaquin Valley of central California, it was and still is an agriculture town. Young Bare showed an interest in film as early as high school and pursued that vocation, enrolling in the University of Southern California film studies program.

Bare is quite the interesting chap and became a legendary Hollywood director. Most people are only faintly aware of him for directing the incredibly successful *Green Acres* television series in the 1960s, but he was so much more. He was a staple of early television and directed Westerns to include: *The Virginian*, *Cheyenne*, *Maverick*, etc. He also directed seven celebrated *Twilight Zone* episodes: *To Serve Man, What's in the Box, Third from the Sun, The Purple Testament, The Prime Mover* and *Nick of Time* with William Shatner. He also directed episodes of *77 Sunset Strip, Route 66, Lassie,* and other hits from the 1950s and '60s.

Fortunately, in later years Richard Bare wrote his autobiography, Confessions of a Hollywood Director. It gives us a first-hand account of his history, thought process, and the time he met Phyllis Coates. He was a Hollywood insider and helped launch the careers of many actors, directors and producers in the business over the years.

Bare made a name for himself early in life by breaking into the business filming and selling his own subjects as an independent. For a while, he leased a cinema in Carmel and showed movies at the Filmart Cinema. It was here that he met and married his first wife, eventually resulting in divorce. He followed up by going to the University of Southern California to study in its film program, and during the war he worked at Fort Roach making army training films.

In 1942, Bare came up with a script for a short comedy. The running title was *So You Want to Quit Smoking*. By then, Bare was teaching film at USC and he involved his students with real experiences about making film and selling/marketing their work. It also kept the production costs down. He was able to find gold in the form of one George O'Hanlon, a professional comedian who cooperated in performing as an "Average Joe," in this case, a characterization of someone who smokes too much. As Joe McDoakes, O'Hanlon lit up the screen with his cigarette addiction/withdrawals and a search for a never-ending supply of tobacco.

Bare intended to sell the script to Pete Smith for his one-reel comedies. The two formats were similar in that a voiceover actor supplied the narration to the action on the screen. Smith loved the comedy parody that Bare produced, but flatly turned down the chance to buy it. Smith's reason was "Big Tobacco" would not approve of even the slightest mocking of the industry. After all, America *needed* their cigarettes, and the country was in the middle of a war.

Bare ultimately was able to sell the product to an independent whose cinematic patrons howled at the screen antics of Joe McDoakes. It was a rough start, but in the late 40s Bare was able to convince Warner Bros. of his desire to make a series of the *Behind the Eight Ball* comedies, running at ten minutes each.

It should be noted that O'Hanlon's "Average Joe" had its roots in Edgar Kennedy's popular *Average Man* series for RKO since the early 1930s. Edgar's character was beaten down by life and family members, culminating in an implosion of some kind. He usually indicated his loss by rubbing his hand over the face as a symbolic "white flag" gesture, called a "Slow Burn." It is there that the similarities between Joe McDoakes and Edgar ends. Joe's character was youthful and snappy. He sometimes broke the fourth wall by talking to the narrator (usually Art Gilmore) and reacting to the advice. It elicited the same kind of sympathy or pathos towards the character. The audience was with him.

So You Want to Quit Smoking turned out to be the beginning of a long series produced by Warner Bros., ending in 1956. And it all happened because Pete Smith turned down what became Bare's initial entry of the series. Bare had originally offered the finished product to Smith for a lousy two thousand dollars.

There might have been further redemption for Bare in that Edgar Kennedy made his own short comedy, *What, No Cigarettes?* in 1945. The basic theme was pertaining to cigarette addiction and the crazy ways to obtain them. No one was offended.

Richard Bare was married six times and died when he reached the very advanced age of 102. He was active his whole life and even met up with Phyllis for a Q&A by Stan Taffel at the annual Cinecon convention at Los Angeles in 2012. (*For more details, see Chapter Eleven*).

Cock 'n Bull Restaurant

By 1947-1948, Richard Bare was now in charge of his own production unit at Warners to make his *Behind the Eight Ball* series. It was noticed that the series consistently made money for the company and always came in under budget. Plus, it was a prestigious compliment to the Warner Bros. package of film fare offered to the movie going audiences. It was inevitable that Bare would get a chance to direct features.

In Bare's book, he described himself as looking "A bit like Cary Grant in those days."[38] He was also pretty sure of himself at spotting talent. In his autobiography, Bare took pride that he "Could scan the room and pick out who he could make a star."[39]

Bare used to go to his favorite watering hole after work at the famed "Cock 'n Bull Restaurant." Or perhaps he considered this home away from home as his lion's lair. This English pub/restaurant was located at 9170 Sunset Blvd. This fine establishment opened in 1937 and was within walking distance of the Sierra Towers and the "Garden of Allah." The buffet always included roast beef and Yorkshire pudding. Hollywood dignitaries such as John Barrymore, Errol Flynn, Orson Welles, John Carradine, Jack Webb, and their peers would sit for hours at the bar to drink and smoke. It also contained an assortment of Hollywood agents and deal makers.

The décor originally had their walls covered with facsimile 19th Century English newspapers, prints of English scenes and autographs of English royalty rather than those of Hollywood-type royalty. For a while, a dart board was in operation next to the bar, but after a few customers were wounded, the missiles were removed. "Celebrities liked to come here because we wouldn't allow autograph seekers to bother them at dinner or wait outside the door."[39]

A 1948 menu reveals that dining at the Cock 'n Bull was also very *pricey*. Lunch was $1.50 and complete dinners cost $3.50; it included salad, entrée, dessert and coffee. An insightful article by Paul V. Coates (no relation to Phyllis) describes the "distinctively smart pub with oak panels and decorated with English hunting scenes." The columnist told his readers: "This fine café has been

---

38 Bare, Richard. Confessions of a Hollywood Director Scarecrow Press, Inc. Lanham, Maryland, and London 2001
39 *Ibid*
39 "Cock 'n Bull Story-Famed Sunset Blvd. Restaurant Closes After 50 Years" Los Angeles Times August 23, 1987

serving excellent food and catering to the sensitive diets of ulcer-ridden actors, producers, agents who frequent the Sunset Strip. [40]

This high-end restaurant was famous for inventing the "Moscow Mule," a concoction of Vodka, lime juice and ginger beer. The full bar offering other cocktails cost seventy-five cents. A night of dining and drinking might add up to a price of a whopping ten dollars that only movie stars or executives could afford. Ten dollars was a whole day's pay for most American's during this era.

Richard Bare boasted in his book that he met three of his future wives at this location. He even divulged, as a mental exercise, how he had scouted the room in the 1960's and saw a likely candidate for "Star" material." After a few Jack Daniels for courage, he approached a stunning blonde and asked if "She ever thought about going into the movies?" The cordial reply was, "Not anymore, I'm Kim Novak." The humiliated Richard Bare slinked back to his scouting stool at the Cock 'n Bull bar.

The last example shows Richard Bare's modus-operandi in full bloom in the 1960's; what was it like in the late 1940's when he met his future bride, Phyllis Coates? This time he noticed a familiar figure. The way Bare described the scene is in his book:[41]

> Jessie Wadsworth, the first female agent in Hollywood, brought a comely young lady into the Cock 'n Bull one evening and introduced her to me. Her name was Phyllis Coates. In short order, she was cast to succeed Jane Harker [the first Mrs. Joe McDoakes], but one thing led to another and soon we were married.[42]

Unfortunately, Bare didn't go into details regarding the "one thing led to another" progression of his and Phyllis's romance and marriage. One can only imagine the circumstances of the first meeting of Phyllis and Richard Bare, he certainly didn't elaborate in his book. It was a proper setting after all, and Phyllis was escorted by her Hollywood agent. And meeting a Hollywood director, well, that's what they are supposed to do. For the record, Jessie

---

40 "Well, Medium and Rare" *Los Angeles Times* Nov. 5, 1949
41 Bare, Richard. Confessions of a Hollywood DirectorScarecrow Press, Lanham, Maryland, and London 2001
42 *Ibid*

Wadworth was part of the Manning O'Conner Agency of 9172 Sunset Boulevard, so it would be perfectly natural and professional to be dinning at the Cock 'n Bull with a client.

It is unknown the exact date when Richard Bare met Phyllis; it is most likely in late 1947 or early 1948. One unverifiable newspaper source identified that Phyllis took a screen test for Bare in late 1947. For some unknown reason, Phyllis was never given screen credit for her numerous roles in this series. Then again, neither did the other screen wives of Joe McDoakes.

Richard Bare already had George O'Hanlon under personal contract to star as Joe McDoakes, did he also have Phyllis under personal contract to play his wife? There are few clues. It might be considered irrelevant because Bare married Phyllis, but before that happened, Warners put out a press release to the papers on March 13, 1948:

Warner Brothers Contract for Phyllis Coates

> Phyllis Coates, attractive and 21 from Wichita Falls, Tex., and UCLA student, has been signed to a long-term contract at Warner Bros. and has been given an important part in *Sunburst*. Phyllis made her stage debut five years ago and has played in a series of film shorts called, "*So You Want to Be...*" During the war she toured with the USO in Europe and did hospital circuits too.

The press release states Phyllis was already connected with the *Behind the Eight Ball* series by March, so it is reasonable to conclude that the series was in production earlier in the year. There was a tight shooting schedule at Warners and they knocked out the year's output earlier in the year, then distributed each title in increments to the cinemas throughout the country.

As the studio was wont to do, they beefed up Phyllis' fictional background of being a student at UCLA. Regarding her "Important part" in an upcoming film, *Sunburst*, there was no film ever released by this title. That is actually a common occurrence in the movie industry, that a title was announced before the release of the film itself. Sometimes the project is shelved, or simply retitled. *Sun-*

burst might have been retitled as, *Embraceable You*, starring Dane Clark and Geraldine Brooks. Phyllis did not make the final cut.

There was another announcement, this time in the trade papers:

> Phyllis Coates signed to a long-term acting contract by Warners. The Texas born actress, 21, toured in *Anything Goes* and *Girl Crazy* on the USO war circuit.[43]

Behind the Eight Ball Series

This short comedy series was first established in 1942 and continued through the years until 1956. There were sixty-three short films during the run for Warner Bros. that served as openers for their features. These were one-reelers credited to Richard Bare for directing and writing; this series was his *baby*. Rubber-faced George O'Hanlon was his star; he capably carried each entry to critical and commercial success.

George O'Hanlon (1912-1989) was born into a family of entertainers, and started in the business as "a Hoofer."[44] He has over 173 credits as an actor in film and television with sixty-four writing credits. After the *Eight Ball* series he was cast as Chester Riley's next-door neighbor for twenty-three episodes of *The Life of Riley*.

Phyllis loved performing in the *Behind the Eight Ball* series, "They gave me a real sense of comedy, and I loved it."[45] Phyllis said the series was the first thing Warners assigned her to do, but it looks very much like Richard Bare had a heavy hand in the casting. Phyllis had a recurring role as Mrs. Joe McDoakes through twenty-nine episodes of the remaining series.

If it is unclear what the exact date Bare met Phyllis, it is also uncertain when Phyllis changed her name from Gypsie Stell. A movie contract at Warner Bros. came around the same time period she met Richard Bare.

As a reward for directing his short subjects under budget and on schedule, Richard Bare was given the opportunity to direct a feature film for Warner Brothers. *Smart Girls Don't Talk was a* crime

---

43 *Showman's Trade Review* March 20, 1948
44 Interview of George O'Hanlon by Leonard Maltin for *Film Fan Monthly* July-August 1974
45 Casual conversation with Phyllis Coates with author

drama starring Virginia Mayo. Bare made sure to cast his new wife in the film, Phyllis played the uncredited part of a beautiful cigarette girl. It was released to theaters October 9, 1948. It cannot be denied Richard Bare helped Phyllis' career along.

Richard Bare Marries Gypsie Stell A.K.A. Phyllis Coates A.K.A. Mrs. Joe McDoakes

The new couple, madly in love, drove to Las Vegas and got hitched on March 28, 1948. Phyllis' new husband was fourteen years older than her. The marriage was covered in the *Los Angeles Times*.

> **Director Weds Actress:**
> The Easter marriage of Director Richard Bare and Phyllis Coates, actress, was revealed on the couple's return from Las Vegas. Bare, former short-subject director recently given his first feature assignment, directed his bride in her screen test last December.[46]

Richard Bare elaborated in his book how the *Joe McDoakes-Behind the Eight Ball* series evolved.

> Jane Harker had played Joe McDoakes' screen wife during the first few years but left the show to get married and live in New York.
>
> We remained good friends and Phyllis continued her role as Joe's wife for several years, until she left Warners to play Lois Lane in the TV version of *Adventures of Superman*.[47]

Richard Bare was still in love with Phyllis and tried to prove it by keeping her in the role as Mrs. Joe McDoakes over the years. It was an amicable working relationship. Both of them moved on with their personal lives. Bare was married five times while Phyllis married four times (not including her annulled marriage). They had a grand reunion at the Cinecon in Hollywood during 2012, sixty-three years after their marriage. (*See Chapter Eleven*)

---

46 *Los Angeles Times* April 2, 1948
47 Bare, Richard L. Confessions of a Hollywood Director Scarecrow Press, Inc. 4720 Boston Wy. Lanham, Maryland.

The "Hollywood" version of Phyllis Coates was written up in a magazine entitled, *So Innocently:*

> The scene is set in California. The sun was painting her satiny skin a delicate bronze…The breeze was gentle—oh, ever so gently. Caressing and kissing her closed lids, her silky hair…She was indeed a picture no artist could duplicate on canvas…She was relaxing when IT HAPPENED! Out of the cloudless sky came the thing that was to change the whole course of her life in the person of a Talent Scout…There she was—this lovely damsel---sunning herself on the beautiful shores of Toluca Lake, never dreaming that two intent eyes were studying her…yes, this is the true tale of Phyllis Coates and how, when innocently picking up a tan---well, to sum it up, Warner Bros. snared her for the kliegs…like we said, it all began so innocently—and ended just like a fairytale.

There were two studio photographs accompanying the undated article. The unknown author was practically drooling. The captions read: "Sitting pretty…yesiree! This is Phyllis Coates who is all set for cinema success. With these sweets, she can hardly miss. She's got everything…and in all the right places, in just the right spots. We like the trend in beauty—wholesome, healthy, vital."

There was another article published featuring Phyllis:

> *Los Angeles Times* March 11, 1948
> **"SHORT Movies Promote Texas Beauty's Career-by Edwin Schallert":**
> Short films, which have often been the "first steps" venture for stars, have evidently lost none of their potency in a high road to studio attention. Latest personality thus registered is Phyllis Coates, who made her bow briefly in *So You Want to Be in Politics*, nominated among one-reelers for Academy consideration.
>
> Miss Coates was the discovery of Dick Bare, who directs the *So You Want To* series, and subsequently appeared in the Joe McDoakes (George O'Hanlon) in two other films. Now Warners has decided to place her in the

second feminine lead of *Sunburst*, with Dane Clark and Geraldine Brooks. She's a strawberry blonde with blue eyes from Wichita Falls, Texas, had experience in USO shows and is 21 years of age.[48]

In addition to appearing in *So You Want to Be in Politics*, Phyllis also portrayed Mrs. McDoakes in *So, You Want to Be on the Radio* during that same year.

Easter Seals

The *Los Angeles Times* printed a photo of Phyllis announcing, "Last minute Reminder-Phyllis Coates, Warner Bros. starlet, poses prettily beside the mailbox to remind you that this is the deadline for buying those Easter Seals."[49] Things were starting to cook.

Harpo Meets Phyllis

In April of 1948 while Phyllis was under contract to Warners, she was assigned with another starlet, Patricia Northrup, for a photo shoot at Toluca Lake. The occasion was for a demonstration of a surfboard powered by batteries, called "The Motorboard." The inventor was Mr. Joe C. Gilpin who invited a publicity crew to document the maiden voyage. What better way than to have two beautiful women showing how it's done? A film crew showed up and *Life* magazine came to record the occasion. Phyllis was prominently displayed standing and in prone position to navigate the rudderless surf board across the natural lake.

The event drew none other than Harpo Marx, whose film persona was the one who chased the girls, usually tooting his horn. This time he caught one, in the form of Phyllis Coates and it was also captured by the camera. Harpo knew Gilpin from one of the Marx Brothers films, *A Night in Casablanca*, and might have been an investor in the new contraption.

This happy event was the feature story for *Life* magazine on June 14, 1948. Unfortunately, the inventor of the Motorboard, Joe Gilpin, suddenly died in March of 1949, he was only forty-four years

---

48 *Los Angeles Times* March 11, 1948
49 *The Los Angeles Times* March 28, 1948

old succumbing to a heart attack. He had been an executive in the movie industry since 1924. The Motorboard was to be marketed to hotels for their swimming pools for $350.00. Needless to say, the contraption was never commercially viable.

"Best Table Decoration of 1948- *Will Phyllis Coates replace the knife and fork?"*[50]

> Beautiful redhead, Phyllis Coates from Wichita Falls, Texas, who has appeared in a few small roles. The Warners think Phyllis has rare promise but needs printed attention. The California Restaurant Associations are gathering in Los Angeles next week and they will label her "Miss Best Table Decoration of 1948." Miss Coates will sit at a gorgeously decked eating board. The fact that she wears a bathing suit will not dampen chances of the photograph breaking into print.[51]

This from the Wichita home newspaper:

> Another Wichita Falls native daughter is climbing the Hollywood ladder in the footsteps of Louise Allbritton to star in Hollywood. Her name is Phyllis Coates. Actually, Phyllis has three names now. She was born in Wichita Falls as Gypsie Ann Stell. Phyllis is her screen name. But recently, Easter Sunday to be exact, she was married to Richard Bare, her studio director, so now she's also Mrs. Bare.
>
> She has three aunts and various other relatives living in Wichita Falls. The aunts are Mrs. Joe Lewis, Mrs. J.T. Carr and Mrs. L.A. Pratt. Her parents, Mr. and Mrs. Robert Rush Stell, now live in Pecos, Texas.
>
> Phyllis went to Hollywood when she was 16 at the request of movie talent scouts whom she attracted with her dancing and singing while still in high school. She was band sweetheart and drum majorette at a number of schools including Odessa High. Her work in USO-spon-

---

50 *Valley Times* May 28, 1948
51 *Dallas Morning News* June 10, 1948

sored shows led directly to her first screen appearance as "Mrs. Joe McDoakes" in some of the series of short subjects made at Warner Brothers. Before entering the USO work, Phyllis was in *Ken Murray's Blackouts* stage shows for almost two years. Later she was a line captain for the *Earl Carroll's Road Show*, and still later went to Chicago where she modeled for the Al Seamon Agency.

Phyllis had a bit-part in *Where Do We Go from Here*, a movie that starred Fred MacMurray, and information received by her relatives here indicates that she soon will be signed up for secondary leads with June Haver and other top stars.[52]

Actress Louise Allbritton was born in Oklahoma (1920) but was raised in Wichita Falls. She had some forty-seven screen and television appearances before she died in 1979. She is best known for her roles in *Son of Dracula* and *The Egg and I*.

For Phyllis, 1948 marked a high point in her early career. And there *was* such a thing as going back home, this time with a new husband.

Starlet to Odessa
On July 2 motion picture starlet Phyllis Coates will fly from Hollywood to take part in Odessa's Independence Day festival July 5. The Odessa Chamber of Commerce said Friday.[53]

Miss West Texas to Be Selected
Phyllis Coates, Hollywood movie starlet, will crown the winner of a Miss West Texas beauty contest as a feature of the Independence Day Festival here Monday. Miss West Texas will enter the state-wide-contest at Port Arthur, from which miss will be chosen to compete in the Miss America competition at Atlantic City, N.J.[54]

The next day there was a news update:

---

52 *Wichita Daily Times* April 22, 1948
53 *Abilene Reporter-News* July 3, 1948
54 *Dallas Morning News* July 4, 1948

> Phyllis Coates, movie actress, a former Odyssean, and her husband, Dick Bare, director, arrived yesterday from Hollywood. Miss Coates, known locally as Gypsie Ann Stell, will speak this afternoon and will judge in the beauty contest. She is now under contract to Warner Brothers. She will crown the winner in a beauty review tonight at the county auditorium.[55]
>
> A whole schedule of events was featured by the townsfolk, starting at 6:30 a.m. for the breakfast and followed by a mile-long parade, exhibits, a softball game, races, an amateur show all leading up to a litany of speeches by dignitaries by local politicians.
>
> The bathing beauty contest at the pool was judged by all the mayors in the surrounding towns, to include Miss Coates. This was followed by a dance in the auditorium, a merchant's display. Of course, a midway carnival was in progress all day and when night fell, fireworks entertained the crowd. The highlight of the day for most people was the "Crowning of Miss Odessa" by Phyllis Coates.[56]

According to the local newspaper, 10,000 people attended the festivities. Phyllis made a speech to the crowd, but it is unknown what she said. Lots of pictures were taken of the events and were displayed on the newspaper the following day. Phyllis was shown crowning Enid Loftus as beauty queen climaxing the event of the Independence Day Festival.

This homecoming of the one-time Gypsie Ann Evarts Stell must have been truly rewarding. All the people who she knew, including those who didn't think she would amount to anything, greeted this "Hollywood Star" with heartwarming receptions. Even her accomplished husband had to take a back seat in the festivities.

By this time Phyllis' father, Rush Stell, was released from prison (1944) and re-married to Melvina Stell. They were living in Pecos, Texas during this time, but it is unknown if he made the festivities. Apparently, Phyllis kept in touch with his family over the years.

---

55 *Odessa American* July 5, 1948
56 *Ibid*

When her father died in 1978, the local newspaper ran an obituary; among the many relatives listed (including a son) was Gypsie Ann Press (Phyllis' married name in 1978).

Photographer's Model

At this time in her career, Phyllis became featured in picture layouts for advertisement firms. She was the focus of a hand care column.[57] Warners also used her to promote an upcoming film. "Five Minutes Daily-Phyllis Coates soon to be seen in Warner Bros. *Kiss in the Dark*, is taking no chances on losing her youthful figure. Once every day she exercises to keep her waistline, abdomen and hips trim."

A Kiss in the Dark is a 1949 film starring David Niven and Jane Wyman. Phyllis had a non-speaking part as a neighbor, but this was a feature film with big stars. It was just the thing young starlets had to do to get noticed for bigger things.

Even the *Los Angeles Times* showcased Phyllis as an excuse to pictorially link her with *A Kiss in the Dark*, and her "exercising regiment for her waistline, abdomen, and hips."[58] This was followed by an article entitled: "Beauty-Why Not Be S-L-I-M?" The photo layout featured a whole article by the Beauty Editor, Betty Clarke, highlighting a routine of "breathing, walking and the correct methods of "a pretty bust-line."[59]

The San Fernando Valley newspaper, The *Valley Times*, featured Phyllis in a bathing suit with a sash identifying her as "Miss Gladiron." The nation's electric iron manufacturers showed Phyllis in a pose "holding a Chinese iron used about 500 B.C. On the table are other antique irons, heated with illuminating gas, iron slugs, gasoline and charcoal."[60]

Phyllis' face was also prominent in an ad for one of the LA newspapers. "Phyllis Coates, film and TV actress, wears a coiffure created by Pierre Alex expressly for the new 'Way back hats.'"

---

57 *Sacramento Bee* September 1, 1948
58 *Los Angeles Times* October 13, 1948
59 *Press Democrat* November 16, 1948
60 *Valley Times* December 2, 1949

The apparel featured rhinestone-spangled vine leaves and green veiling.[61]

Early Television

It may come as a surprise to Phyllis' fans, but in 1949 Phyllis appeared in an early filmed television program called *Your Show Time*. It featured Phyllis as an Egyptian Queen and Herbert Anderson, who later became better known as television's *Dennis the Menace*'s dad.

The Screen Director

Produced in cooperation with the Motion Pictures Arts and Science a short film, *The Screen Director*, featured how the Hollywood directors do their craft. Richard Bare is in a few precious moments going over a script with a brunette-haired Phyllis. The film, shot in 1951, is viewable on YouTube.

> **Actress Wife Sues Producer, Mate:**
> Phyllis Coates, 22, screen actress, began suit for divorce in Superior Court yesterday against Richard L. Bare, 36, film producer, whom she accused of cruelty. The actress, who sued under her legal name, Gypsie Ann Evarts Bare, asked for $400.00 a month alimony. The couple were married in Las Vegas last March 28 and separated November 15, 1948. She sued through attorney Harold E. Sokolov.[62]

The press had a ball with this turn of events. The below article was picked up by the wire services and printed in newspapers across America, this one being in the Milwaukee newspaper.

> **His Movie Titles Bares Ironic Note:**
> Film director Richard L. Bare, 35, recently directed his wife, Phyllis Coates, 22, in a short entitled *So You Want to Hold Your Wife*. Monday, he lost her through a divorce decree. The blonde actress told Judge Jessie Frampton

---

61 *Los Angeles Evening Citizen News* Dec. 23, 1951
62 *Los Angeles Times* December 2, 1948

that her husband objected to her friends and sulked so much she became nervous. After the decree, she returned to the studio to resume work in her husband's short, entitled *Behind the Eight Ball*.[63]

In actuality, *So You Want to Hold Your Wife* was indeed a title in the film series, it was shot and released in 1947 before Richard Bare met Phyllis. His screen wife at that time was Jane Harker. Obviously, the lead-in to the story made the separation and divorce facts a bit ironic to the readers. If that wasn't ironic enough, later in 1950 the pair made another in the series called *So You Want to Hold Your Husband*.

Another aspect of the court appearance for both hit the *Associate Press* wires repeating the basics. *The Fort Worth Star-Telegram* picked up the story:

> Just by way of proving that there is absolutely no similarity between love in the movies and in real life, Film Director Richard L. Bare and Actress Phyllis Coates were divorced Monday. She was awarded the decree but as she was walking out of the courtroom, Bare asked: "Can't we be friends?" She answered with another question: "Why not?" As in the movies, they kissed. The 22-year-old Mrs. Bare told the court that she and the director, 35, got along splendidly in the films, but at home it was another matter. She's going to continue in a series of movie shorts directed by Bare.[64]

An "International Soundphoto" also circulated an image of the two recent divorcees, "Just a Kiss of Friendship" showing Richard Bare kissing Phyllis' cheek after their divorce. The wire photo made most of the newspapers of the day. Everyone deserves a different story, and Richard Bare had his. In Bare's autobiography, he recounts that time period with Phyllis:

> Seven months later [after marriage] we were divorced, but this time I filed first as the dissatisfaction was mine. I even picked her up at her apartment and drove her to

---

63 *Milwaukee Journal* January 22, 1949
64 *Fort Worth Star-Telegram* January 11, 1949

the courthouse the morning of the trial. That night our pictures were on the front page of the *Herald-Express*; we were kissing each other while holding up the divorce decree.[65]

According to the existing divorce decree, it was actually Phyllis who originally filed for divorce on the "Grounds of cruelty." She proclaimed that Bare caused her "great mental suffering and anguish."

The point was made that Phyllis had her acting friends over during the late night, while Richard Bare was an early riser. According to the complaint, "It made Bare grouchy and anxious." Through her attorney, Phyllis claimed "the defendant is well able to pay the plaintiff a reasonable sum for counsel and maintenance the plaintiff for $400.00 per month and the sum of $1000.00 for attorney fees." The presiding judge agreed and it was so ordered with a final judgment of divorce on January 11, 1949.[66]

In later years Richard Bare told his young friend, Jeff Vilencia, some more details about what led up to the split. When Bare started writing his memoirs back in 1983, he told Vilencia a few details he didn't want to put in his autobiography. He described Phyllis as a "Party girl" and she regularly invited her friends over for fun. They stayed up late and played records while early-bird Bare had to get up early for work the next day. One night while Bare was asleep, Phyllis and one of her gal friends sneaked up on him and started tickling him in bed, waking him up. Bare told Vilencia, "It was cute the first time, but they did it again on other nights and he had enough." He warned her, "If you do that one more time, I'm filing for a divorce."[67] The verbal threat in front of her friends mortified Phyllis. She turned cold to him. Only seven months into the marriage, Phyllis decided to cut her losses and filed for divorce.

Just friends they were as the *Behind the Eight Ball* series continued to the theaters until it wrapped in 1956. Phyllis was used as Joe McDoakes' wife as needed because as Bare said, "Phyllis

---

65 Bare, Richard. Confessions of a Hollywood Director Scarecrow Press, Lanham, Maryland, and London 2001
66 Judgment of Divorce January 11, 1949
67 Jeff Vilencia in email to author March 27, 2024

looked good on the screen and had perfect comedy effectiveness, she was a talent."

The late John Field of San Diego and *Superman* series expert told this author that he had the opportunity to visit Richard Bare at his office one day. Field said, "Bare had still photographs from the *Eight Ball* series decorating the walls." He told me that Bare wanted to keep Phyllis Coates on because "she had perfect comic timing." Field offered his own perspective; "Yeah, and she was a babe." Bare answered, "Oh yeah!" While at the office, Bare pulled out a script from one of his file drawers. It contained an old unused work-up that served as a reunion of the cast for one final *Behind the Eight Ball* film featuring George O'Hanlon and Phyllis in their established roles as husband and wife. It was never to be.

Phyllis Coates on Set After Collapse:
Through the spunk of film starlet Phyllis Coates, 22, who collapsed from heat prostration on an outdoor set at Warner Brothers in Burbank yesterday. Miss Coates, who co-stars with George O'Hanlon in the *Joe McDoakes* series of short subjects, insisted on returning to work after the studio's first aid station administered salt tablets.[68]

Translation: Now that Phyllis was a contract player for Warners, the old studio system of getting their stars' name in the paper was an important cog for publicity. In this case, women faint and male stars save people's lives. In a few short years, Phyllis would be working on location in Death Valley. She withstood the challenges without drama.

Robert Nelms-Phyllis' Husband #2

With Phyllis' recent divorce, she was free to pursue other interests. And vivacious Gypsie /Phyllis Coates was never *want* for suitors. Enter musician Bob Nelms into her life.

Robert Lee Nelms was born May 24, 1925 in Quincy, Illinois. Considered the "Gem City," it was a rural area in the southern portion of the state. St. Louis is closer to this municipality than Chicago. The mighty Mississippi roars past its boarder.

---
68 *Los Angeles Evening Herald and Express.* September 2, 1949

When WWII came to America, Robert Nelms joined the Navy until he was discharged in 1945. Nelms was a professional piano player and specialized in jazz piano. According to their daughter, it is believed that Phyllis met the talented musician during a performance. During this time, Nelms served as musical accompaniment to "The Three Dons." A whirlwind romance followed and the two drove off to Las Vegas to get married on January 23, 1950.

According to the federal census of 1950, the new couple lived at 4130 Riverside Drive in beautiful Burbank, California. Bob Nelms is listed as a musician working in an unnamed orchestra.

Their daughter, Christopher Ann Nelms (current name, Zoe Christopher), was born May 21, 1950 at Cedars of Lebanon Hospital in Los Angeles. It was a difficult birth and she was born with a hip displacement. The baby had to wear a cast for the next year and a half. One thing was sure: money was tight, especially since Nelms took to the road as a working musician.

Phyllis as a freelance actress

The old studio system was winding down and Phyllis was no longer protected by the umbrella that Warner Bros. provided for their contract players. It appears that the studio dropped her option after one year; she certainly wasn't the only one in that era. With marriage and a baby to take care of, Phyllis rolled up her sleeves and plunged into the film industry starting at the bottom at Monogram studios.

Outlaws of Texas

This is a Whip Wilson feature that has Phyllis in an important role as "Anne Moore." The pressbook that accompanied this release has some interesting insight to Phyllis' background:

> Phyllis Coates, streamlined redhead, who, as a member of a war time USO troupe, danced before two million soldiers, has the feminine lead opposite Whip Wilson in Monogram's *Outlaws of Texas*. A professional dancer since the age of fifteen, she got the role when Wilson, an ex-G.I., remembered having been entertained by her on

his way home from the Orient after the war. While she does no dancing in the film, Phyllis considers this a turning point in her career. After a long succession of sweet ingenue roles, she finally is given the opportunity to play a heavy, the leader of a gang of holdup men, as ruthless as any killer in her crew.[69]

The pressbook also gave a plot synopsis:

> Action fans from six to ninety-six are having the time of their lives at the…theater these days where Whip Wilson is currently dishing out the thrills in Monogram's *Outlaws of Texas*. Whether he's matching fists or gunfire with bad men, Whip is a tough one to handle.
>
> A fresh story twist finds a pretty girl, Phyllis Coates, as the principle heavy of this film. As the daughter of a famous outlaw, believed to be dead, the girl has gathered her father's crew together, and leads them in a bold series of bank robberies, stage holdups, and cattle raids, and just about anything else that provides exciting screen fare.
>
> As the incognito ranger, Whip Wilson was never better on the screen, being one of the most believable western stars on films. Comic side-kick Andy Clyde is in for his share of action, as well as laughs. As the pretty leader of the outlaw gang, Phyllis Coates gives an excellent account of her work, demonstrating she should go a long way in Hollywood.

This film was directed by Thomas Carr, who in the months to come would be directing Phyllis in *Adventures of Superman*.

Blues Busters (released October 9, 1950)

In this Monogram feature, the Bowery Boys were the series star. Though this can be considered a low budget film, it shakes the rafters with hilarity. Huntz Hall becomes a singing star after a throat operation and croons in a soft smooth voice (dubbed by John Laurenz). The contrast between Sach's real and singing voice is like

---

69 *Outlaws of Texas* Pressbook 1951

comparing Perry Como to Alfalfa. The film is a comedy musical romp and is one of the highest-rated entries in the Bowery Boys series of films.

Phyllis plays Sally Doran, the young girlfriend of Slip (Leo Gorcey.) She is a chorus girl, and gets to perform a solo dance sequence. She is all legs and motion as she taps out her musical number and into the consciousness of every male with life in him. It's the type of number that Phyllis performed at the Florentine Gardens back in 1945. It is regrettable that this seems to be the only film in which Phyllis gets to showcase her dancing talents. The term "fresh face" is most applicable in this entry. Part of the plot entailed a rival club beckoning Sach away with the aid of their vampish female nightclub singer. Her manager husband puts the moves on Sally, and gets slapped across the face for his efforts. Phyllis really let him have it.

Early Television
Cisco Kid

Also in 1950, Phyllis was the leading lady in a *Cisco Kid* TV episode called, *Wedding Blackmail* (as Marge Lacey). Phyllis looked striking in these color adventures of the "Robin Hood of the Old West," starring Duncan Renaldo and Leo Carrillo.

Through 1951 Phyllis was featured in three more episodes with the Mexican crusaders and champions of good versus evil. She played JoAnn Dora in *Haven for Heavies*, Miss Lacey in the *Phony Sheriff*, and a recurring named character in an episode entitled, *Uncle Disinherits Niece*.

Phyllis' four roles in the *Cisco Kid* series established her as a dependable female of strength, determination, and a good sport. She could work quickly and without complaint. Scenes had her on horseback, and since she was from Texas, Phyllis was a natural rider, right? Not so said Phyllis. "I was a lousy rider, I only got on the horse if the script called for it." And if she wanted the part, i.e., paycheck, she kept her mouth shut.

Stars Over Hollywood

Also in 1951, Phyllis co-starred with Buddy Ebsen of all people, in a TV anthology program called, *Stars Over Hollywood*. This installment was named: *Nor Gloom of Night*, an abbreviation of the U.S. Postal Service creed: "Neither snow, nor rain, nor *heat, nor gloom of night stays these courageous couriers from the swift completion* of their appointed rounds"

In this program, Buddy Ebsen is part of the unofficial U.S. Postal Service for their mail carriers. Buddy solves a murder in the small town where he works. The TV listings of the day pointed out that Phyllis Coates was his "co-star."

The Sun Was Setting

A surprise television role for Phyllis, also in 1951, was *The Sun Was Setting*, directed by none other than Ed Wood Jr. This is the same Ed Wood that later directed such classics as *Plan Nine from Outer Space* and *Glen or Glenda*. This fifteen-minute soap opera focused on a young lady who is dying and is being supported by her best friend, Rene (Phyllis). It was filmed pretty straight on and it is quite certain Phyllis never realized that the director came to be the celebrated man as depicted in the Oscar-winning film, *Ed Wood*.

Canyon Raiders

This was a Whip Wilson feature (1951) with Fuzzy Knight and Phyllis Coates as the sexy sheriff. She is kidnapped, then rescued by the star who says to her, "By the way, it's a good thing there aren't too many law officers like you, I'd be in deep trouble all the time."

Oklahoma Justice

Phyllis is cast as "Goldie" in this Johnny Mack Brown horse opera. The star, operating out of the U.S. Marshall's Office, poses as a bank bandit and stage robber. He is trying to learn the identity of a gang that has been operating for several months. Goldie is engaged to the bank cashier hired to help thwart the outlaws. Goldie and her fiancé are given the reward as an advanced wedding present.

The Longhorn

Released in November of 1951, this Monogram feature film starred Wild Bill Elliott and supported by Myron Healey and John Hart. Phyllis plays Gail Robinson, a daughter to the chuck wagon cook. The plot centers on Elliot hiring a band of outlaws to drive his longhorn cattle along the Oregon Trail to Wyoming where he has a ranch. The film contains plenty of stock footage of cattle that is edited in.

Phyllis assists her father cooking on the month-long venture and even getting a compliment by someone suggesting she make a chocolate pie (not sure how she could accomplish that). It was warned in the beginning not to bring her because, "Whiskey and women don't mix on a cattle drive." Another great quote came during a bar scene when one of them actually yells, "You no-good yellow-bellied sidewinder."

Phyllis fends off the Myron Healy character because she fancies Bill Elliott. At the ending scene they are about to kiss when their attention is diverted to a new calf. It was O.K. that the two main characters are talking about marriage, but no kissing (little boys didn't like mush scenes).

This was the first film where Phyllis and Bill Elliott worked together. The two of them would be in three more pictures together: *Fargo, The Maverick,* and *Topeka.* Elliott had been a cowboy for many years and in 1938, he starred in a Columbia feature as *Wild Bill Elliott.* The moniker stuck. Of note, in this film was John Hart, they would be working together in the near future.

This was also the first time Phyllis worked with Myron Healy (*The Longhorn, Fargo, The Maverick,* and *Panther Girl of the Kongo*). He was a journeyman actor of 323 acting credits in film and television. Phyllis had affection for him and sighed when mentioning his name. Those rugged males looked out for Phyllis on location and treated her as a lady.

Ex-Dancer Dons Jeans in Movie

Phyllis Coates featured in Monogram's Whip Wilson starrer *Wild Horse Canyon* now before the cameras, was a night club dancer before going into pictures three years ago. She not only dances well, but she has pretty legs. "But apparently Hollywood doesn't know that. I've been in fourteen pictures-five of them Westerns and when I haven't had to wear riding breeches or jeans, then I have to wear long flowing gowns," Phyllis said.[70]

---

70 *Los Angeles Times* February 6, 1951

Chapter Four
Superman

WITH THE ADVENT OF the miracle of television into America's homes in the early 1950s, there was a big demand in programs for the family to watch. Some of the shows were broadcasted live, others were pre-filmed, then beamed to the boxed receptors and monitors across the airwaves. This new version of home entertainment provided escape into fantasy and entertainment with grainy black, grey and white images. The cultural impact of this new medium was instant.

The fictional character of Superman was born out of the comic books of Action Comics in 1938. The front cover featured a caped man with superhuman strength lifting a car overhead. The script was written and drawn by Jerry Siegel and Joe Shuster, and in so doing created the images of America's first super hero. The progression of comic books introduced characteristics of his superpowers, told of his origin and the cataclysmic events that blasted him to earth. It took years, but a whole industry was established that included not only comic books, but radio, cartoons, and even two movie serials. Superman was everywhere, even fighting the Nazis in cartoon form.

The character of "Lois Lane-girl reporter" was invented for additional plot and a possible love interest with Superman. She first appeared in the very first edition of Action Comics. Eventually her character was so essential and strong, a spin-off version of the *Superman* comics introduced "Lois Lane-Superman's Girlfriend." This all happened before the feature film and television series, so the timing was right and every American knew who and how prolific Superman was. One couldn't actually get away from it, Superman had entered the consciousness of every kid on the schoolyard. The next big step to cement the industry was a movie feature version and television series. That was not only a huge leap in a single bound, it was a financial gamble.

> **Phyllis Wins Role of Lois Lane July 6, 1951**
> Screening of more than 300 applicants left pretty Phyllis Coates, 21-year-old brunette western actress as the choice of Producers Bernard Luber and Robert Maxwell for the role of Lois Lane in their Superman TV series. She'll play opposite George Reeves in the films scheduled for shooting beginning July 10 at RKO-Pathe studios. Western fans will remember her for leads opposite Johnny Mack Brown, Whip Wilson and Bill Elliott.[71]
>
> After running through some 200 candidates, they finally signed George Reeves as Superman and Clark Kent. "Good looking Phyllis Coates, a graduate of Hollywood horse operas is doing Lois Lane (girl reporter) role."[72]

---

71 *Los Angeles Times* July 6, 1951
72 *Los Angeles Times* October 19, 1951

During an interview Phyllis did for author Gary Grossman for his *Superman Serial to Cereal* book, she said she competed against ninety-five other hopefuls for the part.[73] Other contemporary descriptions printed she was in competition with some 300 other female candidates, certainly an exaggeration.

In later years, Phyllis told me the directors for the first year of *Adventures of Superman* were Lee Sholem and Thomas Carr, and they had a say in casting. Carr previously directed Phyllis in the Western *Outlaws of Texas*. Phyllis described the two readings she did for the part before Carr chose her for the role of Lois Lane. However, Phyllis apparently had a leg up on her competition. She explained to me that the producers Robert Maxwell, Barney Sarecky, and Bernard Luber] "Knew what I could do."

It should be noted that Carr also directed the two *Superman* serials in 1948 when Noel Neill played the "Lois Lane" part. Is it possible that decision makers rejected Noel for the television series? Or was it a case to recast everyone from the serial? Regardless, Noel Neill permanently held a grudge against Phyllis for the rest of her life. Phyllis always regretted that Noel refused to be at the same place as Phyllis.

"Well kid, welcome to the bottom of the barrel" – George Reeves on meeting Phyllis for the first time.

Superman and the Mole Men began filming on July 10, 1951 and continued through July 21st. The cast worked more than quickly, in only twelve days the crew and principles churned out good footage for a feature film. Then, with just one day off, Sunday, July 22, the cast and crew began working on the twenty-six episodes that would comprise the first season on television. Episodes were shot at the RKO-Pathé back lots known as Forty Acres. This is the same area that King Kong was filmed among other well-known features in the 1930s and 40s.

---

73 Grossman, Gary. Superman Serial to Cereal. Big Apple Film Series Popular Library Publishers 600 Third Ave. New York, N.Y. 10016, 1976

Phyllis remembered that *Superman and the Mole Men* was shot in a hectic schedule, twelve-hour days for six days a week. "George had a small trailer with a bar and had the cast and crew drinking up a storm by eight in the morning. George hid it well, but I didn't. At 4 p.m. George would open his bar regardless if the day's shooting was done or not."

"My mother was an alcoholic and I couldn't be one." – Phyllis to author

Harry Thomas did all the make-up for *Superman and the Mole Men*, applying bald-caps and hair for the midgets who played the mole men. Thomas stayed on to serve his craft for the crew and had a good working relationship with them. Phyllis remembered him distinctly.

> My makeup man was Harry Thomas, who made up every monster in Hollywood [sic]. He could tell when I was drinking the night before because my skin would sag. He told me, you should watch your drinking with them, it's affecting your beauty—Phyllis Coates to author

Thomas made a career for himself applying makeup for the Hollywood independent studios; his idol was Jack Pierce who was an institution at Universal. Thomas claimed he hated working for the major studios and considered himself an *artist*. He eventually found himself at the Hal Roach Studios in the 1930s and even did a little work as an anonymous actor. Thomas played one of the prisoners in Laurel and Hardy's *Pardon Us*.

Superman and the Mole Men was the first feature film of the Man of Steel, it was released to the theaters on November 6, 1951. It was a bare bones production, but it had its own charm and intensity. We first see Phyllis Coates and Clark Kent together as journalists who were assigned to investigate the deepest oilwell ever drilled, almost six miles down in the fictional mid-Western town of Silsby. There had been reports of glowing nocturnal creatures that surfaced from the largest oil well in existence.

The locals are literally up in arms at the perceived intentions of these aliens, and they aim to stop them before harm is done. Lois and Clark check themselves into their separate rooms at the local hotel and sense the growing dangers. Lois' first recorded words while surveying the town and denied a story: *"Isn't that just ducky?"*

As the tension builds, old Pops drops dead of an alleged heart attack inside his working shack, Clark and Phyllis discover the body and Clark decided to investigate further, leaving Lois to telephone the Sheriff. In a dramatic scene, we see the curious little men (Jerry Maren and Billy Curtis who actually played munchkins in MGM's, *The Wizard of Oz*). They are described as looking like "mole-men," are void of hair on top, and they peer into a window inside where Lois was on the phone. She shrieks in startlement, and drops the phone. Without realizing it at the time, Phyllis established her character as a screamer of great range.

The townsfolk hear of this and rush to judgment fearing an invasion and the contamination of their water supply. The Sheriff, Clark, and Superman urge caution towards the aliens until they know more. The leader of the vigilante committee, Luke Benson (Jeff Corey), wants to barrel through the red tape and, with his dogs, shoot first.

The armed townsfolk confront Lois and Clark in front of their hotel to intimidate them to stay where they are. Benson warns Lois to "stay inside." Apparently, he didn't know who he was talking to. Lois says, "I'll go back inside when I feel like it, BUT I DON'T FEEL LIKE IT." She then slaps and punches the vigilantes at will. Superman then arrives, picks up Benson and throws him into the crowd, justifying it while saying, "You're too stupid to use guns."

The mole men return to the base of their towering oil-well and return down under. They set fire to the oil so they can't be followed. As Superman and Lois look on, the last line of the movie ends with Lois murmuring, "It's almost as if they were saying, 'You stay in your world and we'll stay in ours.'"

Now with *Superman and the Mole Men* in the film can, the producers went right into production for a hopeful television series. George Reeves and Phyllis Coates starred with their names prominently in the credits. The rest of the series regulars were hired:

Jack Larsen as "Jimmy Olsen, the cub reporter," "John Hamilton as the Chief," and "Robert Shayne as Inspector Henderson." It is an odd fact that all the people mentioned above were at one time or another a Warner Bros. property.

The Adventures of Superman made its television debut on September 19, 1952. It was a syndicated release owned by National Comics. While Phyllis Coates' character is a full-grown independent woman of twenty-four years, Jack Larsen was referred by everyone as "The Kid." He was only one year younger than Phyllis, but acted it as a younger man with a higher-pitched voice.

Phyllis worked six days a week on the *Superman* TV series, and had to memorize twenty-four pages of dialogue a day. She loved working with George Reeves and the crew. Phyllis was allegedly paid $350.00 per episode. She had only one outfit to wear (as did the other permanent cast members) so the scenes could be freely edited.

We shot four episodes at once. All the indoor scenes were shot, then the exteriors. We didn't know what was going on. –Phyllis Coates to author

In historical perspective, Phyllis Coates' "Lois Lane" for television in 1952 might be the first serious professional female portrayed in the new medium. In later years, Phyllis admitted she didn't realize she was "Blazing a new trail" for womanhood.

The fact Phyllis was playing an ace investigative reporter gave her certain allowances beyond the norms of housewives of the period, or even Eve Arden's comic portrayal of a teacher in *Our Miss Brooks*. In 1952, newspaper reporters were mostly a man's world and female reporters in the newsroom would ruffle feathers. And Lois Lane was no social society columnist. Her character can be described as "**Abrasive, aggressive, assertive, bullheaded, competitive, confident, curious, feisty, go-getter, gutsy, headstrong, inquisitive, intrusive, indiscreet, meddling, mercurial, nosy, plucky, prying, pushy, sassy, scheming, smart, snoopy, spunky, strong-willed, tough-as-nails,** and an **A-list screamer.**"

In later years on TV, *The Mary Tyler Moore show*, also in a newsroom office setting, Ed Asner (boss to Mary) told Mary that she had a lot of "spunk." Mary took it as a compliment until Asner said, "I hate spunk." If he had worked with Phyllis Coates' "Lois Lane," he would have seen *spunk in spades*.

In the first year of *Adventures of Superman*, the Lois Lane character was no "damsel in distress." She got herself in jams, but considered herself self-reliant. Lois often shook off Clark Kent's journalism partnership and even mocked him. She would often ridicule Clark for scurrying away before Superman arrived to save the day.

When Lois Lane enacted her primal screams, it was reaching a decibel level designed to repel dangerous men. That may have been her first line of defense, but Phyllis' Lois Lane was not afraid to try and sock her way out of trouble.

It should be emphasized that in the making of *Superman* episodes, everyone knew it was directed fast and furious. It was an action-filmed series after all. The actors had to find their spots so fists could come flying in the close settings, and it had to look real. The objective was for the actors to be out of harm's way, but create an illusion of them receiving a punch. For most of the stuntmen, this was their specialty. In the episode *"Night of Terror,"* Phyllis missed her mark and got knocked out cold! Everyone was stunned and the production ceased while they carried Phyllis out to recover. The director apparently shrugged his shoulders and encouraged his crew to get Phyllis ready to resume the sequence.

Phyllis actually remembered the incident years later. She claimed it was her fault for not being in the correct place when the bad guy threw his punch at her. There was no time for coddling, "Everyone get back to work." The scene was used without edit and was as real as it gets. They didn't call the director, Lee "Roll-em Sholem" for nothing.

Author Tom Weaver sought out Lee Sholem for his book *Return of the B Science Fiction and Horror Heroes*. The director of *Superman and the Mole Men* and the first season of *Adventures of Superman* had the utmost respect for Phyllis. Weaver interviewed Sholem and specifically asked how he liked working with Phyllis Coates.

She was a very, very nice gal, willing to do anything. I'll tell you an anecdote: We had stuntmen doing fights on that show often. We had both George Reeves and Phyllis Coates in fight scenes in one day—and this one day was not a lucky day for us. Both of them got knocked cold. These stuntmen would throw a right or a left hook, and if their timing was off, "Look out." That day one of the stuntmen accidently actually punched Phyllis and knocked her out![74]

Superman's Girl Friday

There was an incredible article about the success of the show on television for the magazine, *TV People*, December 1953. The author of the piece was Jim Warren and he set it up nicely. "Phyllis Coates plays the role of Lois Lane, star girl reporter and Superman's romantic interest." [*sic*] In reality, the romantic interest was only in the comic book version, "Lois Lane-Superman's Girlfriend."

Phyllis regretted that she and George couldn't flirt with each other on camera in their roles. It would have stretched their characters out a bit, but it was considered taboo for early TV. Phyllis said that director Sholem's wife was always on the set "acting as a spy. If we did anything I'd hear about it." Phyllis told author Gary Grossman that it was Sholem's wife who made her cut her hair into "the kinky Lois Lane bundle."[75]

> *There was no play between George and me, I would have enjoyed the situation, it would have expanded our characters* –Phyllis Coates to author

---

[74] Weaver, Tom. Return of the B Science Fiction and Horror Heroes. McFarland & and Company, Inc. Publishers Jefferson, North Carolina, and London 1991

[75] Grossman, Gary. Superman from Serial to Cereal. Big Apple Film Series Popular Library Publishers 600 Third Ave. New York, N.Y. 1976

Video Actress Can't Convince Daughter - by Walter Ames Phyllis Coates the blonde actress has played many roles in her movie career but she admits she's having trouble being convincing to her own daughter, Christopher, 4-years old, in her television role as Lois Lane, girl reporter in the Superman series. "Christopher just can't understand why I can't see through Superman's disguise in the telecasts. She thinks I'm quite stupid about the whole thing."

For those who haven't caught up with Superman, the title role is played by George Reeves. His disguise consists of removing the glasses he wears as the newspaper reporter and donning an abbreviated cloak and tights outfit to float gracefully through the air to troubled spots. Phyllis revealed that she didn't have much hope for the Lois Lane part. The producer said I was too short," she recalled. "I've lost other movie roles for various reasons but never for being too small. After all I'm 5 feet 4 inches tall and I could stretch the point by wearing high heel shoes.

Besides her regular Superman role, Phyllis has become a real television veteran, having appeared in most of the top telecasts filmed in our midst, but she doesn't quite know how to convince her own daughter that Superman really doesn't fool her—except in the television screen.[76]

The TV show was a rousing success, much to the surprise of Phyllis Coates:

> Less than a week after the program went on the air in Los Angeles, I had to change the coloring of my hair from auburn to blonde. I couldn't go anywhere without being mobbed. Not only boys and girls but big, grown-up women. They'd spot me in a supermarket.[77]

---

76 *TV People,* December 1953
77 *Ibid*

Walter Ames got Phyllis to talk about her background and informed his readers:

> She was discovered back in New York by the eye of a Warner Brothers talent scout. Phyllis added, "They shipped me in a cattle train, nobody met me at the station. I spent my last three dollars taking a taxi to the studio and where did I end up? Playing opposite George O'Hanlon in the "Joe McDoakes Series." That series was her entrance to the big screen and developed her comedy chops under the tutelage of Richard Bare.[78]

It is dubious at best that Phyllis was "discovered" in New York since we have a full account from Richard Bare's autobiography. Her mentioning of a "cattle train" to transport her to Hollywood is probably the idea of the writer or a publicity agent. It made a good "rags to riches" story.

According to the article, there were ninety-four other actresses vying for the part of Lois Lane. Phyllis was signed for the role forty-eight hours after auditioning. For the TV series, Phyllis said:

> We'd shoot a complete Superman in two and a half days. Nights I bone-up on the script, I'm up at six-thirty…at the studio at eight…home by seven…asleep by eleven… up at six-thirty. That takes care of twenty-four hours.[79]

Phyllis was described in the article as a "devoted mother and spending her off duty time with her daughter 'Crinker'" [Christopher]. She articulated that the child was born with a congenital hip deformity and spent the first year of her life in a plaster cast.

> It was when we were making the first Superman picture [feature film], I couldn't get a sitter, so I had to take Crinker to the studio with me. I left her on the back seat of the car near the stage where we were shooting. She couldn't fall out. In fact, she couldn't move. But she never cried or complained. Everybody on the lot stopped by at one time or another and kept her company. John Wayne,

---

78 *TV People 1953*
79 *Ibid*

and Bob Mitchum and Barbara Stanwyck. Even Charlie Chaplin. He put his autograph on her cast. I keep the cast just in case I get too big for my britches.[80]

Chaplin was indeed on the RKO lot shooting an interior theater scene for his *Limelight* feature film. The set was also utilized for a scene in *The Case of the Talkative Dummy* in *Adventures of Superman*.

With her husband gone, Phyllis hired a live-in assistant named Della. She had double duty as a babysitter for Crinker and as Phyllis' stand-in at the set. On sunny Sundays the three of them headed down to the beach in Santa Monica. The warm sand was very therapeutic.[81]

When asked if she enjoyed playing Superman's girlfriend, Phyllis told the interviewer:

I've played in dozens of westerns. I'm always the nice girl who gets rescued from the bad guys by the hero. But in those pictures, even when the hero arrived, I was never quite sure I would be rescued no matter what the script said. With Superman it's different. The minute he comes on the scene, I can just sit back and relax.[82]

Scream queen Phyllis has been recognized with her distinct shrieks by all discerning viewers of *Superman*. She has often been compared to Fay Wray (King Kong's reluctant girlfriend). Randy Sadewater compiled a list of Phyllis' screams from ten of the *Adventures of Superman* television episodes:

Mystery of the Broken Statues
The Monkey Mystery
Night of Terror
The Deserted Village
Treasure of the Incas
Mystery of the Incas
The Runaway Robot

---

80 *TV People*
81 *Ibid*
82 *Ibid*

The Human Bomb
Ghost Wolf
Unknown People

There has always been interest as to why Phyllis would leave *Superman*. The truth is the series was in hiatus until the show had a sponsor, and that took almost a year to nail down. (Kellogg's breakfast cereals came through). Phyllis had a series of answers; at first, she just alluded to not wanting to be typecast. Another that she was drinking too much, but at the Charlotte Film Fair one year, she told the audience she "Had the hots" to continue comedy and the opportunity presented itself by joining up with Hollywood movie star Jack Carson and Allen Jenkins for a television series.

It would seem to be an instant hit sharing the small screen with such a confirmed star. In those early days of television, the movie studios let it be known that to jump into a rivalry for the American entertainment would border on desertion.

Phyllis had the professional respect of her fellow actors and most prominent was George Reeves. It was he that insisted to the producers that the name "Phyllis Coates" was right below his on the ending credits. Phyllis had no idea of that and was surprised when Reeves accomplished it.

Author Gary Grossman interviewed *Superman* director Tommy Carr for his book: *Superman Serial to Cereal*. He praised Phyllis:

> Phyllis read those lines with great arrogance; she had a strong sense of the bitchy character that was important for Lois Lane's credibility. She was a much better actress than the part or lines called for. I used her in westerns, and I'd tell her just once and she'd get it. She could handle most anything.[83]

While everyone was waiting for the TV debut of *Adventures of Superman*, Phyllis kept herself busy. She had to; money was not coming in from her husband the musician who was still overseas swinging it with the band. There were whispers that Mr. Nelms

---

[83] Grossman, Gary. Superman from Serial to Cereal. Big Apple Film Series, Popular Library New York. 1976

was having an affair with an Egyptian woman somewhere in the hot sands of Africa.

As a result of untold expenses, Phyllis committed herself to many television and movie roles; she didn't have the time or money to see if the new *Superman* series would amount to anything. One of those examples was *Craig Kennedy- Criminologist (Fugitive Money)*. For one day's worth of shooting, Phyllis made $55.00 (per day according to a contract she signed pertaining to June 21-June 28, 1951). While that may seem like a mere pittance in today's economy, $55.00 was not bad for a day's work when many in the work force would be fortunate to earn $8.00 per day.[84] The minimum wage in 1952 was only .75 cents an hour, and $55.00 could buy you a whole month of groceries for the family. Or, depending on one's priorities, a $55.00 dollar payday could buy fifty drinks for everyone at the Cock 'n Bull restaurant along with leaving a big tip.

To further the perspective of wages earned by actors in that era, Producer Kit Parker of Kit Parker Films said that independent producer Robert L. Lippett Jr. was "Very tight in salary for his limited productions."[85] Parker has seen contracts for as little as $3.00 an hour and the "actors were happy to get it."[86]

The *Craig Kennedy-Criminologist* television series starred Donald Woods who scientifically solved his cases. He didn't have to use a gun but got confessions and solved cases by matching scientific evidence. Woods had a long career in film starting in the 1930s and was prevalent in radio as well. The medium of television was perfect for him although *Craig Kennedy-Criminologist* only lasted one season.

In viewing this episode of *Fugitive Money*, Phyllis plays the role of Natalie Larkin, a gun moll. She must have been working simultaneous with the *Superman* series because she is wearing the same outfit as her Lois Lane character, albeit with a "tough egg" persona.

---

84 Contract for Phyllis Coates artist July 1951
85 Conversation with Kit Parker with author 2023
86 Ibid

Chapter Five
Life Gets in the Way

With Clayton Moore in "Jungle Drums of Africa" (1953)

1952 WAS ALSO THE YEAR of the long-awaited debut on television of *Death Valley Days*. This series had a long run on radio for fourteen years. Phyllis played one of the pioneer women (Virginia Arcane) in the first episode called, *How Death Valley Got its Name*. It was shot in the 120-degree heat of Death Valley in July. The pilot episode was based on the original autobiography of William Manly who wrote *Death Valley in '49*[87] This program aired on

---

[87] Manly, William Lewis <u>Death Valley in '49</u> The Pacific Tree and Vine Co. San Jose, California 1894

October 3, 1952 and was introduced by "The Old Ranger." In the years ahead, Phyllis would perform in seven different episodes of this long-lasting series until 1964.

On May 5th of that same year, *The Files of Jeffrey Jones* premiered. This was a new filmed series of a private detective, starring Don Haggerty. The innovated plot line took the viewers with him from the crime to the solution in each case. Phyllis Coates was in two of them: *The Healthy Corpse* and *No Weeds for the Widow*. Phyllis was the widow.

Phyllis also lent female support for the western TV series, *The Range Rider* which starred former stuntman Jock Mahoney and child actor Dickie Jones. Phyllis was in two of the half-hour filmed shows: *Trail of the Lawless* (as Doris Burton) and *Pale Horse* (as Jane Tracy). Phyllis remembered "Jock" as a fun-loving guy and a prankster."88 Mahoney's character was described as having "a reputation for fairness, fighting ability, and accuracy with his guns and was known far and wide, *even by Indians.*"

As usual, Phyllis co-starred with George O'Hanlon for three more entries of the *Behind the Eight Ball* film series: *So You Want to Go to a Convention, So You Never Tell a Lie, So, You Want to Wear the Pants.*

In addition, Phyllis was in the following feature: *Invasion USA.* This is a quasi-science fiction- themed yarn that takes place at a bar where people sitting around exchange "what if" scenarios if the United States was under attack by a nuclear war. It was almost like a future *Twilight Zone* episode in that the viewer wasn't sure if the predictions were true or not. In one of the scenarios, Phyllis played Mrs. Mulfory, a mother with many children, who was in a car when catastrophe hits. The car is upended by a tsunami and as the camera tilts, we hear screaming and can assume death awaits. Ironically, Noel Neill also had a small role. However, the two Lois Lanes of *Superman* fame did not share a scene, and it is likely they didn't know the other was in the same film.

Phyllis continued making western features through the year. She made two with Whip Wilson: *The Gunman, Wyoming Roundup,* and two more with Wild Bill Elliott: *Canyon Ambush* and *Fargo.*

---

88 Conversation with author

Supporting Elliott in *Fargo* was Myron Healey, Fuzzy Knight. Phyllis (as Kathy MacKenzie) played the daughter of a rancher.

In an interview by Joe Collura, Phyllis told him: "The quickie B-westerns I made at Monogram were each shot in about six days each. The main concern there was to light the cowboy star's hat and his horse—the heck with the leading lady."[89]

An exception to Phyllis' steady diet of westerns is *Flat Top*. This is a war picture that took place on an aircraft carrier. It was another Monogram production; this time, as Dorothy Collier, she is married to the star of the picture, Sterling Hayden. Phyllis was only in one scene for a whopping thirty seconds, holding their new infant while reading a letter from home. When this film was released, the country was relishing *Adventures of Superman* on TV. Phyllis certainly didn't want to look like "Lois Lane" for this color feature. She had chopped most of her hair and dyed it blonde.

The inclusion of Phyllis is noteworthy only because *Variety* informed their readers that Phyllis Coates made a personal appearance at the Four-Star Theater in Los Angeles. As part of the promotion there was a 45-foot model aircraft carrier as a lobby display for the film.

It was big doings for the premier of the picture: it was held in San Diego aboard the aircraft carrier USS Princeton. Phyllis Coates, who was the only female player in *Flat Top*, lent a hand in the promotion aboard the special Santa Fe train taking a Hollywood entourage of "100 movie personalities" to San Diego and was met by the mayor.[90]

> Scheduled to accompany Phyllis Coates were Sterling Hayden, Richard Carlson, Scott Brady, Hillary Brooke, Dan Duryea, Wayne Morris, Virginia Grey, Gale Storm, Peggy Castle, Rita Moreno, Donna Reed, Karen Sharpe, Helene Stanley, Elena Verdugo, and Helen Westcott.

In the independent feature film *The Maverick*, a rampaging story of the old West and shot at the Ray Corrigan Ranch in Simi Valley, California, Wild Bill Elliott starred as Lt. Pete Devlin, Myron

---

89 *Classic Images* September 2015
90 *San Diego Union* Nov 11, 1952

Healey as Sergeant Frick, and Rand Brooks as Trooper Barnham. Phyllis played Della Watson, and Florence Lake (Edgar Kennedy's wife in dozens of his *Average Man* comedy film series) is "Grandma Watson," Phyllis' mother.

Phyllis' character drove a covered wagon and tries to merge with Elliott's unit, but Elliott refuses to allow them to accompany the detail. Feisty Phyllis throws out the line, "It's a free country" and joins anyway, citing freedom to travel the same road. Lots of drama ensues but it is the old formula: "Boy meets girl-boy arrests girl-girl redeems herself-picture ends with a hint of a budding romance."

The Maverick was helmed by Thomas Carr who was directing the TV series episodes of *Adventures of Superman* during this year. It was released on December 14, 1952 and mostly relegated to a companion feature in a double bill.

Clothes Stolen from Actress Phyllis Coates.

In real life, sometimes even little news items can tell us what was going on in people's lives. This incident was no publicity stunt; Phyllis was victimized by crooks stealing her belongings from a parked car. The details were taken from a Sheriff's Office log.

> Television actress Phyllis Coates yesterday reported to deputy sheriffs that thieves who broke into her automobile stole nearly $800.00 worth of clothing and luggage she had packed for a trip to Las Vegas. The actress who lives at 1016 N. Hudson Avenue said her car was parked at a restaurant at 27380 W. Pacific Coast Highway, Malibu, at the time of the theft. The thieves gained entrance to the 1950 convertible coupe by breaking a window.[91]

Marriage Trouble

It was apparent early that this new marriage had its challenges. Phyllis was working almost daily in the business and when work did present itself to Robert Nelms, it was during the evening. They

---

91 *Los Angeles Times* November 3, 1952

had a special needs child that they both loved, but differences of opinion flared.

Nelms left home on November 19, 1951 ostensibly to work as a musician in Europe. It is unclear if he traveled with a band or was a solo artist. He headed east and on December 6 of that year departed New York on the SS Ile de France. The vessel was described as a luxury ocean liner.

In that article "Superman's Girlfriend" from 1953, Phyllis told the interviewer about going to the "Santa Monica Beach every sunny Sunday" with her young daughter. She still brought her wandering husband into the conversation. "The Pacific Ocean is the best swimming pool in the world. When Bob gets back, we may rent a cabana."[92]

Nelms had been gone for over a year before he returned, and Phyllis was way past holding a candle in the window. Their daughter had been missing out of daddy's presence, and Phyllis had to work full time to pay the bills. The *Los Angeles Times* informed their readers:

> Lois Lane, of television's "Superman" series, yesterday divorced jazz pianist Robert Nelms, because, she said, he told her he needed his freedom to develop his art. The attractive blonde said Nelms took a generous sampling of freedom a year after their marriage by dashing off to Europe for several months, and sending her letters detailing his romances with other women.[93]

The peripatetic Robert Nelms returned from Europe on the S.S. Neptunia from Bremerhaven, Germany. He arrived in New York on July 13, 1953. There was no welcoming committee to greet him. More specifically, he was not allowed into the house. The two were only married one year, nine months and twenty-seven days when Phyllis (under her legal name of Gypsie Ann Stell) and her attorney maintained that such conduct constituted cruelty. While her husband was touring Europe he wrote her about his love life with other women, including an Egyptian dancer.

---

92 *TV People December*, 1953 Mark Goodman publisher
93 *Los Angeles Daily News* October 2, 1953

Miss Coates told Superior Court Judge Allen T. Lynch that her husband wanted her to live with him permanently in Europe because "he felt artists had greater freedom there and the public better appreciated musical effort." Phyllis said, under prompting by Attorney S.S. Hahn, that she believed America held equal promise for artists and that she wanted to raise her daughter as an American"[94]

Nelms did not answer the complaint. Since the defendant didn't contest or show up to court, it was easy for the judge to make his ruling: "A default on cruelty grounds." Judge Allen Lynch ordered the defendant to pay the plaintiff for the support of their minor child $60.00 a month.[95] Nelms actually got off easy. Phyllis was making her own money and didn't need the musician's unstable income; she waived alimony payments. Phyllis was awarded custody of their child and reasonable visiting rights were set up. The final judgment of divorce was dated October 1, 1953.

Phyllis was quoted in the press:

> He thought no musician should be burdened by the responsibility of married life. He returned two months ago, but only to tell me he had no intention of coming back to me. I think he is now in South Africa.[96]

Daddy Nelms did keep in touch with his daughter, Christopher, the rest of his life. He continued a music career and professed a never-ending love for her mom. He died in 1994.

Once again, Phyllis would be more than busy in 1953. She was cast in a Paramount picture that starred Bob Hope in, *Too Many Girls*. Paramount put out a press release on the subject:

> Phyllis Coates has been signed as a wise-cracking chorus girl in Paramount's new musical comedy "Here Comes the Girls, the studio announced yesterday, October 29, 1953. She will play the role of Phyllis, backstage pal of Rosemary Clooney in the colorful, star-studded movie.

---

94 *Los Angeles Herald Express* October 1, 1953
95 Interlocutory Judgment of Divorce October 1, 1953
96 *Los Angeles Times* October 2, 1953

A well-known movie and TV actress in Hollywood, she landed the part after racking up impressive credits in television's "Superman" series, the film shorts, "Joe McDoakes series" with George O'Hanlon, "Flat Top" with John Hodiak, and "Back to Broadway" with Virginia Mayo.

She joins a cast at Paramount headed by Bob Hope, Rosemary Clooney, Arlene Dahl and Tony Martin. Also set for the Technicolor musical is Millard Mitchell, Robert Strauss, Johnny Downs and Fred Clark. Paul Jones produces "Here Come the Girls" for Paramount with Claude Binyon directing.

It should be noted that I watched an extant version of this film, but the scene describing Phyllis as a, "wise-cracking chorus girl" was not in the version I saw. It is also likely that the scene was cut. Phyllis is undistinguishable from the many other chorus girls in the rest of the movie.

One of Phyllis' TV appearances this year was again on *Death Valley Days*: "Solomon in All His Glory." Phyllis played Margie McMahon, a woman's columnist in an old western town. The leading man was played by James Griffith who at one time was an editor for another newspaper. He succumbed to alcohol and chronic drunkenness; he redeemed himself in Phyllis' character's eyes as he risked his life to save a boy who fell down a shaft.

The "Old Ranger" vouched at the beginning of this episode that it "was a true story." It was good to see Phyllis as a journalist, something her Lois Lane character excelled in. This was broadcast on October 27, 1953, right when *Adventures of Superman* found itself back on primetime.

Newcomer Makes Western

Despite *The Rocky Mount Telegram*'s interesting lead-in to the article, Phyllis was no longer a newcomer to westerns. It is absurd to characterize Phyllis at this point in her career as a "newcomer." She had been in the movies and TV since 1948. In 1950, she was the leading lady in *The Cisco Kid* (TV) and a Whip Wilson film before, but this was a Republic Studio release and they apparently didn't acknowledge the other westerns in town.

The Rocky Mount Telegram (North Carolina) mentioned this film and described Phyllis as "beautiful and blonde, who portrays the leading feminine role opposite western star Rocky Lane in Republic's new thriller, *Marshall of Cedar Rock*."[97]

Interestingly, Phyllis divulged in that *Rocky Mount Telegram* newspaper article that her early ambitions were in the writing field and she served an apprenticeship on her high school paper. That fact is unconfirmed, but a future career in journalism sounds like the perfect fit for the future "Lois Lane."[98]

Marshall of Cedar Rock was another Republic western that runs just under one hour. It stars Allen "Rocky" Lane. Phyllis plays Martha Clark. It was released February 1, 1953 right in the middle of *Adventures of Superman* television run. Ironically, this picture had half the cast of *Superman*: John Hamilton (The Chief) and Robert Shayne (Inspector Henderson). The only ones missing were Jimmy Olsen and the big guy himself. Perhaps an alternative title could have been: "Rocky Lane Meets Lois Lane" ... or perhaps not.

It seems that westerns were Phyllis' bread and butter during the early years; but they weren't her favorite genre. Nonetheless, it was work. In *El Paso Stampede*, Phyllis is Alice Clark. In this one, Allan Lane goes undercover to find cattle rustlers. In the meantime, he romances Alice and saves her from kidnappers.

Topeka has Bill Elliott, Fuzzy Knight, and a Davy Crocket character. Phyllis plays Marian Harrison, Fuzzy Knight's character's daughter. This is the last movie where Phyllis' character was someone's daughter.

In April of 1953, it was announced in the show business bible *Variety*, that a new series was slated for the fall season called: *Here Comes Calvin*. The situation comedy starred Jack Carson as an old vaudeville actor, "Calvin Potts," with Allen Jenkins his manager. Phyllis was to be a regular on the show as Calvin's long-time suffering girlfriend, Connie. It also had in the cast Mabel Albertson

---

97 *The Rocky Mount Telegram* May 10 1953
98 *Ibid*

as Phyllis' stern mother who was suspicious of Calvin's hesitancy to marry her daughter. It was produced by Desilu ... so what could go wrong?

This only one episode (actually a pilot) featured Calvin trying to make some easy money in a goldmine venture. He coaxed everyone in for a "sure thing," then pulled out at the last second only to realize it wasn't a scam after all.

Phyllis felt certain this was the way to go in her career with an established Hollywood leading man and solid character actor support to make for a lasting television program. This series was a chance to shed her "Superman/Lois Lane" association and establish herself with a different role; she even dyed her hair blonde for the part. Phyllis told this author that Jack Carson "got sick" and couldn't commit to the rest of the series. It finally aired in 1954 under *General Electric Theater*, where it died a painless death. Of note, Jack Carson continued steady work without missing a beat. Later that year he starred in his own TV variety program, *The Jack Carson Show* that lasted two years.

The Lone Ranger

Actor Clayton Moore has always been associated with the television role of "*The Lone Ranger*" (1949-1951 and 1954-1957), but during the television season of 1952-1953 he was in a contract dispute with the producers of the show. The suits thought that all they had to do was hire another actor, put him in the same outfit of mask and horse, and no one would know the difference. They hired John Hart as the masked man and saved a few bucks by not giving Moore a raise. The switch was well publicized so it was no secret. One thing they didn't count on was the viewing public noticed the difference, the voice was all wrong. The sponsors noticed the difference as well.

Phyllis was in two episodes of *The Lone Ranger* during this time with John Hart in the lead. Hart had the right physique and possessed a solid background in westerns. He was born in 1917 and started his acting career on stage at the famed Pasadena Playhouse. After the war, the WWII veteran landed a leading role in Columbia's "*Jack Armstrong*" serial in 1947. This was after the radio version, and Hart played a more mature "All American Boy" in science fiction exploits.

Hart performed in fifty-six episodes of *The Lone Ranger* and Phyllis was in two of them, *The Perfect Crime* (as Naomi Courtwright) and *Stage to Estacado* (as Ann Wyman). Phyllis and Hart were also in the same film, *The Longhorn*, in late 1951 but they didn't share a scene. However, they did share a brief romance and it appears it was during the time after Phyllis' husband (Nelms) was absent from his husband obligations.

In the book *Jock Mahoney: The Life and Films of a Hollywood Stuntman* by Gene Freese, it was briefly mentioned that Phyllis Coates was "John Hart's girlfriend."[99] Further proof comes from the Lone Ranger himself, Clayton Moore. In his autobiography published in 1998, he wrote that John Hart visited Phyllis on location and wound up in the movie himself.

Phyllis' first daughter, Christopher, told me she fondly remembered John Hart's grandmother. She was often her babysitter over at the house, and she sat in her lap while being read to.

Jungle Drums of Africa (1953)

So just what was Clayton Moore doing while absent from his iconic role of the Lone Ranger? He took the leading role in a Republic film serial, *Jungle Drums of Africa,* and it co-starred Phyllis Coates. This time she played "Carol Bryant," the daughter of a medical missionary in Africa after her father died. There were twelve chapters to this serial and if anyone was curious what the Lone Ranger actor looked like without his mask, this is the place. His character in full-faced glory is named "Alan King." Clayton went by the name of "Clay Moore" in references to the film. In the years after, Phyllis always called him "Clay." In this cliffhanger, he is a mining engineer developing a uranium mine.

In addition to the film footage, there were plenty of movie posters and lobby cards prominently on display featuring both of the lead stars. One of the taglines to the original poster read, "Jungle Thrills and Voodoo Madness in the Heart of the Dark Continent."

---

99 Freese, Gene. The Life and Times of a Hollywood Stuntman McFarland& Co., Inc. Jefferson, North Carolina, and London. 2013

There are a couple of crooks after uranium, secret agents after oil, and the requisite witch doctor tying the plots together.

As with serials of this type, there were snakes, beasts, spear-chucking natives, quicksand and lots of stock footage from earlier Republic serials. One such example was footage from "Perils of Nyoka." Each serial chapter featured a cliff-hanging segue to the next. It is a chuckle to see Phyllis' character save Moore from certain doom in a couple of the chapters; I don't think he was particularly keen to that image. However, Moore certainly had opportunities to save Phyllis a few times as well.

This serial was shot in fourteen days in September and October 1952, with most footage filmed at Republic Studios and the Iverson Ranch in Chatsworth. In his autobiography written in 1998, Clayton Moore mentioned working with Phyllis on this serialized entry.

> My co-star was Phyllis Coates, we both knew how silly *Jungle Drums* was, and we frequently broke up at the ridiculous situations. The special effects consisted of prop men just out of camera range throwing earth and arrows and spears at us. In one scene Phyllis was supposed to be sucked through a wind tunnel. They just tied a rope around her ankles and pulled her through.[100]

Terry and the Pirates - *The Green God* ... Georgia Pettigrew

This was a half-hour TV show starring John Baer brought to the small screen from the comic pages of newspapers since 1934. The main character was named Terry Lee: "A wide-awake American boy." He was a pilot during the war and afterwards worked for the government in the post-war territories. In this episode Phyllis' character is Georgia Pettigrew, a local dancer at the Blue Dragon, and a sweet talking "Gorgeous doll." Actually, she is a gun-wielding embezzler who pulls a gun on Terry for a showdown at the conclusion. She wants the priceless black necklace and warns him and his co-pilot, "*I not only can sing and dance; I can shoot and fly a*

---

[100] Moore, Clayton. Thompson, Frank. <u>I Was That Masked Man</u> Taylor Trade Publishing 1998

plane too." Phyllis hits all the notes here as a terrific actress in this little seen entry.

Perils of the Jungle 1953

This is a feature production from 1953 taking advantage of a jungle set, starring famed lion tamer Clyde Beatty. The set looks like *Gilligan's Island* and most of the wild beasts were filmed from someone other than the crew and edited into this. The only exceptions were when Beatty uses his stock-in-trade-whip and chair to get the lions to escape a fire. He also traps a gorilla in a in a man-made pit. Phyllis is "Jo Carter" here; she is in the business to sell wild animals that she has caged. She looks like Lois Lane as though she walked into this set from *Superman*. They don't give her much to do and she is gone during the second half of the film.

This film was made at the height of Clyde Beatty's career. He was not only a performer, and animal trainer, he owned several circuses. He also had a radio show and was in nine films over his career.

Myrt and Marge

Another unusual entry in Phyllis' career was the filmed half-hour television show, *Myrt and Marge*, a popular radio soap opera during 1931-1946. The radio show had a good run but ran its course. This was a show that Phyllis had followed through her growing up years, so she was thrilled to play the part of "Marge" (the younger sister) for the camera. She was associated with the project as far back as April 4, 1949 when the *Los Angeles Evening Citizens News* printed: "Phyllis Coates has been signed to play Marge in the video film version of *Myrt and Marge*." It is unknown when this project was shot, but it surfaced on television during the summer season of 1953.

TV listings of the day identified this program thusly: "The newest radio veteran to be readied for television is Myrtle Vail's familiar *Myrt and Marge*." And another description: "*How Myrt Met Marge*," and a further description from a TV listing: "Some soap opera addicts might find this one to their liking; *Myrt and Marge-*

--it has everything from Franklin Pangborn to a stray horse. It's a tale of a stage-struck young lady in New York, based on the famous radio pair of the 1930s."

There are filmed copies of this one-time program in existence and it featured a delightful sequence of Phyllis dancing. It is believed to have been shot at the old Hal Roach Studios.

Abbott and Costello Show- *Cheapskates*

The old Hal Roach Studios was also the place where Bud and Lou filmed their television series. In 1953 during the second and last season for the show, Phyllis Coates brightened up an episode called *Cheapskates*. As "Millie," Phyllis is a gun moll who vamps Lou Costello in search of hidden diamonds. She is cheek to cheek with Lou trying to get him under her spell.

Las Vegas

Phyllis told me in later years that shortly after making this guest appearance on their show, she was in Las Vegas at the same time Bud and Lou were performing. There they were at a crap table at one of the hotels. Phyllis said they were blowing money playing the game; she said she counted $22,000 in losses in the short-time she was watching. At one point they recognized her, "It's Phyllis!" and gave her a big hug. She said they were pleasantly sloshed and started "pinching my boobs." She was distressed about how much money they were losing, but Abbott tried to reassure her. "This isn't our money, it's the house's money. We're entertaining the people." When recounting this story, Phyllis said to me, "What I could have done with that money."

Return to Stage Work

In 1954, Phyllis had an opportunity to return briefly to her true love: performing in front of an audience on the stage. The play was called, *Blaze of Glory,* and it was performed at the Laguna Summer Theatre, at Laguna Beach, California on July 27th of that year.

This play was reviewed by Edwin Schallert of the *LA Times* who hated the play, but not the actors. It involved a returning veteran of the war, murder, and labor disturbances in which "commies" were involved. Phyllis was lumped in with the other actors in the reviewer's assessment, "The cast headed by Alex Nicol, Lynn Bart, Olive Blakeney, and Phyllis Coates do notably good work for the most part. Miss Coates achieves a sympathetic impression."[101]

Blaze of Glory was a common expression back in those days. Interestingly, Lou Costello in his solo period of 1958 performed in *Blaze of Glory* as a plumber in a television appearance. It had no relation to the play plot.

Gunfighters of the Northwest

This is another film serial that Phyllis was in and shared billing with Jock Mahoney (as Sgt. Ward) and Clayton Moore (as Constable Braum Nevin, Sgt. Ward's sidekick). It pits the Canadian Mounted Police against "The White Horse Rebels" and was filmed at Big Bear Lake. Phyllis plays Rita Carville and John Hart played Sgt. Dan Wells.

The fifteen chapters featured all the usual cliffhangers, pitfalls and dangerous perils, all shot entirely outside with no interior sets. Constable Ward is assigned to track down a dangerous criminal known only as "The Leader." Trying to locate a gold mine, The Leader pits the Mounties against the Indians.

The whole production was shot within thirty days. Clayton Moore had nice things to say about the experience in his autobiography.[102] "The whole cast and crew lived in a rustic hotel. Everyone became close, like a family."[103] What Clayton Moore said about the experience of closeness with everyone is exactly the sentiment Phyllis had with her fellow actors and why she was drawn to the profession. She lamented that fact years later when she "settled down" as a doctor's wife.

Continuing onto television, in the hopes of being part of a solid continuous part, Phyllis was part of the cast of *Professional Father*. It debuted on CBS February 26, 1955 and was a family situation comedy. It starred Steve Dunn as the father and professional child

---

101 *Los Angeles Times* July 30, 1954
102 Moore, Clayton. 1998 I Was the Masked Man Taylor Trade Publishing
103 *Ibid*

psychologist. His wife was Barbara Billingsley (obviously before her *Leave it to Beaver* role). Phyllis played Nurse Marge Allen in four episodes to the doctor's character. The show was trashed by the critics who weren't entertained that this professional father could manage his office patients but couldn't handle his own children. It lasted one season.

Also in 1955, Phyllis landed what looks to be a one-day gig in a famous early television program called *The Millionaire*. In this one, Phyllis plays a fiancé to an "innocent man" who was condemned to death for a murder. He has a few hours left of his life to prove he's not guilty. A check that comes to him for one million dollars gives him funds to "outwit his unethical lawyer."

Norman Tokar (1919-1979)

Director Norman Tokar was of Russian heritage and born in New Jersey. He had a busy life acting on stage and behind the camera. As a child actor, he performed on Broadway and played Henry Aldrich on the radio when the original actor went in the service. After wartime service, he helmed many early television shows after which he specialized in Disney movies for the big screen. Tokar was married before and had one child with his former wife.

In 1954 Phyllis and Tokar met and started dating pretty seriously. Phyllis was eight years his junior. Things didn't exactly start off on the right foot as Tokar's over-protective mother tried to influence her son against Phyllis. "She even hired a private investigator to investigate [Phyllis'] past."[104] According to family lore, Norman's mother was suspicious of Phyllis and tried to interfere with the relationship. It didn't work.

The two got married on August 27, 1955 at the director's spacious residence overlooking the Pacific Ocean.

> Phyllis Coates, co-star* of *The Great Gildersleave*[sic] and *Superman* television shows, today was married to Columbia Broadcasting System producer-director Norman

---

104 This according to Phyllis' second daughter, Laura Press in an interview with the author

Tokar in his home at nearby Malibu Beach. Scores of motion picture and TV celebrities will be on hand for the ceremony and reception.[105]

*Phyllis was in only one episode: *Gildy Goes Diving*. She gives the star a kiss for his new political ambitions.

Director Norman Tokar had a wide and varied career on television to include the first ninety-three directing duties of the *Leave it to Beaver* episodes (1957-1960). Phyllis was on one entry: *The New Neighbors*. The plot spotlighted Beaver having a crush on Betty Donaldson (Phyllis), the wife of his new neighbors. Phyllis' character rewarded the Beaver with a kiss on the cheek after he gave her a box of chocolates. Wally's friend, Eddie Haskell (in his first appearance in the series), lets the Beaver know that her jealous husband is going to "cream him." According to Phyllis, there was talk of keeping the neighbors as permanent characters, but somehow it didn't work out.

During the time of their marriage, Phyllis and Norman enjoyed a substantial income and were living at 9884 Carmelita Avenue in Beverly Hills. The house was built in 1942, had four bedrooms and five baths with 4,086 square feet of living space, all on 30 acres on land.

The Frontier - *King of the Dakotas*

Tom Tryon and Phyllis played the Marquis and Marquise de Mores. It was a two-episode drama telling the story of a French nobleman who carved a feudal empire out of the Dakota Badlands in the 1880's. He amassed a huge fortune before being driven out by avenging cattlemen whose lands he had appropriated. Alan Hale Jr. and Raymond Bailey who became famous in the 1960's for their roles as "The Skipper" on *Gilligan's Island*, and as "Mr. Drysdale" on *The Beverly Hillbillies*, were in this production.

---

105 *The Pomona Progress Bulletin* August 27, 1955

Lassie/Jeff's Collie *The School*

Phyllis played the new schoolteacher (Miss Vernon) in this half-hour staple television show in 1955. It takes place in a rural school that the local kids go to. The conflict begins when the new teacher assigns different desks for the students, and it becomes more of a challenge when the teacher bans all their dogs from sitting in the classroom. Misadventures ensue when the schoolhouse almost burns down, but all is well when the teacher allows the children to bring their dogs back in, to include the teacher's own little collie puppy happily sitting in the teacher's desk drawer.

Of interest in this episode is Robert Maxwell, listed as a co-producer. *Lassie* was his series to produce, and he undoubtedly hand-selected Phyllis for the part. Maxwell was also one of the producers for the first season of *Adventures of Superman*.

Phyllis continued pouring into her work on television; in 1955 she was in a 30-minute comedy called *Willy and El Flamenco*. Phyllis didn't get to play an ethnic character very often, but in this one she played Betty Estrada and is married to Romon Estrada. The comedy starred June Havoc as "Willy Dodger," who in this case tries to solve the marital problems of a Spanish dancer and his wife.

Also in the same year, Phyllis was cast in the popular situation comedy *Topper*. This was actually a spin-off of a film of the same name made by Hal Roach Studios from 1937. The TV version starred Leo G. Carroll as Cosmo Topper, the vice-president of his bank. He is constantly and mischievously bothered by a couple of ghosts whose afterlife he is responsible for. The ghosts mean well, but they always seem to complicate matters for the old boy.

This episode was called, *King Cosmo the First*. The plot slightly borrows from Mark Twain's *The Prince and the Pauper* in that there seems to be a strikingly resemblance to Topper to the fictional King of Borokovia. The King's loyal executive (played by the always entertaining Phil Van Zandt) maneuvers Topper to a local hotel suite to substitute for the King; there is danger involved, and that is why the King has relocated.

As Topper is getting comfortable getting on with getting bank papers organized, a visitor's door opens from the suite's boudoir. Enter the King's royal mistress; it is a brunette-haired Phyllis Coates wearing a robe with exposed legs. She is determined to distract the King to play with her, and she is not discouraged. Phyllis is a standout while vamping the alleged King until it all becomes clear this was a merry mix-up. Phyllis loved playing comedy and this was a good example.

The Lone Ranger-*Woman in the White Mask*

This episode is one of the most popular and it was dusted off from the original radio broadcast with the same title but different actors. Phyllis is the white-masked villainess who robs stage coaches to supplement her expenses running her ranch. To help with the disguise, she dons a brunette wig, large earrings and speaks with a Mexican accent. She in financial disarray when she was cheated out of money that her late father was a victim of. She has employed loyal cowboys to help with the ranch…and also robbing. One of her cowhands had an itchy trigger finger and shot the stagecoach rider in the shoulder despite Phyllis' character's (Jane Johnson) directions to "not hurt anyone."

Clayton Moore as the Lone Ranger is more than brave and resourceful, he figures out the villainess' horse tracks and confronts her, leading to this almost flirtatious exchange:

> **The Lone Ranger**: *"Perhaps we'll meet again?"*
>
> **Phyllis as Jane Johnson** (disguised in her white mask): *"It is entirely possible. But in the meantime, Senor, if you are wise, you will chase something that you can catch."*

A happy ending ensues when the masked man saves one of Jane's cowhands from certain death, and finds that she actually has money owed to her from her late father's estate. This was the third episode where Phyllis lent her talent to the series.

Chapter Six
Panther Girl of the Kongo

This Republic serial featured earthquakes, snakes, apes, escapes, cheesecake, outbreaks, outtakes, retakes, mistakes, headaches…and chaffed legs.

It is now 1955 and Phyllis is an in-demand talent. One could conceivably go to the cinema and see Phyllis Coates on the screen in a serial, short film, and feature. She was cast in one of the last film serials ever made, *Panther Girl of the Kongo*. Though it was not her first serial, it was the first time that Phyllis was the "star" of any production.

Panther Girl of the Kongo was one of the last movie serials ever put up on the screen. Serials, once a staple of the movie going experience, were definitely on the way out with double features taking up the bill; television further encroached on the moviegoers' experience.

Phyllis Coates played Jean the Panther Girl, an anthropologist and wildlife photographer, the main character in this series. The natives call her "Panther Girl." Dr. Morgan uses his crawfish mutations to scare people away from his diamond mine. Giant crawfish claws were prominent throughout the series and are almost laughable. Phyllis had to be a good actress to register fear at these subpar effects.

As the star, Phyllis had to work hard and was in almost every action shot. Though, admittedly, a lot of the footage of Phyllis swinging through the vines and doing somersaults in the air was carefully edited with stock footage. The scenes of lions, snakes and the inevitable quicksand were deliciously on display.

Phyllis has often since been referred to as "The Last of the Serial Queens." It began shooting on August 16, 1954 and ended on September 4th. The twelve chapters often utilized stock footage to reduce production costs. Phyllis wore a short "Jungle costume" that would make most mini-skirts look conservative. In fact, it was the same costume worn by Frances Gifford in the 1941 *Jungle Girl* serial. Both serials were shot at Republic Studios. The idea of slinking through the jungle without leggings makes one itch.

One of the uncredited stars of *Panther Girl of the Kongo* was the elephant, Emma. She was first on screen for *Soul of the Beast* (1923) in which she was named "Oscar." She was housed at the Selig Zoo and used in numerous Tarzan movies and others.

Phyllis loved the animal and it bonded with her. She was expected to ride on Emma throughout the serial, so Phyllis insisted to shoot all her scenes with the elephant out of sequence. "Once I got on top of her, I wasn't going to get off and on again." With her short dress, Phyllis felt the coarse hairs on her thighs which chaffed horribly.

In an interview with author Gary Grossman, in regards to the infamous man-made swamp at Republic Studios, Phyllis told him: "The assistant directors took health precautions when they dragged us out and gave everyone a shot of penicillin. And believe me, that didn't make the swamp any more popular."[106]

"Who knew elephants had hairs?"
—Phyllis Coates to author

One of the most memorable scenes from the serial was when the natives tie Phyllis Coates to a tree to sacrifice her to a killer gorilla. The gorilla was played by Steve Calvert and when the gorilla closed in on her, Phyllis' daughter Zoe Christopher, bolted from behind the set to rescue her mother. She pounded on the feet of the gorilla demanding that he not hurt her mommy. To appease the youngster, the actor took off his gorilla head, which according to Zoe, "did not help at all."

Phyllis said that the black actors playing as natives were actually jazz musicians who had to play into the wee hours of the night/day and be on the set at daybreak.

If there was an Academy Award for "Best Performance of an Actress Battling a Giant Paper- Mache Lobster Claw," Phyllis would have been triumphant.

The Man Who Beat Death

Phyllis was in an interesting TV production in January 1956 as part of ABC's *Reader's Digest* program. It starred Bill Talbert who at the time was the top champion tennis player of the era. Talbert was diagnosed with diabetes at the young age often and rose in the ranks of tennis champions during his adult years. Talbert didn't have any acting experience, but played himself in his life-long battle with his disease. On the telecast Phyllis played his ever-loving wife, Nancy.

---

106 Grossman, Gary. 1976 <u>Superman Serial to Cereal</u> Popular Library, New York

Girls in Prison

Despite the titillating title, there's no erotica in this film. Phyllis' character "Dorothy" played it as a deranged prisoner. Richard Denning played the chaplain, and Jane Darwell (Ma Joad from *The Grapes of Wrath*) was cast as the warden. An interesting footnote is that actress Adele Jergens played an inmate, she shared the screen with Phyllis back in 1950 in *Blues Busters*.

Girls in Prison was a routine prison themed genre production with clichéd characters of this ilk. It was filmed in June of 1956 when Phyllis had just found out she was pregnant.

New Son Born

Phyllis and her husband welcomed their new offspring, David Tokar born on December 18, 1956. The new addition to the family was an early Christmas present. Now Christopher (Crinker) had a baby brother to share with their parents.

Conclusion of the Behind the Eight Ball Series

1956 also marked the end of the *Behind the Eight Ball* series. It was a wonderful association with Richard Bare and George O'Hanlon. Phyllis was in twenty-nine of these funny short films, and it satisfied her craving to do comedy. She was good at it, after being broken in by Ken Murray back in 1943. Phyllis didn't play a clown, like Lucille Ball or Joan Davis. Her roles were written to provide comedy contrast to the star. She had her moments to shine, but never upstaged the main character. In *So You Want to be Pretty*, Phyllis matches comic scenes adeptly with her screen husband with hideous overbite teeth.

In the series, Phyllis could play the nagging housewife with gusto when called for. She could also be as pretty as a dream walking. A best example of that was in one of the last episodes, *So You Want to Play the Piano*. As Mrs. McDoakes, Phyllis is elegantly dressed in evening wear and glides in and out of scenes enraptured by the neighbor's classic piano playing.

There was talk of the series going to television, but nothing became of it. The creative forces would have had to put together shows of nearly one-half hour compared to the ten-minute entrees done for the cinema. They would have had to pad the content while sacrificing concentrated hilarity. O'Hanlon might have been stuck being a dopey dad, and it wouldn't have worked in the mid-1950's. Sponsors would have demanded the head of the family be of stoic stock. George O'Hanlon was a funny man and continued his career in support fashion on TV and the movies. He was awarded a star on the Hollywood Walk of Fame in 1960 for his work. Ironically, O'Hanlon did get cast as the head of the family in cartoon form. He was the dad in the futuristic TV show, *The Jetsons*, debuting in 1962.

Director Richard Bare also continued in the business helming many of the TV episodes of the 1950's and 60's. It included such standouts as *Cheyenne*, *77 Sunset Strip*, *The Twilight Zone*, *Petticoat Junction*, and *Green Acres*.

1957
Pepsodent Commercial

Phyllis was modelling on the side, including making commercials. There was a magazine photo spread of her for Pepsodent toothpaste. It also featured her daughter, Crinkle (Christopher), now seven years old. They both shared the same sink and toothy smiles while they brushed together. It was an adorable pose for both of them.

Chicago Confidential

In this feature film Phyllis played Helen Fremont, who was married to Detective Brian Keith, the star of the flick. Support was provided by Beverly Garland. A good film but Phyllis was mostly window dressing to the proceedings.

I Was a Teenage Frankenstein

> *"Whit Bissell? What you see is what you get"*
> – Phyllis Coates to author

This was a follow-up to the success of *I Was a Teenage Werewolf,* made by America International. It was not a sequel even though Whit Bissell played the same mad scientist/God-like creator, introduced as an English medical doctor bearing the surname of Frankenstein, only there is not a hint of any English or European accent. This is a fun film from beginning to end with all the campy elements of nothing making sense. Phyllis plays Whit's fiancé; why those two were romantically matched stretches credibility in itself. Whit slaps her around and treats her like a dog. He had more affection looking after his ungodly creation of a teenager already deceased from a car accident and brought back to life, albeit hideously disfigured. The good doctor has a reluctant but loyal assistant who helps him with body operations, buying equipment and tending to all matters of running a private morgue and crocodile mote.

Phyllis' character, shuttered upstairs as the doctor's secretary, is forbidden to see or inquire about the ghoulish goings on in the laboratory. Disgruntled over the lack of attention from her fiancé, she becomes curious while the doctor and his assistant are temporarily gone. In a "Pandora's Box" sequence, she makes a key and snoops around the lab and opens a morgue drawer where the teenager and his mutilated head pops up into a sitting position. Cue a Phyllis Coates' patented scream. Not sure why a now living creature was stuffed back into a morgue drawer, but the scene elicited a memorable sequence.

Now that she saw the monster's face (not a bit like Universal's Jack Pierce's make-up, which was copyright protected in any case), Phyllis' character fesses up to her insane fiancé and reassures him of her loyalty and love. Does he deserve it? No. Proving that the real monster in this picture is Whit Bissell; he feigns approval of her assertiveness, and then promptly sets her up to be killed by the monster.

The doctor summons Phyllis to help with medical assistance in the form of an injection in the teenager's arm. Her words are comforting, but she didn't know that the doctor conditioned his creation to convince him that she means to put him away for good. Having a taste of life now, Frankie Jr. doesn't want to go back to where he once belonged, and sees Phyllis as his enemy. When the doctor conveniently excuses himself from the room, he lurks just outside the door listening in to make sure his evil plan to kill his fiancé is dispatched down the hatch without a hitch.

Phyllis talks soothingly to the monster but he is hellbent on destroying her. The monster grabs her and we hear blood-curdling shrieks as she is cornered. The camera is on the doctor's face as we have to imagine what is transpiring inside the locked room. When the screaming stops, the doctor enters the room and discovers the monster was a good boy and dispensed with the fiancé by shoving her through an opening into the crocodile-infested habitat. We see the remaining clothes of hers left over from what the crocodile consumed.

All does not end well for the doctor, however, because the monster destroys its maker the same way it disposed of Phyllis. The last seconds of the movie are featured in color and also show the remnants of the doctor's garments. I think the crocodile was smiling.

During the time Phyllis was making *I Was a Teenage Frankenstein*, her alcoholic grandma was living with her. She got an unexpected call from the police and learned, "My grandmother was passed out drunk on the neighbor's front yard and I had to go get her."[107]

1958

Richard Diamond - *Another Man's Poison*

In this hit TV series starring David Janssen, we get to see Phyllis in one of her sexiest roles as Monica Freeborn. She even assertively and tantalizingly kisses the private detective and then pushes him away. Of course, Richard Diamond returns for more as the episode ends. It does spark some imagination.

Perry Mason - *The Case of the Black-Eyed Blonde*

Phyllis plays Norma Carter in this first TV version of *Perry Mason*, and she is a stinker. More specifically, a murderess, who also acts her own death scene. As Phyllis lies in a hospital bed, she

---
107 Phyllis in conversation with author

performs without makeup emphasizing her near death state without any inhibitions. Some vain actresses can't do that.

Cattle Empire

This is an "A" film western in color. It starts off with the townsfolk amusing themselves by dragging the star of the picture, Joel McCrea, though the dirt roads by a horse. It's O.K. though, because he emerges with only a scratch on his shoulder. Phyllis, as Janice Hamilton, looks after him. She is married to a prominent cattle owner who is blind. McCrea's character is John Cord and he is promptly hired by Mr. Hamilton to drive his cattle to Ft. Sumter where the herd can be sold. To accomplish this, Cord must hire the cowboys who tried to kill him, to aid him in driving the cattle. Simple.

Janice tags along to keep an eye on her husband's investments and starts to admire Cord. There are subtle overtones between them, but this is a family picture. Phyllis had certainly graduated from being a serial queen to a featured leading lady. Color enhanced her beauty.

> I admired Joel McCrea on *Cattle Empire*, but I was not comfortable in the role of a western heroine. I was a lousy rider. I only got on a horse when I had to, and got off as soon as I could. One time after a chase scene, I couldn't get my horse to stop. It ran through the cameras, the lights, the reflectors—everything![108]

In 2002, authors Michael G. Fitzgerald and Boyd Magers interviewed Phyllis for their book: *Ladies of the Western*. She had an anecdote to share about Joel McCrea during the time they were making *Cattle Empire*:

> Joel and Frances Dee had a long and happy marriage. Joel was very cute. He asked me to go to dinner one night and you don't turn down the leading man. It was really funny. He said, "I want to apologize to you." I said, "For what? Whatever could you have done to offend me?" He said, "I wanted you to know I wouldn't offer to take you to bed."

---

108 *Classic Images* September 2015

Well, my jaw dropped down. I didn't know what to say. He said he was very much in love with his wife, and he always made that clear to his leading ladies." I thought I'd die."[109]

Blood Arrow

Phyllis plays a young Mormon woman (Bess Johnson) in this feature western. Her mission is to deliver a smallpox medical serum to a Mormon settlement through warring Indian country. She meets Dan Kree (Scott Brady), a down and out scout; Brill (Paul Richards), a gambler who thinks there is gold in the Mormon Valley; and Gabe (Paul Haggerty), who is trying to find his-trapping partner. Bess promises to pay them $600.00 in gold if they escort her despite the dangers. Paul Richards plays the bad guy of the bunch, as usual for his career characterizations.

This is Alice

Phyllis landed the job as a series regular as Alice Howard's mom (who speaks with a southern accent) for this TV series filmed at Desilu. *Variety* wrote a review and instantly dismissed it. Alice was the child actor, Patty Ann Gerrity. She played a nine-year-old daughter to her parents: Tommy Farrell and Phyllis Coates. They live in the fictional town of River Glen, Georgia. In the initial episode, veteran actor Charles Coburn guests as a runaway millionaire who is mistaken for a tramp and brought home to Alice's family.

The unnamed reviewer was downright rude in panning the child actress, but mentioned "Phyllis Coates was attractive as the mother of the irritating social prodigy." In later years Phyllis described Patty Gerrity as "a very talented child actress." It was a reunion of sort for Phyllis and Tommy Farrell, who played her husband in this series. They had both worked together in a feature Western, *Outlaws of Texas* back in 1950, and in the serial *Gunfighters of the Northwest*.

---

109 Fitsgerald, Michael and Magers, Boyd. Ladies of the Western: Interviews of Fifty-One More Actresses from the Silent Era to the Television Westerns of the 1950s and 1960s. McFarland & Co. Inc. Publishers Box 611 Jefferson, North Carolina 28640. 2002

TV Guide Nov. 8, 1958

Phyllis was also in a photo spread of all the television moms in a *TV Guide* program. In a color group shot, these 1958 moms were all pictured serving or drinking coffee. They were: Barbara Billingsley, Virginia Steffen, Phyllis Coates, June Lockhart, Nan Leslie, Sallie Brophy, and even Sammee Tong from TV's *Bachelor Father*, a domestic servant for the widowed man of the house and his daughter.

Gunsmoke *Wild West*

Marshall Matt Dillon believes a little boy who tells him his pa had been kidnapped by a couple of hombres and then goes into action. Phyllis Coates was cast as "Hattie Kelly," the boy's stepmother. She had these choice words to say to Murray Hamilton (as Webb Cutter):

> **Hattie Kelly:** [upset about being left behind] You dirty rotten coward.
>
> **Web Cutter:** That's about enough Hattie.
>
> **Hattie Kelly:** I hate you. Get out. Get out! Go on, both of you get out! I wouldn't have either one of you.
>
> **Web Cutter:** Either one of us?
>
> **Hattie Kelly:** Why, you didn't think I cared did you? I would have had one of you shot the other before I was through. Mister, pie don't cut three ways.

Marriage Trouble

The marriage of Phyllis and Norman Tokar was faltering and they separated on July 28, 1958. The period from marriage and separation was only two years and eleven months. Son David was twenty months old and Christopher was eight.

Phyllis was the petitioner. The grounds for divorce were because the defendant, Norman Tokar, treated her with "extreme cruelty and has wrongfully inflicted on her grievous mental suffering so as to make living with defendant no longer tolerable."[110]

In addition to the custody of David Tokar, Phyllis and her attorney [Paul Hutchinson] petitioned for monetary support. The court document gives an insight to the real property and monies in their community assets.

> Defendant is employed as a producer and director of television programs from which he derives a substantial income in excess of $50,000.00 per year. He is well able to support the plaintiff and their minor child. Said child has no property or income of his own, and plaintiff has no property or income except her interest in the community property and except her earnings from time to time as a freelance actress on television.
>
> Plaintiff has been encouraged by her husband during their marriage to engage in such freelance acting, and at the present time she is employed. Her income from such employment consists of fees paid to her for each show in which she appears, but her contract in that regard expires September 30, 1958, and plaintiff is unable to state whether she will receive any income henceforth.[111]

Phyllis sought $1,250.00 per month for alimony and $250.00 per month for the support of their son. She also petitioned to keep the home and their 1956 Mercury station wagon (value of $2,000.00). The couple also had an interest in a shopping center at Covina, California. The house they owned in Beverly Hills was appraised at $135,000.00. The monthly payments of which were $1000.00 per month. In addition, she petitioned the court for an additional amount of $300.00 per month for gardening and swimming pool service, utilities and housekeeper, necessary in maintaining the property, the paying of taxes, insurance, utilities, and housekeeping so that "their son may have a home in which to reside."

Furthermore, a Restraining Order was asked for based on an incidence on June 1958 when the defendant committed physical

---

110 Divorce petition filed August 27, 1958
111 *Ibid*

violence on Phyllis. She described herself as "Being afraid" of Norman Tokar. The R.O. was administered immediately.

This case went to trial in Santa Monica before the honorable Judge Mark Brandler. The final divorce decree dissolving the bonds of marriage was finally granted on May 2, 1960. Phyllis essentially got all that she asked, including the defendant's costs to the attorney representing her. The house on Carmelita became the home that Christopher (and David) grew up in during their most impressionable years exploring the Beverly Hills neighborhood.

1959
Live Theater *Circle of Wheels*

This was a play that had an unusual science fiction theme and starred Gene Saks and Phyllis Coates as husband and wife. It debuted at the Horton Theater on Melrose Avenue March 6, 1959.

The *LA Times* did a small piece on it: The meaning of *Circle of Wheels* cannot be explained at this time without unveiling the intricate plot. Its director, Joseph Sargent, defines it enigmatically as a "lighthearted version of the hidden and more violent aspects of modern marriage." [112]

According to a *Variety* write-up from their opening night, it pertained to two healthy mates who "grow cogs in their livers"! "When the couple discovers their insides are being replaced by mechanical apparatus, they conclude that it's in payment of a past sin."[113] The unnamed reviewer remarked that "the actors played their roles straight and missed opportunities for laughs."[114]

There was a really cute article that columnist Allen Rich of the *Valley Times* wrote after interviewing Phyllis; it was all done tongue-in-cheek for the reading pleasure of his readers. It's a hoot.

> Miss Phyllis Coates has a regular role in *This is Alice*, seen every Tuesday night on television. She's played feature parts in practically every big network at one time or another and she currently has a well-paying job on one of

---

112 *Los Angeles Times* March 1, 1959
113 *Variety* April 1, 1959
114 *Ibid*

the top commercials. Also, a big home in Beverly Hills, complete with two children, Oriental servants, and a dog.

So, when I interviewed her, what did she want to talk about? Not TV, not commercials, but a forthcoming little theater play she is rehearsing for…it will pay peanuts.

Allen Rich: "You will never become a tycoon like Miss Lucille Ball that way," I told her.

Phyllis Coates: "Please let me tell you about the play. It is called…" She began.

Allen Rich: "This," I interrupted, "is a TV column. "Perhaps someday I will introduce you to Mr. Len Boyd, our drama editor, and he will listen to your glowing story." I considered her career. I slyly told her "I thought she was great as the girl reporter in 1953 on *Superman*."

Phyllis Coates: "Oh that," she smiled. "I've been on the really big dramatic shows since, with one exception. That exception is 'Playhouse 90'and I'm really on that, too. I also do Kleenex commercials. Well, we do three or four each shooting day. Some are 60 seconds. Some are 90 seconds. The schedule is just like for a dramatic series. I have to be at Cascade Studios at 6:30 in the morning for makeup. We start filming at 8 a.m. and we don't get through until 6 p.m. or later."

As already indicated Miss Coates appears to love her art more than money but I did manage to pry from her the information that it is not unusual for a performer to make perhaps $5,000 to $6,000 per annum for showings and reruns of each commercial. Multiply this by the three that are produced in single 12-hour span and you come up with a figure somewhere in the fancy neighborhood of $18,000…not bad for a single day's work.

Allen Rich: "And how much will you be paid for the play?"

Phyllis Coates: "Never mind. Money isn't everything. Little theater gives one a chance to grow professionally. On a TV series there's never enough time to rehearse. Why, on this play we are rehearsing six full weeks. It opens March 6 and will be seen for four consecutive weekends."

Allen Rich: "You rehearse six weeks, then only play on weekends? And you do all this for a sum I won't even mention?"

Phyllis Coates: "Yes, but you would not understand. After all you are not an actor. If you had any of the milk of human kindness you would mention the name of the play. Think of all the work these fine actors are doing. Think of the hopes we all have."

With all the bugs worked out, the play surfaced again on May 18, 1959 at the El Capitan Theater. It was the same venue where Phyllis started her career on stage with Ken Murray in 1943. The El Capitan was one of the leading theaters on the West Coast up until 1951 when NBC took a lease on the building for their national telecasts of such shows as *This is Your Life* and *The Bob Hope Show*.

The *LA Times* wrote: "Stars of the show are Tommy Noonan and Phyllis Coates. Each of them seems to bring to their role sincerity and finesse. They are both to be congratulated on jobs well done."[115]

In May the *Hollywood Reporter* quoted Producer Gertrude Marks who announced there were "negotiations for a four-week engagement coast tour,"[116] but terms and commitments weren't realized.

George "Superman" Reeves Dies June 16, 1959

"The boy is dead." Such were the cryptic words from George Reeves' ex-girlfriend Toni Mannix. Being very close friends with Phyllis, she called her at 4:30 in the morning not only to let her know, but also to recruit her to come to George's house with her.

---
115 *Los Angeles Valley Times* May 26, 1959
116 *The Hollywood Reporter* Vol. 154 issue 46 May, 1959

"There was no way I was going," Phyllis said. "I suggested she get Jack Larson to go, I had to be at the studio at 8 A.M."

Phyllis knew all the players involved; she considered George to be a close personal friend, and had good experiences with Toni Mannix who was married to Eddie Mannix, long time executive at MGM Studios.

Back in 1951 when the *Superman* series was being filmed, Toni took Phyllis under her wing, treating her for meals and health spas. She also inserted herself into Reeves' life by buying a house for him and keeping his liquor and bar well-stocked. Toni was seven years older than George and according to Phyllis, "was looking very matronly." There is no doubt that George was feeling like a "kept man." The Mannix's had championed George's career and most recently, Eddie Mannix pulled strings to get George into the Director's Guild. Eddie Mannix was now very old, suffered from health problems, and was confined to a wheelchair. He had his own mistress and according to Phyllis, "Didn't give a damn that his wife was mixed up with George." There certainly were no ill feelings toward Reeves.

George was a long-time drinker, but in those days if you weren't Ray Milland in *The Lost Weekend*, you weren't considered an alcoholic. Phyllis remembered George had an open bar in his trailer during the filming of *Superman* and was drinking "eye-openers" at 8 a.m. Worst of all, Phyllis was starting to drink as well, though nobody could keep up with George.

There were a lot of things going on in George's life leading up to his death; it was sometimes described that George suffered from chronic depression and that his moods could be higher than high or lower than low.

George Reeves died at his house, in his own bed at 1579 Benedict Canyon in Los Angeles after bawling out visitors who were partying downstairs in the wee hours of the morning. He was angry and once he retreated upstairs, he impulsively reached for his loaded firearm, aiming it at his temple. It was discovered that two bullet holes on the floor were done before that day. One of the holes was explained as a "hesitation shot," a phenomenon fairly common of suicides of this nature. The coroner's office ruled it a suicide by a single shot to his head.

The guests downstairs included the new love in his life, Leonore Lemmon. She was a dynamic and shapely young figure of a woman from New York. They were planning to get married. Leonore observed George's unsettled manner and cryptically predicted that George was "going to shoot himself." Things seemed suspicious indeed until the coroner's examination findings. How ironic is it that Leonore Lemmon's initials were "LL"? The same initials as "Lois Lane" and, for that matter, "Lana Lane," and the Lex Luther character from the *Superman* comic books.

Newspaper headlines across the country printed the actor's death on their front pages along with pictures of Superman. Phyllis went to George Reeves' funeral, and reportedly, Noel Neill did also. They neither nodded nor spoke to each other. Remarkably, there was a very low turnout. It seems incomprehensible compared to nowadays that there was so little fanfare about the memorial service. Perhaps it was because most of his fans were not adults, and certainly because of the absence of media hype. It was a period of mourning.

In happier days, Reeves was often a guest for dinner at Phyllis' house. This is confirmed by Zoe Christopher who was a young child during the 1950s. She said that the table discussion never touched on *Superman* or the series. The last time Phyllis saw Reeves was when he brought a script to her that he was going to direct. Phyllis said, "George Reeves always had faith in me, he told me that 'One day I'll help prove you can really act.'"[117]

The Incredible Petrified World (1959)

Phyllis is Dale Marshall in this clunker, and boy did she regret it. Jerry Warren directed this low budget "thriller" starring John Carradine. The water scenes were shot off the coast of Catalina. The plot had them shoot inside the Colossal Cave in Vail, Arizona. According to Phyllis, the production (such as it was) incorporated

---

117 Grossman, Gary. Superman Serial to Cereal Big Apple Film Series Popular Library New York 600 Third Ave. New York, N.Y. 1976

every member of Warren's family. She had bad memories of making this movie.

> I was talked into being in this picture as a favor to Jerry Warren; we dated when I was sixteen. Jerry assured me that no one will see this picture in California, so I did it for him for old time's sake. The cave was full of bat excrement; it was a horrible, horrible experience. I wasn't even paid. I was up for a few more parts, but this movie sunk me. I never talked to him again.–Phyllis to author

Death Valley Days - *One in a Hundred*

Phyllis gets top billing in this memorable episode. As Mary, she is a recently widowed pioneer with a sickly child. The wagon train through hostile country is supposed to be protected by an assigned cavalry officer who was just given a new repeating rifle by his supervisor. He is just a little too affectionate with his new "toy" and shoots at anything to excess, including an Indian. Mary is disgusted with him. She is more concerned with the lack of water they are all suffering from. Mary becomes sick with worry and dehydration and heads out to a nearby waterhole that is identified as poisonous. She is spotted almost reaching the pond, and in an unbelievable plot devise, the cavalry soldier is ordered to shoot at Mary, but only to "Wing her." She collapses after being hit from behind by a bullet and is carried back to camp. A very strange way to prevent her obtaining water to say the least.

1960

Now divorced, Phyllis' primary responsibilities were not as an actress, but as a mother. She joined the elite Malibu Beach Club, a mountain retreat that promoted "good food and good health," with fruits and vegetables grown in Malibu. It was designed as a center of activity, "where women may relax and refine balanced living." The club was designed for women to spend a weekend or a week." This exclusive club hosted lectures about art, literature, music, and the spirit."[118] Phyllis had a lifelong appreciation of the arts.

---

118 *Los Angeles Evening Citizen News* September 3, 1960

The ranch club facilities had a dedicated arts and crafts building along with a private steam room and workout facilities. Phyllis not only frequented this place on the weekends, she was friends of the husband-and-wife owners. She was part of a photo layout for an article in the *Los Angeles Evening Citizen News* expounding the amenity offerings.

Adjacent, but under separate programming was the Gerson's Calamigos Star C Ranch for boys and girls. It featured a pool, activities, riding stables and was properly supervised. It sounds much like the fictional *Triple K Ranch* of the *Spin & Marty* series Walt Disney produced for the *Mickey Mouse Club* during that same era on TV.

For the year, Phyllis guest-starred in four different TV shows: *The DuPont Show* hosted by June Allison (with David Niven), *The Best of the Post* (as Mollie the murderess), and *Hawaiian Eye*. Most prominent was *The Untouchables*.

1961

Send Me No Flowers was a comedy play Phyllis Coates and John Newton starred in at the Gallery stage on May 22, 1961. This romantic comedy had previously been on Broadway. Phyllis played Judy Kimball; the part Doris Day played in the 1964 film version. A critic from the *Los Angeles Evening Citizens News* wrote a review and singled out the wife character (Phyllis). He described her as, "Not only pretty, she has the comedy timing that is markedly unusual in good-looking actresses."[119]

Perry Mason - *Case of the Cowardly Lion*

This is a really fun one, though pretty farfetched. Phyllis played the mistress to a veterinarian who works at the San Diego Zoo. Her married beau winds up dead in the lion's den with scratches on his face. An accident? No, it's murder and guess who did it? Phyllis' character as Frieda Crawson. In an elaborate scheme that must have looked good on paper, Perry Mason deducted that the man was scratched not by the lion, but by a lion rug that was in the

---

119 *The Hollywood Reporter* Vol 164 issue 27

den. It had attached claws and that's how she was able to render him helpless and scratch him with the claws of the lion rug. Then somehow, she threw him into the lion's den so that it would appear the real lion did him in. A pretty elaborate murder, and the type of role Phyllis loved.

The Untouchables

Phyllis was in three episodes of this very popular crime drama series starring Robert Stack as Eliot Ness. The first one was made in 1959. *Ain't We Got Fun.* Phyllis was cast as a sexy gun moll assigned to oversee a young speakeasy comedian named Johnny Paycheck, played by Cameron Mitchell. Big Jim Harrington was the mobster (and a look-alike to Guy Lombardo) who took the kid into his payroll and invested in him for bigger things in a classier joint. The young comedian, however, couldn't keep off the bottle and descends into disfavor with the big cheese and his pyromaniac henchman. Phyllis played it to the hilt as a cold, calculating dame who spews out criticism to her assigned victim. Phyllis never looked better.

In *The Frank Nitti Story* shot in 1960, Phyllis turned informant and was knifed in the back as she attempted to call Eliot Ness. Actors love death scenes and this was a good one, though she collapsed quietly to assassin Frank de Kova. It was very unusual to see a beautiful woman getting "rubbed-out" on TV in the early 60s; no wonder this series had a reputation for being gritty.

It is 1962 and it is Phyllis' final appearance on *The Untouchables* series in an episode entitled *A Fist of Five*, directed by Ida Lupino. It is a noteworthy entry for many reasons. Phyllis played a beautiful disabled patient confined to a wheelchair. It took place in 1929 in the south side of Chicago where the mob smuggled in drugs through the produce wholesale market. Lee Marvin starred as a disgruntled fifteen-year veteran of the police force who was fired for his violent tendencies. So naturally, he recruits his five brothers (one of whom is a young James Caan) to form a gang of vengeful vigilantes against the underworld.

The backstory, as narrated by Walter Winchell, shows Phyllis' character was a former showgirl who suffered the use of her legs in a bombing of a speakeasy three years prior. She was angelic in this role and fiercely protective of her criminal husband, Anthony 'Tough Tony' Lamberto (Frank de Kova). She practically spits in Eliot Ness's face when he tried to pry information from her. As Mrs. Lamberto, she told Ness: "I know how long you've tried to destroy my husband; do you really think I would tell you anything? My husband and I have a very good marriage, and I believe in the vow I took to honor him…goodbye."

Phyllis said this was one of her favorite roles because Ida Lupino was at the helm. Lupino had a staunch background as an actress and director, and was well-admired in Hollywood. It must have been comforting for Phyllis to be directed by a female with a solid background of successes. Phyllis revered the talent Lupino brought and who suggested tips that Phyllis was most grateful for. Phyllis was always open to better her craft.

"I watched her render men impotent and open pickle jars like a goddamned Marine. – Zoe Christopher (Phyllis' first child)

Chapter Seven
A Doctor's Wife

"The Baby Maker" with Barbara Hershey (1979)

Marriage to Dr. Howard Press

Howard Press (1932-2018) was born in Brooklyn, New York. At the age of ten, he moved to Los Angeles with his parents. He was a serious boy and attended the University of Southern California receiving a D.O. degree from the College of Osteopathic Physicians and Surgeons and an M.D. from the California College of Medicine at UCLA-Irvine. Dr. Press practiced medicine in Los Angeles from 1959 to 1975.

Phyllis met her future husband by way of an introduction of a roommate of his. He was already a practicing physician in Los Angeles when Howard and Phyllis started courting. Now thirty-five years old, Phyllis found herself an ideal mate with a future and not attached to Hollywood. Howard was attracted to Phyllis' enchanting beauty and found her incredibly interesting. Like a couple of love-starved kids, they impulsively decided to drive to Mexico and were married on October 3, 1962. After protests from Howard's mother that the marriage was not legal, the two made it so by getting married in a civil ceremony in Los Angeles on November 16.

Birth of Laura Press August 16, 1963

Laura was born in Los Angeles and shared her young life with her older half-sister, Christopher, and her half-brother, David. Phyllis had still retained custody over her children. There was also a child in the house from the Tokar family coming and going.

Death Valley Days - *A Gun is Not a Gentleman*

Now at 36 years old and a mother of three, Phyllis could still pull off the role of a saloon girl/mistress to, of all people, Carroll O'Connor's character (as Senator Broderick). The Senator and Justice Terry engaged in a legal duel in San Francisco. Phyllis, as Lois Bouquette, stands by her man even though he is shot to death. The episode was loosely based on a real incident between the two named combatants with the appropriate referee in 1859. As an interesting plot device, Phyllis foretells doom by noticing her man's holding his card hand of "Aces and Eights," and identifies it as "Dead Man's Hand." The card sequence has been historically attributed to the legend of Wild Bill Hickok who was shot holding this hand, a full fifteen years after the 1859 date of the duel.

Gunsmoke - *The Homecoming* (1964)

This was one of Phyllis' favorite roles of her career as Edna. Her first husband returns from seven years in prison for killing Edna's lover, vowing to reclaim his house and business. Edna tries to goad her new husband and her son into a plot to kill her first husband. Then she tries to run away with a new lover, a traveling salesman.

Her character lies and cheats through the whole episode. This was the third appearance of Phyllis in this award-winning series.

Death Valley Days (1964)

The Left Hand is Damned was the title of this episode. It had a double meaning harking back to some cultures that the left hand was perceived to be sinister or evil (defined, of course, by right-handed people).

The main antagonist in this is a right-handed cowboy that gets his hand shot up. Phyllis is a saloon girl that witnesses the out-of-town gambler who is shot by the proprietor of the establishment. She scolds him for being insensitive to the badly wounded boy, then helps him recover. The incident did little to quell his anger at the proprietor and instead swells more hate, announcing revenge on him. His right hand incapacitated, he starts practicing shooting with his left hand. The cowboy seeks retribution and thinks he sees his adversary's silhouette through the window. Instead of hitting his intended victim, he shoots Phyllis' character, Dora, in the back. She gives a surprise expression, and then drops down for one of her infrequent death scenes.

I actually viewed this one with Phyllis when it was first released on videotape. She told me, "A whore with a heart, those are the *best* kind of roles."

Perry Mason - *Case of the Ice-Cold Hands*

Perry defends a woman accused of murdering a man from whom she allegedly stole money. Phyllis played the wife of the deceased with contempt for the victim. Her courtroom testimony was extra snarky.

1965

Phyllis still kept her options open for acting whenever the opportunities came. There was a summer replacement series called *Moment of Fear*, a weekly suspense drama with different actors each week. Phyllis co-starred with the always interesting Fred

Clark. In this episode, a newsman enlisted the aid of an eccentric bachelor to solve a murder.

1966

Summer Fun - *Thomson's Ghost*

This was another pilot for a potential TV series by Bing Crosby Productions. It borrowed heavily from the "Canterville Ghost" story penned by Oscar Wilde. It starred the iconic Bert Lahr of Cowardly Lion fame. Instead of England, this ghost tries to help an American family, but his bumbling does more harm than good. Phyllis played the mother of the family that also featured Tim Matheson as her son. It did not catch on as a series because Bert was very ill and couldn't continue…and he was the whole show. It was aired as a TV movie in August of 1966. Bert Lahr died five months later.

1967

These were family years for Phyllis and she was out of the loop as far as fan mail requests and responses. Since the studio system was non-existent and the fact that Phyllis was not in a contemporary series, it would be very hard for enthusiasts to reach her. A one-page letter has surfaced from April 12, 1967 from a fan, and it briefly captured what was going on in Phyllis' life during this time.

> *Dear Joan,*
>
> *Thank you for your nice letter—I'm not much for answering letters, but decided to drop you a quick note with information you requested.*
>
> *Yes, married-have three children: Daughter 17, boy 10, daughter 3 ½*
>
> *Haven't much time for hobbies, live at the beach and go to the mountains a lot. I'm 5-3 ½ birthday is Jan. 15, 1927. Who knows when I'll make another film, but doing some advertising.*
>
> *Best to you, Phyllis Coates*

It should be noted that "the mountains" usually meant the area above Malibu Beach where Phyllis was a member of their exclusive club. Phyllis also enjoyed visiting the desert oasis Joshua Tree National Park, east of San Bernadino and north of Palm Springs. It was very true that Phyllis had no spare time while raising a family; she also had to care for her mother who in her words was "in and out of mental institutions," and an alcoholic grandmother. It was a full-time job in itself and the responsibilities never ceased. It was a welcome and happy occasion when Phyllis' daughter Christopher graduated from Mira Costa High School in Manhattan Beach in Los Angeles proper in 1968. She was enroute to her own life experiences.

The Baby Maker (1970)

This is the last theatrical movie that Phyllis was in. It starred Barbara Hershey as free-spirited Tish Gray who lives with her boyfriend. She is hired by an upper-middleclass couple who couldn't conceive, so they hire Tish as surrogate mother to carry the biological fetus of the husband. There is only one scene where Phyllis played Tish's mother. The daughter comes to visit her mom who is living in a trailer home with her own mother. We see Phyllis who is forty-three-years-old here and wearing her naturally long dark hair. This was the new age of the sexual revolution and it contrasted with traditional norms from the past. This film is a reflection of the times, at least in some parts of California.

For those living as an older adult in 1970, culture shock had set in compared to the past years and decades. This was true for any American. The years between 1960 and 1970 ushered in cultural changes in music, politics, fashion, social mores, and Vietnam. To those who lived through WWII, things were moving too fast. To quote singer/songwriter Bob Dylan, "The Times Are-A-Changin."

It was time for Phyllis' daughter, Christopher, to go to college and she chose the University of Oregon. She came back with a new sense of self-awareness and embraced the woman's liberation movement. Not impressed, Phyllis told her: "I've been liberated my whole life."

Relocation to Big Sur/Pfeiffer Ridge and Beach

Ever since Phyllis visited the Monterey Peninsula with her first husband, twenty-five years prior, she fell in love with the Monterey area and secretly wished she could move there if the right circumstances came along. It was back in the year 1950 that she and Richard Bare drove to Carmel to see his mother and he took the opportunity to take Phyllis on a whirlwind tour of Big Sur, Carmel Highlands, Carmel, Carmel Valley, Monterey, Pebble Beach and Pacific Grove. That opportunity finally came to be in 1975 when the family moved to Big Sur. They bought an exquisite piece of property and built a home on Pfeiffer Ridge where it led to Sycamore Canyon Road, and on to the beach and the Pacific Ocean. The natural arched rocks were a place where filmmakers would shoot dynamic scenes. There were many film and music people from Hollywood and other VIPs living there, ever so discreetly.

Just down Highway One is the world class resort Esalen Institute. It's described as a retreat with hot tubs and unparalleled views of the Pacific Ocean. It also featured music and "alternative education." Also, on Hwy. One is the famous Nepenthe restaurant nestled naturally into the sensitive woodland areas. It was once owned by Orson Welles and Rita Hayworth. There is also the Ventana Inn, an exclusive resort and restaurant.

Laura was now only twelve-years-old, and Christopher by this time was married and had relocated. Phyllis' son David was now twenty-years-old and loved being able to surf the waters of the Pacific Ocean. He also got a job working at the Fernwood Restaurant, and fit right in as a local connecting him with all that Big Sur had to offer.

Fernwood in Big Sur was the quintessential woodsy, earthy, laid-back, casual dining place and bar for locals and tourists. There was a chess game always going at the front window with customers sitting at handmade wood table and chairs. In the 90 miles of Big Sur between the San Luis Obispo County line and Carmel, Highway One bisects the Pacific Ocean and the Los Padres National Forest. There is no "downtown" in this vast stretch of land and if a tourist asked where it is, the locals might say: "Big Sur is not as much a place as it is a frame of mind." Big Sur had a reputation as "Marijuana Heaven." The locals all had sources for the golden grow, most were highly suspicious and paranoid of strangers…and cops.

When living in Big Sur, Dr. Press had to commute twenty-six miles to Monterey proper where he had his practice. The road north to Monterey is California State Highway 1, and makes up part of the most scenic route from San Francisco to San Diego. It is a slow, winding road and sometimes the fog, ocean, wind, and steep cliffs can make it a treacherous drive. Bixby Bridge, a landmark prevalent in so many film and TV shows, connects Big Sur to Point Lobos. It's just south of the Carmel Highlands, and on to Carmel and Monterey. This area has sometimes been described as "The greatest meeting of land and sea."

Dr. Press was a general practitioner and was holistic in his approach. Even at home, the doctor did not allow Coca-Cola in his house, much to Phyllis' chagrin. His office of practice was on El Dorado Street, sometimes considered "Doctor's Row" of professional offices in Monterey. He also served on the staff of the Community Hospital of the Monterey Peninsula from 1976-2005. As the doctor's wife, Phyllis helped out performing office duties and interacting with patients. They had no idea she was the former Lois Lane of early television; Phyllis had a friendly and professional demeanor and genuinely cared for her husband's patients.

For all intents and purposes, it appeared that Phyllis was now content; she was securely married to a solid professional, had a beautiful home near the beach and it was easy for Phyllis, (known by the locals as Gypsie) to make friends easily.

Local Big Sur resident Tori Chesebrough-Buckles filled me in on her friendship with Phyllis:

> I always knew her as Gypsie. She and her husband, Howard, lived up Pias Road on the ridge between Wreck and Pfeiffer beaches during the Mid 70's. Gypsie was the sweetest person and was always happy with a smile and laugh. They were close friends with my parents and would socialize at either their house or ours. Gypsie was basically a stay-at-home mom to Laura during those years. David also lived there. I would stay at their house some-

times to take care of the dogs if they were away. Sometimes Gypsie would call and ask "did you just get home?" She did this because all of a sudden, the dogs, Lady (long-haired dachshund) and Primo (pit bull mix), would jump up and take off. She said that they could hear my car going up our road across the canyon, and run down their road to Sycamore Canyon, then up our road to greet me! Then I'd drive them back home.

The last time I saw her, she was living in a small house behind Howard's office in Monterey after they divorced.[120]

Never Too Late - Cause of friction between spouses, by Emily Kratzer.

The hit farce *Never Too Late* will come to the stage of the Center Theater beginning Feb 8 for a three-week run through Feb 26. It stars Robert Shayne and Phyllis Coates and has been hailed by critics as a three-act show that leaves us in a state of crazed satisfaction…it is a mad, mad, mad, mad show. *Never Too Late* is a story of a middle-aged couple whose family has grown and the lady of the house finds that she again is in the family way.

Phyllis Coates, who plays Edith Lambert, the dutiful, obliging and sometimes cunning wife, gives the play a lot of zest. Her calm announcement about being pregnant, which is ignored as the family fights, drew guffaws from the audience.

Robert Shayne, plays Harry Lambert, the fretful, demanding husband.

Bart Williams plays Charlie, in a role reminiscent of Mike Stivic in *All in the Family*. He punctuates the humorous dialogue with comical antics, and is most ludicrous when chasing Mayor Crane around the darkened living room draped in a blanket.

---

120 Interview with author March 21, 2024

Stephanie Shayne ably plays Kate to the hilt. Kate finds herself the lady/drudge of the house when mother Edith's condition gets her the royal treatment Kate's effectively sloppy costuming would make Phyllis Diller blink. Robert Shayne (father of Stephanie Shayne) played a drunk character for comedy relief. Shayne, who played Inspector Henderson in *Adventures of Superman*, had a delightful reunion with Phyllis during the three-week run-in Palm Springs.[121]

As a result of this play, it kindled a long-repressed urge for Phyllis to perform again in front of an audience. There was talk that this play could go on tour, but Phyllis' husband forbade it. Resentment grew and it was the beginning of the end for the marriage; however, they sputtered forward. Phyllis missed the camaraderie of show business people and the nurturing reinforcement it gave.

"I Love acting on stage, they generally give you three weeks to rehearse which is like Heaven. With those quickie westerns, there was absolutely no time to practice. We just did it."
– Phyllis to author

Bart Williams

Phyllis' dearest friend at this stage of her life was fellow actor Bart Williams. They had met and acted in the 1978 play *Never Too Late*. Their friendship lasted the rest of their lives.

Bart was a roly-poly man of thirty years who enchanted everyone who knew him. He was an expert at Hollywood history and in his younger days took care of Buster Keaton's widow. Bart grew up in Keaton's neighborhood; one day he knocked on their door and asked Eleanor Keaton if "Buster could come out to play." That endeared him to the couple. Bart was encouraged to make a career out of show-business and he stuck with it.

---

121 *Never Too Late* February 9, 1978 *Desert Sun* Palm Springs, California

Bart was a confirmed bachelor but made himself available whenever Eleanor needed him. The same could be said for Phyllis; she and Bart were as close as girlfriends. Bart lived and worked in Los Angeles, but came up north often. Bart owned Stan Laurel's original 1947 Chrysler and enjoyed showing it off in parades and car shows. Bart even came up for Pacific Grove's "Good Old Days" parades in the mid-80's with Phyllis as a guest celebrity. She was always announced as the "original Lois Lane."

Marriage Trouble

The marriage between Phyllis and Dr. Press continued to crack further over the years. There were many reasons for this to happen. Foremost was the fact that Phyllis was now drawn to the stage like a magnet. The experience of performing in *Never Too Late* was so invigorating it made her have a taste for more. Phyllis never forgave her husband for giving her an ultimatum of giving up showbusiness for good. Howard's point of view was that his wife was needed in his doctor's office. The resentment brewed and, according to their daughter Laura, they were arguing more and more and contempt opened wider. "Gypsie" had many social friends in Big Sur and Monterey, and she spent more time with them. The doctor built a little house in back of his offices at 111 Lane Street in Monterey for use in the middle of his work week ostensibly to ease his commute to Big Sur. It also might be that he used the well-equipped home as a respite.

Phyllis had long, lingering doubts to confront every day. It was she who originally wanted to return to the Monterey Peninsula as a doctor's wife. She had security and money, but now she was looking at the rest of her life and what she might have missed.

Separation and Divorce

Married for twenty-four years now and with kids matured into adults, Phyllis started thinking of a divorced life and returning to her first love, acting in varied roles. Phyllis and Howard Press physically separated on the third of January of 1986. Their daughter Laura knew it was coming, "They were arguing about everything at that point." Through the couple's representative attorneys and a judge, a Petition for the Dissolution of Marriage in Monterey County for Irreconcilable Differences was filed. All court documents pertaining to Gypsie Press were also listed as A.K.A. Phyllis Press vs Howard Press. The final divorce decree came in on December 22, 1988.

Dr. Howard Press eventually settled in Walnut Creek, California after a remarriage. When the doctor died in 2018 the local newspaper on the Monterey Peninsula printed his obituary:

> Howard Press was considered an "Old School" physician, dedicated to his patients, and became known as a skilled diagnostician who drew upon both traditional and alternative medicine to find answers. He was a man of many interests-a student of Buddhism, a lover of literature, classical music, and an avid gardener. He could often be seen around Monterey with his beloved dachshund, Blueberry. [122]

---

122 *Monterey Herald* March 25, 2018

Chapter Eight
Meeting Phyllis

Phyllis Coates

LIKE ANY MALE BABY BOOMER, I was certainly aware of the actress Phyllis Coates while growing up watching *Adventures of Superman*. Her name was emblazoned right below George Reeves on the opening credits. *Superman* repeats could be seen on an almost daily basis, and then there were all those television programs in which she performed character roles.

In the San Jose area, of Northern California, there was an independent television station "KICU" called "The Perfect 36." They showed old movies, old TV shows and locally-produced commercials. Every Labor Day weekend in the mid-80's, they hosted a "Superman Marathon," and they hired Phyllis Coates to tape segments of her introducing the programs. It was a big success to have someone from the original cast presenting each episode chronologically.

In those early days video cassette recorders (VCR's) were the new king of home entertainment. KICU was a U.H.F. station and had limited reach with their broadcasts. The marathon was a new concept in programming and Superman fans across the nation were hungry to see the series broadcast in consecutive order. Some of the film collector magazines/newspapers printed pleas from viewers outside of the broadcasting range to record the programs. This was a "thing" in the early 1980's for TV buffs to record and exchange home-made video recordings in different regions of the country. It was amazing to read all the requests for the Phyllis Coates lead-in of the program from interested viewers from across America. This is when I first learned that Phyllis lived nearby in Monterey County. However, I never had reason to try and look her up in Big Sur/Carmel where she lived.

Meeting Phyllis

I first met Phyllis in 1987 while she was living in Carmel proper on 8th Street. She had just divorced her doctor husband and settled comfortably into this village of an arts community. It was only one square mile but was comprised of charming homes, businesses, and restaurants, some of which were individually crafted like an old European hamlet.

Carmel had always been a draw for people of the arts and bohemians who were inspired by the Pacific Ocean, Carmel Beach and the Monterey Cypress trees. Actors, artists, writers, and photographers made this place their home to world acclaim. Movie celebrities and dignitaries quietly lived here. It was a mecca for golfers. Doris Day had a hotel in town called The Cypress Inn, and they welcomed dogs. In 1986, the voters of Carmel elected Clint Eastwood to be their mayor. Phyllis just adored him.

In this same year, I was "Grand Sheik" for the Midnight Patrol tent of the Laurel and Hardy Appreciation Society (Sons of the Desert). Myself and two other law enforcement officers picked the name "Midnight Patrol," as that was the name of a short comedy L&H made.

We started the chapter (tent) in 1984 in Monterey and made a lot of friends throughout the organization and visited other "tents" in other cities. One couple that really took a liking to us was Lois Laurel Hawes (Stan's daughter) and her husband, Tony, a British gentleman and professional comedy writer. They invited me over to the house in Tarzana, California, and an instant and long-standing friendship began.

At some point Lois encouraged me to communicate with an old friend of hers: Phyllis Coates. I certainly knew the name already. Our tent had yearly banquets with guest celebrities. Tony and Lois pledged to come to Monterey for our annual banquet and to communicate to Phyllis about me.

I was soon invited to meet Phyllis at her elaborate townhouse in Carmel. I later learned she had just relocated there from Big Sur; she was going through a divorce with Dr. Howard Press. Phyllis' son, David, from a previous marriage lived with her; he was in his late 20's. Phyllis was very cordial to me; I am sure that Tony and Lois told her that I was a deputy sheriff. I was there to introduce myself and to explain about the banquet and a reunion with Lois Hawes.

Lois had known Phyllis for years; she met Phyllis since acting school (The Bliss-Hayden) in the late 1940's. In that class was an unknown: Marilyn Monroe. (*See chapter Two*)

Phyllis surprised me one afternoon while talking about her early-stage act that opened the Ken Murray Show in 1943. She reenacted how the chorus girls bounced out to introduce the star while singing Murray's opening theme. Phyllis even recreated the lively steps by extending her raised arms and sashaying with open palms. The spontaneous performance was done in Phyllis' bare feet. Phyllis matter-of-factly pointed to her hammer-toes and explained they were caused by wearing glamour shoes that were too small when dancing all those years ago.

Sons of the Desert Banquet

Our 1987 Midnight Patrol banquet was to celebrate our local tent/chapter of the Laurel and Hardy Appreciation Society in the Son's organization. It was our second anniversary and our tent officers were very excited to invite our special guests: Stan Laurel's daughter, her husband Tony Hawes, actor Henry Brandon (whom we idolized for his role of "Barnaby" in Laurel and Hardy's *Babes in Toyland*), book author Randy Skretvedt (who had just written *Laurel and Hardy the Magic Behind the Movies*), and local gal, Phyllis Coates as our celebrity line-up.

Our banquet venue was the California First Theater; it really was California's first theater dating back to 1849. It was quaint and rustic with bench seats for the 100 attending members. Laurel and Hardy films were shown, but the most exciting aspect of our second year of existence was welcoming our celebrity guests. Bart Williams escorted Phyllis to the stage where she got a big round of applause. I had previously edited onto videotape some highlights of Phyllis' career, and there was a montage of opening credits of many of the TV shows she was in. It was thrilling as well to see the reunion of Lois Laurel Hawes and Phyllis.

At the conclusion of the banquet, Phyllis asked if she could borrow her highlight tape to show her children. Pleased at that request, I happily gave it to her. A friendship evolved between Phyllis and me. More than a few times I would stop by and visit Phyllis, sometimes watching a movie together. Whenever Tony and Lois came north, we always included her.

David Tokar

Phyllis was having problems with her son, David. Big problems. He was a chronic heroin addict and had a history of stealing valuable items for drugs. According to Monterey County Courthouse records, he had twenty-three criminal entries since he was an adult. Once, I asked about the highlight tape I made for her and she frantically looked for it. She later found out that David had stolen it and sold it. He had a bad habit of stealing her things, but

I couldn't figure out who would want to pay for a homemade videotape of edited clips. Phyllis was both embarrassed and furious.

Clint Eastwood

Clint lived quietly in Pebble Beach with his first wife, Maggie, since the early 1960's. He bought the place with money he'd made in the television series *Rawhide*. Phyllis had two acting roles in the series, but unfortunately never shared a scene with Clint. It was in 1986 that Clint surprised the world by throwing his hat into the ring for the election of Mayor of Carmel. Only 4,000 people lived in the village and Clint won in a landslide. Phyllis was a big fan of his, she told me that Clint had offspring all over the peninsula, "and he pays for every one of them."

1987 Sons of the Desert Banquet

At our annual Son's banquet in Monterey, we enjoyed the presence of celebrities, Lois Laurel Hawes, her husband, Tony, Virginia O'Brien, Phyllis, and Tommy "Butch" Bond. Tommy was a child star acting in the *Little Rascals/Our Gang* film series at Hal Roach Studios in the 1930's; he is best remembered as the neighborhood bully who menaced Spanky and Alfalfa. He was also notable in films when he was cast as "Jimmy Olsen" in the Superman serials of 1948 and 1950.

Phyllis and Tommy had never met before so it was a rare privilege to call them both on stage as "Lois Lane meets Jimmy Olsen." They spontaneously hugged each other beaming their smiles as photos were taken. Tommy shared his experiences as "Jimmy Olsen," recounting one of the serial chapter's scenes. His character was knocked unconscious and placed on a conveyer belt slowly rolling him to a furnace of real fire and flames. He was supposed to be motionless with closed eyes waiting for the director to yell "cut" while there were fist fights going on around him. Tommy said he felt the heat getting closer and closer, so he jumped out before he was supposed to, not taking any chances. Tommy laughed at the memory.

We showed film clips of our celebrities including Virginia O'Brien, a former MGM star who is best known for her deadpan expression while singing. When we projected images of the *Superman* serial, we were surprised when Virginia loudly yelled, "Oh No, not him!" During the time the series was filmed, Kirk Alyn played the Clark Kent/Superman role. He and Virginia were previously married.

George Reeves

> *"My friend Bill Cassara, who is with the Sheriff's Department here in Carmel, told me George committed suicide. He saw the pictures."*
> – Phyllis Coates to author Tom Weaver[123]

There was a time when I mentioned to Phyllis that in 1984 our Sheriff's Office combined my status of a Field Training Officer and Deputy Field Coroner. As part of our training, they sent me to an F.B.I. class that was a week-long in Carmel. Only officers who were death investigators were enrolled. It was on a need-to-know basis.

One of the topics of instructions was specific to "Celebrity Deaths." It was fascinating and there was a whole set of checks and balances pertaining to procedures and dealing with the media. The teachers were working agents with many years of experience, statistics and slide photographs. They covered old Hollywood deaths such as the 1935 demise of Thelma Todd. We were shown the death scene photos and coroner's report of that case. The instructors were the consummate professionals in their field with high credibility; talking confidently to other specialists, they weren't selling anything.

My ears particularly perked up when the agents specifically covered the George Reeves' case, calling it right off as a "classic suicide." This case was unusual in many aspects. On slide projected pictures, I had seen the black and white photos of the autopsy

---

[123] Weaver, Tom. *Science Fiction Stars and Horror Heros.* McFarland & and Company, Inc. Publishers Jefferson, North Carolina, and London. 1991

where they pointed out important facts. I respected that Phyllis was friends with George Reeves, so I didn't fill her in graphically of the scenes. I do remember that she didn't flinch when I told her of the confirmed suicide. She just stared wide-eyed ahead.

Phyllis explained that George and she had talked about doing a movie together. George had been very excited about the project, because he was going to direct it. She said he seemed very happy. I calmly reiterated to Phyllis that the class was put on by the FBI to professionals. I told her, "They had nothing to gain or sell by distorting the facts."

I don't think we talked much more about it for years. I later became aware of an interview that Phyllis gave a sci-fi magazine. In 1991 renowned author Tom Weaver sought out Phyllis for his book: *Science Fiction Stars and Horror Heroes*, Phyllis gave a great interview touching on many topics and the subject eventually came around to Reeves.

> **Weaver** asked: What's your opinion about George Reeves' death?"
>
> **Phyllis**: I don't think we'll ever know. I do know that my friend Bill Cassara, who is with the Sheriff's Department here in Carmel [Monterey County Sheriff's Office], told me George committed suicide. He saw a photograph of George Reeves, showing the bullet hole. They had examined that photograph and took into account the angle at which the bullet had entered the head, and definitely determined that it was self-inflicted, that he was not murdered."[124]

It seemed to me that interviewers always asked George Reeves' fellow *Superman* actors their opinion about his death. It was a shock that they never got over it and they found it hard to comprehend. Even casual fans would ask Phyllis about her beliefs about the circumstances. How was she to really know?

---

124 *Weaver, Tom. Science Fiction Stars and Horror Heros. McFarland & and Company, Inc. Publishers Jefferson, North Carolina, and London. 1991*

Phyllis Hosts Senior Citizen's Day at Eastridge Shopping Center in San Jose May 3, 1987

This was an all-day affair that honored Phyllis and was co-hosted by Jane McMillan of radio station KLIV in San Jose. There was a reception with prize giveaways, a fashion show, a variety show, and a sweepstakes with over 1,000 prizes. Eastridge at one time was the largest shopping mall west of the Mississippi.

Phyllis' mother's death

Phyllis' mom died on June 19, 1988, in Pacific Grove, California. She passed away in a rest home in this quaint community adjacent to Monterey. Born Jackie Luzzie Teel, she had been married at least three times, the last to a Mr. Rappee. She reached the age of seventy-eight before she finally succumbed to Alzheimer's disease. Phyllis took care of her mother most of her adult life.

Retirement

Now at the age of sixty-one and with the death of her mother, divorced, and her kids grown up, Phyllis was now free to pursue her own personal interests. She was very comfortable on the Monterey Peninsula having lived there since 1975, but resisted the temptation to go to Hollywood for film work. To quote Phyllis: "Been there done that." Phyllis happily corresponded with many of her fans throughout the years. She was invited to meet her public at various film events and conventions all over the United States. It was now her opportunity to attend them.

Children and Animals

Finally, being retired and free from marriage allowed Phyllis to also explore new acting opportunities. She had been absent from the screen for many years. Though anxious to get to work and make some income, she refused to go to Los Angeles to seek opportunities. She was settled comfortably in her Monterey home now, and sought a companion. Phyllis went to the S.P.C.A. and picked out a small mixed breed dog and named him "Lucky." He went with her wherever she went.

Phyllis had always been drawn to animals. Her first child, Zoe Christopher, remembers that there was always a pet in the house. Zoe elaborated to me in an email:

> Wounded animals brought out her kindness, but everyone fretted she was too cold for children. Thankfully all her children *were* wounded animals from birth, and that's literal. I was born without a right hip socket, my brother with a 'cauliflower ear,' and my sister with a tumor on her nose!

Zoe expounded with more pleasant memories:

> When I was little, I always had a dog. She'd take me to the pound and we'd choose one. She had a dog named Mu for years (I think she buried him in the garden in Manhattan Beach) and she loved my brother's dog, Primo, that they had in Big Sur.

1988 Charlotte Western Film Fair-Three-day event July 7-9

Phyllis addressed an enthusiastic audience at this film fair in Middle America. She was pressed to answer a question pertaining to her favorite acting role. She answered, "Over the years, I've done many things professionally. I'd be hard-pressed to pick one actor, director or project I liked best."[125] She elaborated further by saying, "I didn't leave *Superman* because I was mad or anything like that. I loved George and I loved the crew."[126]

1988 Commercial

In the late 1980s, Phyllis was hired by the Del Monte Shopping Center in Monterey for a local commercial. The thirty-second spot featured Phyllis in casual dress with a costumed 20-year-old "Superman" actor. As she was pitching the finer points of shopping

---

[125] *Classic Images* #483 Sept. 2015 "Phyllis Coates-That Feisty Lois Lane" by Joe Collura
[126] *Ibid*

there, Superman swept her up in his arms and "flew" away with her, *cheesy* as it was, the locals loved it.

1988 Comic Convention in San Diego

Phyllis was invited as a special guest to the prestigious mother of all comic conventions. Established in 1970, it welcomed thousands of excited attendees for all the festivities. 1988 was significant in that it was also the 50th anniversary of the first *Superman* comic book. To help celebrate, the convention head extended a welcome to Phyllis as well as to Robert Shayne, who played Inspector Henderson in *Adventures of Superman*. People were thrilled to meet them. At the podium, Phyllis entertained the crowd by sharing her memories making a commercial for Kleenex. The late John Field, a nationally known "Superman" and the golden age of comedy expert, informed me Phyllis recounted the scenes for the camera by explaining she was at the studio all day for take after take. She said the Kleenex had to pop up a certain way before the director was happy. Everyone got a laugh over that one.

The convention was a nice reunion for Phyllis to see Robert Shayne and his daughter; they had all acted together in the 1978 stage play *Never Too Late*. Phyllis often stayed with Shayne's daughter when she was visiting Los Angeles. Robert Shayne died November 29, 1992.

1988 Sons of the Desert Banquet – *Phyllis gets "slapsticked"*

Our Midnight Patrol annual banquet was again held at the California First Theater in Monterey (established in 1849). That year we featured Phyllis, of course, and movie stars Anthony Caruso, and Henry Brandon. The event was emceed by the one and only British comedian and husband to Lois Laurel, Tony Hawes.

It was quite a day of festivities starting with a barbecue steak lunch outside the historical grounds; we then adjourned inside to the pub leading to the chairs in the balcony. While members were milling around talking and drinking, Bob Zeroun, our illustrious Sergeant of Arms, reprised a gag that Charley Chase victimized Laurel and Hardy in their feature film "*Sons of the Desert*."

In that movie, Chase laid a trap in the form of a wallet stuffed with money and placed it on the floor as if someone had lost it. Oliver Hardy waved off Stan and discreetly bent over to pick it up…then WHAM, Charley Chase let him have it with a slapstick paddle to his butt. Most of our attendees were aware of the joke so when Zeroun placed his own wallet on the floor of the pub with currency plainly sticking out, everyone was watching to see who might fall for the gag. Most of us were standing around trying not to act conspicuous when Phyllis walked up, spotted the wallet and said, "Oh, someone dropped their wallet." She bent over and… CRACK, she got slapped on her backside. Most of us turned our heads as the scene was unfolding, but Zeroun was steadfast and let her have it. Phyllis was sixty-years-old at this point, but like a *Twilight Zone* sequence, she was in the world of Laurel and Hardy. She, of course, popped up, then realized the comedy aspects and laughed hard at herself. What a trouper.

We reconvened to the theater inside and took our chairs. Our stars were seated at tables near the stage for easy access. On stage was where Tony Hawes was most comfortable, he had previously been an emcee at the London Palladium and events all over America. He was a member of *The Masquers* organization in Los Angeles and reveled in show business events.

One by one, Tony called each celebrity up to the stage, but not before showing film clips of some of their most notable scenes of their respective careers. After traditional toasts and drinks, Anthony Caruso was first to be summoned. Preceding this, we showed film clips of perhaps Caruso's most famous role as a safe-cracking gangster in *The Asphalt Jungle* (1950).

We also showed clips of Anthony Caruso who starred as a gangster in *Adventures of Superman-Czar of the Underworld*. Though it was shot in season one of the series, Phyllis unfortunately was not in this one.

Then, we showed the complete episode from the *Joe Piscopo TV Special* featuring Caruso in a *Godfather* skit. Tony introduced him as his character in the short as "Tony DiNono." Anthony was quite the dignitary in showbusiness circles; he was the "Harlequin" in the

Masquers club. Caruso was indeed the highest-ranking officer in that organization and it was an honor to have him up in Monterey.

Next up was Henry Brandon and we showed clips of him starring as "Chief Scar" in *The Searchers* (1956). He was the main antagonist against John Wayne in this heralded film. Also shown were wonderful clips of Henry as "Barnaby" in Laurel & Hardy's *Babes in Toyland* (1934). His melodramatic characterization always elicited "B-o-o-s" from the audience. This was followed by the complete 20-minute short film comedy of *Our Gang Follies of 1938*.

Henry reprised his role of "Barnaby" as a young man and "twenty years later" as the evil impresario who signs Alfalfa to a singing contract. This two-reeler featured musical numbers at "Club Spanky." A highlight for Phyllis watching this was the little girl (Annie Ross) who sang the *Bonny Banks of Loch Lomond* number. She got the biggest kick out of Annie throwing her hips to accent a note. Phyllis reached over to her accompanying female guest and enthusiastically remarked, "Oh, isn't that wonderful?" It might have been something Phyllis could have done when she was dancing swing-style on stage in her yearly years.

It was now Phyllis' turn to come to the stage, but not before showing edited clips of her in various western roles, and as Lois Lane in a montage from *Superman and the Mole Men*. It was followed by edited segments of Phyllis' screams in her Lois Lane character. With a round of applause, Tony reached out his hand to help Phyllis up. She told us that the ray gun the mole men were using was actually an Electrolux vacuum cleaner with a funnel glued to the end.

Sons' member, Gary Cohen, was called to the stage to show her and the audience an original one-sheet poster of Phyllis and Clayton Moore in the serial *Jungle Drums of Africa*. Phyllis was happy to sign it.

At the event's conclusion, Henry Brandon approached Phyllis to undoubtedly compare notes. I overheard him, "You should talk to my agent, he likes the old-timers."

1989

The sad ordeal of Phyllis' son, David, finally caught up to him as described by a newspaper account from *The Salinas Californian*. Phyllis always tried to go to bat for her son, and this time she even testified on his behalf. It wasn't enough to sway the jury. Phyllis couldn't bear to go to the sentencing proceedings.

David Tokar's Heroin addiction/Phyllis' appeal to Judge Phillips

> David Press was convicted by a jury last month of possession of stolen property. Press was also charged with a residential burglary, but the jury hung 10-2 for conviction. One of the defense witnesses was his mother, Phyllis Coates, who appeared as Lois Lane on the *Adventures of Superman* in 1952 with George Reeves. Coates shares the apartment with her son, but was not present in court during the sentencing hearing on Wednesday.
>
> Monterey County Superior Court Judge William Curtis chose the maximum sentence for Press, who according to a pre-sentencing report is a painting contractor and former heroin addict, with a long record of drug offenses. Press was on probation for a crime in Santa Cruz County when he was arrested by Carmel police April 24. According to the report, Press was taken into custody after a burglary in a nearby apartment near San Carlos and 8th Streets in Carmel. A couple said they returned from a few days' holiday on April 5 to find two sets of silver flatware, and other silver items, missing.
>
> Later, a second-hand dealer reported someone who resembled Press sold him some silverware, according to the report. Police said they searched the man's apartment and found silver items, including a silver cup inscribed with the name of one of the burglary victims. Press, who lived in the same building as the couple, denied any involvement in the burglary, according to a probation officer who interviewed him. Press said he found the

items in a pillowcase in the building, and admitted he was "stupid" not returning them, according to the pre-sentencing report.[127]

Phyllis was outraged at her son's continuing theft to support his habit. She was the victim of numerous stolen items she had collected over the years. Nevertheless, she appealed directly to Judge Curtis to try to keep her son out of prison. She made the point that prison would not benefit him in any way and that his life would be in danger. This sentiment is not unusual for mothers who appeal on behalf of their children. She offered to place David in a rehab facility to insure a better outcome. Phyllis convinced the judge who let David face his own demons. Both let him know that this was his last chance. Phyllis wound up spending thousands of dollars on him throughout the years.

One afternoon on my day off, Phyllis called me at home to come over. She was distraught because her son took her car without permission…again. This time she was afraid he would try and sell her car to get money for his habit. I explained her options. Since I was off duty and in another jurisdiction (Monterey P.D.), I let her know she could make a stolen vehicle report with them. Doing that would enter the vehicle number and description into C.L.E.T.S (California Law Enforcement Telecommunications System) and would register the car and suspect into the computer system. I made it clear that when police do spot the car, that it is handled as a felony car stop. The driver gets taken out of the car with a shotgun trained on him. There are always risks, and accidents have been known to happen when things don't go smoothly.

Phyllis feared for the worse not knowing what her son would do under stressful circumstances. I let her know of the option of hiring a private investigator to find the car and bring it back. She asked for a recommendation. I suggested a retired detective turned private investigator that I had previously worked with.

Phyllis engaged the P.I. and his working partner in the days to come; they had dealt with him over the years and knew his habits. They also knew where he would score his fix, China Town in

---

127   The *Californian* (Salinas) September 14, 1989

Salinas. It was an old dilapidated section of town built many years ago, but after the war, families and businesses slowly moved to the suburbs. The only thing left were old restaurant fronts, a soup kitchen, a flop house and railroad tracks. The blighted area drew prostitutes, "johns," and drug dealers, not to mention their customers. It was the place to obtain heroin and other illicit drugs. Many homeless and the addicted lined the area.

The private investigators found Phyllis' car abandoned in the area, and had the disabled car towed back to Phyllis. She was incensed, and vowed that was the last time she was ever going to deal with her drug addicted son. Phyllis called and filled me in. I came right over when I was off duty.

Already present was Phyllis' daughter, Laura. She too was caught up in the ongoing drama with her half-brother. No one knew David's whereabouts when all this was going on. Then, as if on cue, the wayward son came through the front door with a jovial greeting: "Hi Mom." Phyllis spit out her words: "**Your** *mother* **is drugs.**" It shook David up. "No mom, don't say that." I'm not sure Phyllis ever confronted him like that before, but the tone of her voice underscored she was fed up. Phyllis banished him from the house with words to the effect of, "and never darken my door again." I stood shoulder to shoulder with Phyllis but didn't have to say a word, this was strictly a family matter. There was no use in a rebuttal or for David to appeal to her maternal instincts. There was no other confrontation, he left the same way he came in, albeit with a new reality. He returned to Chinatown in Salinas and got a part-time job at Dorothy's Kitchen.

Shortly after this incident, Phyllis moved to the little house on 111 Davis Lane in Monterey. Phyllis obtained the dwelling as part of her divorce settlement. In the new arrangement, only Phyllis and "Lucky" lived there. It was warm and cozy.

Kiss Shot

It was also in 1989 that Phyllis responded to a call for her acting skills for a made-for-TV movie called, *Kiss Shot*. It starred Whoopi Goldberg and Dennis Franz and fortunately this production was shot in San Jose, just over the hill from Monterey. Phyllis had always retained her Screen Actors Guild membership and found an agent closer to her than Los Angeles. The San Francisco firm was Stars Agency. They set her up with a studio photographer with a series of different head shots of Phyllis in different characters.

The title *Kiss Shot* pertained to Whoopi Goldberg's expertise at tournament pool playing. The plot entailed she had to come up with a balloon payment of $3,000 to keep her house and a roof over her young daughter's head. This family flick had Phyllis playing an important character, "Ruby," a waitress and co-worker of Whoopi. There are some heart-warming scenes of Phyllis babysitting and caring for the young girl.

The whole film was shot in and around San Jose, but for the climax there was a grand tournament that allegedly took place in San Francisco. According to Phyllis and others, the staged tournament was actually shot at the Fairmont Hotel in San Jose despite edited visuals of the Golden Gate Bridge. The last scene before the fadeout clearly shows downtown San Jose. Phyllis said they only needed her for two days of shooting, but it was very "exciting" for her to work again.

March 30, 1990 *The Salinas Californian*

> Some stayed home in their sweats and swilled beer while they watched the Oscars. Others donned tuxedo, furs and jewels and experienced the evening in style at "Oscar Night at the Plaza." Monday. There was a big screen for viewing at the Monterey Plaza Hotel and plenty of hors d'oeuvres. Glittering from the Monterey County Film Commission (benefactors from the event and supporters attended clapping furiously for their favorite stars and movies).
>
> Even Phyllis Coates of Carmel, the original Lois Lane, was there. She said she hopes she's nothing like the woman she portrayed in the "Superman" series. She's grown up with the times but still looks young."[128]

---

128 *The Californian* (Salinas) March 30, 1990

1990 *Argus-Leader, Sioux Falls, South Dakota*:

> Phyllis Coates "sang a little and danced a little" in a vaudeville show called, *Ken Murray's Blackouts*. She got an agent and went to work for Desilu. She also played a Southern mother with children in *This is Alice*, a TV series in the 50s. To this day, people often recognize her voice in the grocery store she frequents. However unrealistic her role in the Superman series was, Coates has been a mentor to many budding journalists. She gets fan mail daily, and one woman said she was so influenced by Lois Lane that she ended up buying a newspaper business.

KGO Radio Interview

It was around this time period that Phyllis' agency lined her up for an on-the-air interview at San Francisco's premier KGO radio station. It was established in 1924 and became a juggernaut in the bay area with 50,000 watts of a broadcast signal. This was exclusively a talk/news format when Phyllis guested on the Ronn Owen's Show. I listened in.

The host eloquently informed his listeners of Phyllis' career before he invited her to the microphone. Phyllis took to this format like a duck to water. Her natural velvety voice resonated with clarity and confidence. She was instantly recognizable and her vocal articulations were received like hearing an old friend. The switchboard lit up with listeners anxious to share their thoughts and questions with Phyllis. She was so gracious and patient with the callers, it was obvious to me that Phyllis could have made a career in this medium. However, she had a face for the big screen and she chose the right career path.

As I recall, almost all of the callers were females who expressed their gratitude to Phyllis mostly for her "Lois Lane" role. She heard from fans, baby-boomer professionals, teachers, journalists, and one attorney. Most of them told Phyllis that they were inspired by her as a role model and helped them in pursuing their own careers. It was a great show.

Goodnight, Sweet Marilyn (1991)

"The Tom Cats are after you, that's just the way it is, baby."

On paper, this project had potential, even though this was a very low budget film. The subject matter of Marilyn Monroe was near and dear to Phyllis, having known her when both were in acting school. The script emphasized the relationship with Marilyn's "crazy mother" (Gladys Baker), played by Phyllis. She certainly related to that dynamic with her own mom. In one black and white dream sequence, Gladys Baker appears to her daughter in a straight-jacket. To quote Michelle Benton Cassara, "This must have been a catharsis role for Phyllis. She was able to purge her personal misgivings about her own mother."

This flick was shot on videotape, and was never released to the cinemas. It only existed in video format. Despite the provocative title and theme, it was ignored.

1991 Saturday Night at the Movies Sponsored by *The Salinas Californian* Newspaper.

Phyllis was always willing to help a cause and participate as a celebrity for a film event. She was especially interested if she didn't have to travel. An opportunity came up in Salinas, California, only eighteen miles from the Monterey coast. The Children's Miracle Network organization hosted a fundraiser. Phyllis was joined by Walter Reed, who also was in *Superman and the Mole Men* with Phyllis.

> A 1950s science fiction film festival will be held at noon and 7 P.M. Saturday at the Hartnell Performing Arts Center. On the bill are *Flying Disc Man from Mars*, and *I Was a Teenage Frankenstein*. There will be special guest appearances by Phyllis Coates (Lois Lane), Robert Clarke and Walter Reed, with an autograph session. Tickets are $7.50 for adults, $3.50 for children. Proceeds

benefit the Children's Miracle Network Telethon. There will also be door prizes and free popcorn.[129]

Catalina Island

The International Sons of the Desert sponsored an event on Catalina Island to celebrate the 100th anniversary of Oliver Hardy's birth as well as Hal Roach's 100th birthday, both being born in 1892. Tony Hawes was in charge of this event and he pulled out all stops for a weekend celebration. There were many events and celebrities attending as well as Sons across the globe. Phyllis and Bart Williams were some of the special guests. Phyllis came dressed as a gangster's moll, delighting her fans.

1992 Robert Shayne Dies

On November 29th, I learned that Phyllis' long-ago co-star Robert Shayne (as Inspector Henderson) from the *Adventures of Superman* died. He was 92 years old. I stopped by to see Phyllis to check if she knew. Phyllis had always kept in touch through his daughter, and remarked how she would have to send a card to her. They had last seen each other at a convention in San Diego in 1988 and actually played man and wife in *Never Too Late* in 1978.

Love Letters

Bart Williams offered to direct a play starring Phyllis and their good friend, Alan Young, for a fundraiser for the American Lung Association on August 26, 1993. A local committee was organized and a suitable play was decided upon. It was A.R. Gurney's production *Love Letters* at the Monterey Conference Center's Steinbeck Forum. Maggie Eastwood (former wife of Clint) was the angel that produced the show.

The attending audience dressed in formal clothes and the director of the show, Bart Williams, donned a black tuxedo. He also was the master of ceremonies and introduced the play to the audience. The conference center was packed and good will was in the air.

---

129 *The Salinas Californian* May 9, 1991

Everyone was familiar with actor Alan Young who played the male lead, he spent his whole life in showbusiness on the stage, television and movies. Most of the crowd remembered him from his days of "Wilber Post," the owner of the talking horse: *Mr. Ed*, whose TV show was on the air for six seasons. I knew him from his early variety show, and the films: *Tom Thumb*, *The Time Machine*, *Mr. Belvedere Goes to College*, and numerous voices for Disney characters.

The audience members certainly knew the local gal, Phyllis Coates, though most of them only addressed her by her given name, Gypsie. She was a spry sixty-six-years-old at this point, but poured into her role. She emoted her lines like the pro she was and accentuated her character with hand expressions.

Alan Young was seventy-three at this point, and it seemed that his timing was off a bit, but it didn't matter, the audience loved them both.

Calamity Jane Night in Carmel April 17, 1993

I was involved with a fundraiser to raise money to help support The Monterey County Sheriff's Advisory Board and for Crime Stoppers of Monterey County. I was the liaison to the latter as the law enforcement representative. Both were non-profit organizations in need of funds. I approached Terry Melcher about my idea for a fundraiser with a Doris Day theme. Kit Parker had a 35mm print of *Calamity Jane*, the 1951 musical that Doris starred in. She claimed it was her favorite movie.

The event was held at the Golden Bough Theater in Carmel. Both Doris and Clint Eastwood introduced the film to the audience; some had come across America to be there. I invited Phyllis as a guest, and she sat quietly in the front row taking it all in. She told me later, "You have to work hard to be a big star."

It's too bad that Phyllis was not in any of Doris' films even though they were both at Warners for a time. However, in 1953 George O'Hanlon and Phyllis played husband and wife in *So You Want a Television Set* as part of the *Behind the Eight Ball* series. What is notable is that George is driven away from his own TV by intruding neighbors, and he retreats to a movie theater. George settles in a vacant chair right between Doris Day and Gordon MacRae who are watching the movie intently while munching on popcorn. The two were starring in *By the Light of the Silvery Moon*, made that same year. It was a light throw-away gag ending that must have made moviegoers of the time break out in big applause. Unfortunately, Phyllis did not share a scene with them.

Photo Gallery

"Blood Arrow" with Scott Brady

"Wyoming Roundup"

Panther Girl of the Kongo

Superman and the mole Men

39 of the shortest, most delightful half-hours in television Produced for NTA by Desilu

THIS IS ALICE is tailored for the entire family because a house is just not a home without an "Alice."

THIS IS ALICE takes you to a very special world. It is the wonderfully winning world of a wide-eyed, imaginative little girl and her family. It's a happy story. And Alice? She's fun... perhaps that's not the right word. Lovable? Of course, but so much more. Captivating? Certainly that, but yet there must be a better way to describe her.

THIS IS ALICE is *habit forming*. That's the word. But don't take anybody's word for THIS IS ALICE. Make up your own mind. See it... every "funny," "lovable," "captivating," "habit forming" minute in the year.

THIS IS ALICE stars 10-year-old *Patty Ann Gerrity*, a real-life combination of angel and pixie. Wait until you see her nurse a stray camel through the whooping cough. Patty Ann will inch her way into your heart. She's... well, she's *Alice!*

THIS IS ALICE is produced by that house of hits, Desilu. It's the logical successor to "I Love Lucy," "December Bride," "Sheriff of Cochise," and "The Danny Thomas Show."

Phyllis played the mother in this series

I Was a Teenage Frankenstein

I Was a Teenage Frankenstein

The demise of Phyllis in I Was a Teenage Frankenstein

Panther Girl of the Kongo

Superman and the Mole Men lobby card

L-R: George Reeves, Lucien Littlefield, Phyllis, Jack Larson, Robert Shayne "The Runaway Robot"

Panther Girl of the Kongo w/ "Emma"

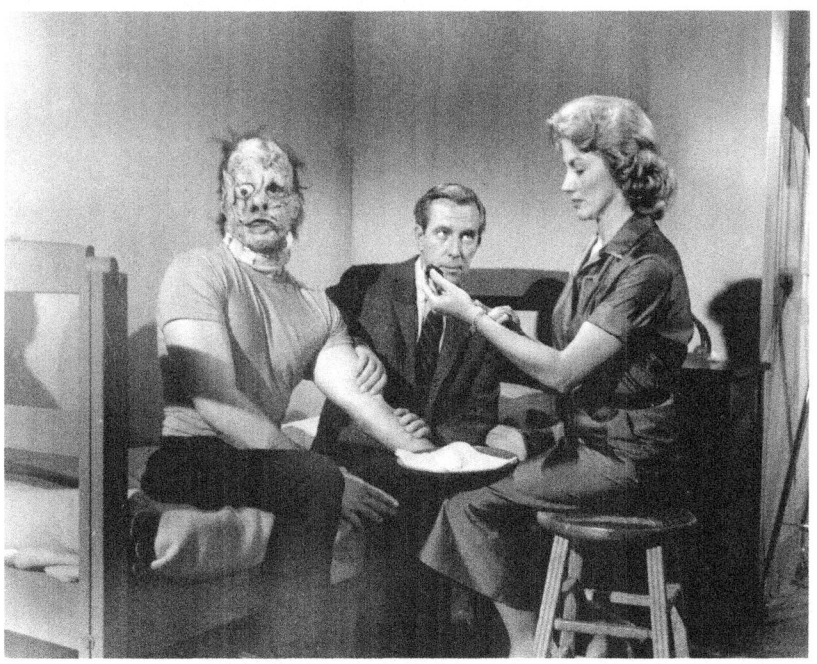

I Was a Teenage Frankenstein w/ Whit Bissell

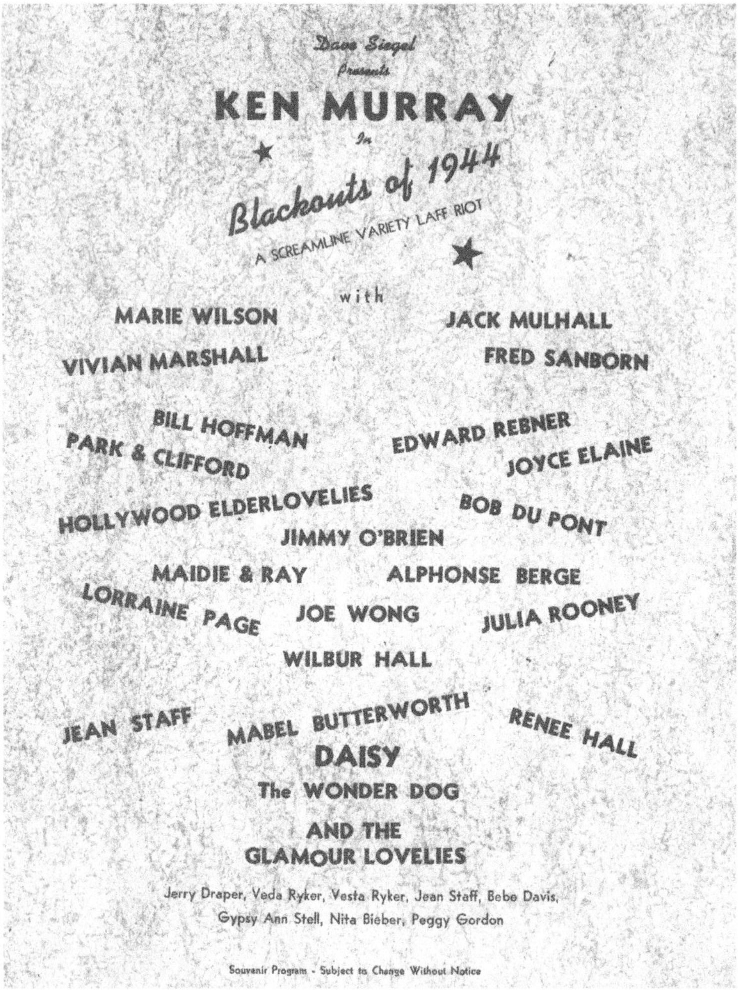

Dave Siegel presents

KEN MURRAY

in

Blackouts of 1944

A SCREAMLINE VARIETY LAFF RIOT

with

MARIE WILSON   JACK MULHALL
VIVIAN MARSHALL   FRED SANBORN

BILL HOFFMAN
PARK & CLIFFORD   EDWARD REBNER
          JOYCE ELAINE
HOLLYWOOD ELDERLOVELIES   BOB DU PONT
JIMMY O'BRIEN
MAIDIE & RAY   ALPHONSE BERGE
LORRAINE PAGE   JOE WONG   JULIA ROONEY
WILBUR HALL

JEAN STAFF   MABEL BUTTERWORTH   RENEE HALL

DAISY
The WONDER DOG

AND THE
GLAMOUR LOVELIES

Jerry Draper, Veda Ryker, Vesta Ryker, Jean Staff, Bebe Davis,
Gypsy Ann Stell, Nita Bieber, Peggy Gordon

Souvenir Program - Subject to Change Without Notice

Gypsie Ann Stell as one of the "Glamour Lovelies"

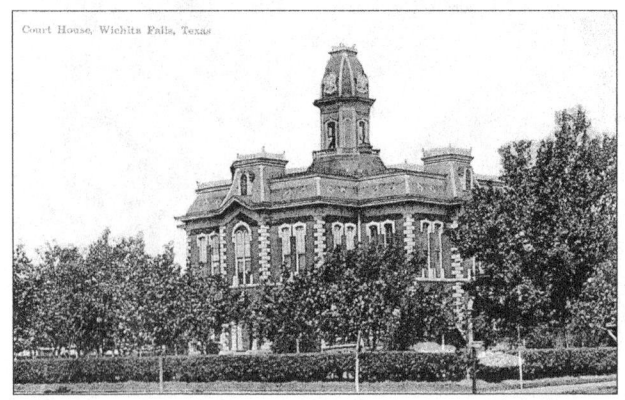

Courthouse where Phyllis' parents were married (1926)

Phyllis and Bart Williams at Midnight Patrol banquet (1988)

Phyllis and George O'Hanlon in "So You Want to be a Cowboy"(1951) Courtesy of Randy Skretvedt

Postcard of "Ken Murray's Blackouts" Where Phyllis got her first professional start in Hollywood

At the Charlette Western Film Fair (1988)

From: John C. Flinn
Monogram Pictures Corp.
4376 Sunset Drive
Hollywood 27, Calif.

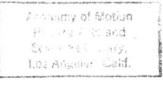

September, 1951

Biography

PHYLLIS COATES

Vital Statistics:

Birthdate..........Jan. 15, 1927   Weight....................110 lbs.
Birthplace...Wichita Falls, Tex.   Color of Hair................Red
Height..................5' 3½"   Color of Eyes...............Blue

Phyllis Coates is a pretty, blue-eyed redhead who came to Hollywood as a dancer and fast is becoming a queen of the Westerns.

Educated in her native Texas -- in Catholic schools at Abilene and Stanton and in Odessa High School by which she was graduated -- she first wanted to be a great dancer.

Her first professional work was done soon after her arrival in Hollywood when she appeared in the famed Ken Murray's "Blackouts" at the El Capitan theatre. Later she was a featured dancer at the Florentine Gardens, then (1944) a popular film and night club.

But as soon as Richard Bare, a Warner Bros., director, saw her, her career changed. She was offered -- and accepted -- a screen contract at that studio, where she remained for more than a year and for which she regularly appeared in a series of short subjects.

During the last two years, Miss Coates has become something of a specialty as the girl who falls in love (but never seems to have a romance) with cowboys -- on the screen, that is.

Miss Coates is married to Bob Nelms, musician now with The Three Dons. They are the parents of a girl, Christopher, born in 1949. They live in a Hollywood bungalow.

        Picture Credits: THE LONGHORN (MONO)
                            BLUES BUSTERS (MONO)
                            OUTLAWS OF TEXAS (MONO)
                            MAN FROM SONORA (MONO)
                            CANYON RAIDERS (MONO)
                            NEVADA BADMEN (MONO)
                            OUTLAW JUSTICE (MONO)
                            THE HOUSE ACROSS THE STREET (WB)

###

The Untouchables "Ain't We Got Fun"

Stage play "Never Too Late" with Robert Shayne (1978)

At the Edgar Kennedy Celebration in Monterey with Our Gang alumni: Dorothy DeBorba, Tommy Bond

At the Edgar Kennedy Celebration L-R: Bevis Faversham, Jeffrey Weissman, the author, Phyllis, Mark Kennedy (as his Grandfather-Edgar Kennedy in a radio reenactment of the "Wedding of Stan Laurel" (1997)

Bottom image: Tyler St. Mark, Bart Williams, Lois Laurel Hawes, Phyllis at at the Sons of the Desert convention in Sacramento (2010)

Phyllis w/ Walter Reed in Salinas (1991)

Posing in Bart Williams 1947 Chrysler (once owned by Stan Laurel)

Phyllis at home in Monterey w/ her dog, "Lucky"

Spiderman captured Phyllis at the New York Collectors Show

Author with Bart Williams and Phyllis As F.D.R. and Eleanor Roosevelt

Author with Phyllis at the Cinecon in Hollywood (2012) Phyllis' last public appearance

Chapter Nine
The Return of Lois Lane

With Bevis Faversham, Jeffrey Weissman, Mark Kennedy (1997)

1994 WAS QUITE THE YEAR for Phyllis and her long association with her most famous character, Lois Lane. There were autograph shows, conventions, banquets and television guest shots based on her fame.

The Hollywood Ray Courts Show

On January 13, 1994, Bart Williams was paramount in arranging Phyllis to attend the first "Ray Courts Show" at the Beverly Garland Hotel in Hollywood. Attendees were charged an entrance fee and could purchase photos of their celebrity favorites directly from each artist. The autograph fees were set by each star.

Phyllis was a guest celebrity along with the following stars:

> Paul Petersen: *The Donna Reed Show,* Brandon Cruz: *The Courtship of Eddie's Father,* and Lisa Loring: *The Addams Family.* Among the heroes of the 1940s-'60s were cowboys Montie Montana, George Montgomery, and Monte Hale; Gordon Scott of *Tarzan,* Phyllis Coates of TV's *Superman,* Hal Smith of *The Andy Griffith Show,* and Edd (Kookie) Byrnes of *77 Sunset Strip.* More than 100 dealers participated in the show, held four times a year. Show hours were Saturday 10 A.M.-7 P.M. and Sunday 10 A.M.-5 P.M. Admission was $5, children free with an adult.

Phyllis said to me later, "I had to be dragged there by Bart, but once I was there, I really enjoyed the experience of meeting and signing for fans."

On April 1994, Phyllis went to Los Angeles to film the latest incarnation of the Superman franchise, this time to play Lois Lane's *mother* in the primetime series aired episode of TV's *Lois and Clark-House of Luther."* It was the last episode of the series of season one.

From the papers came this original announcement:

> **It's the Original Lois Lane!**
> Phyllis Coates, who first played the feisty girl reporter on the classic Superman TV series, will pop up on the May 8th season finale of ABC's *Lois and Clark: The New Adventures of Superman* as Ellen Lane, Lois' mom. In the episode, Ellen attends the wedding of her daughter (Teri Hatcher) to Lex Luther, unaware that the villainous Luthor has trapped the Man of Steel in a deadly kryptonite cage.[130]

For promotion to the episode, Phyllis appeared with actress Teri Hatcher on the *Good Morning America* television show on May 1, 1994. Teri Hatcher told the audience that it was her idea to bring

---
130 *Abilene Reporter News* April 17, 1994

in Phyllis for a wedding scene. "After all," said Teri. "I would want my mother to be there." For the record, as Ellen Lane, Phyllis did share lines with Teri Hatcher's "Lois." In prepping in her wedding dress, and in a state of indecision about going through with the wedding, Ellen tells her daughter, "Just do what your heart tells you." Those were the words she longed to hear, for Lois stopped at the altar to announce, "I can't do this."

From *TV Guide*: **Wedding Bells for Lois?**

> Invitations are sent to the cream of Metropolis society requesting their presence at the marriage of Lois Lane and Lex Luthor in the conclusion of a two-part season finale. Lois' mom (played by Phyllis Coates, TV's first Lois Lane) arrives for the wedding, but Lois' friends from the *Daily Planet* won't be in attendance…some are busy sifting through evidence concerning the fall of the paper; Perry is appealing to a media mogul to rebuild the *Planet*; and Clark is fighting for his life—Superman has been felled by a massive dose of Kryptonite.[131]

In May of 1994, *People* magazine featured Phyllis in an article called "*Fast Pace Lois.*" The photographer and interviewer came to her house for a photo shoot in and around Carmel and Monterey with Phyllis posed at the beach. A number of shots were taken throughout the day including Phyllis with her dog.

I happened to drop by afterward to see how it went. Phyllis remarked that it went "pretty well," but at the end of the session the photographer asked if she could do him "a favor?" He pulled out a "Superman shirt," the one with the Superman emblem on it.

Phyllis was always accommodating in these kinds of things, sometimes to a fault. She put it on and the photographer had her pose as if she is unveiling a costume underneath, much like how Clark Kent is shown in the comic books. When she relayed the story to me, I told her, "You *know* that is the shot he is going to use." And sure enough, it was. Phyllis was a bit dismayed when the issue came out. The picture wasn't exactly flattering.

---

131 *TV Guide* April 8, 1994

Superman Festival in Metropolis, Illinois June 9-12, 1994

Author Chuck Harter reminisces about the festival in an email to author:

> I made my first visit to Metropolis as a guest at the 16th Annual Superman Celebration. The other guests were Kirk Alyn (Superman) and Tommy Bond (Jimmy Olsen) from the *Superman* series. The first season TV *Superboy* (John Haymes Newton) was a guest as well. Phyllis Coates rounded out the celebrities. There were numerous appearances for all over the four days and Phyllis was greeted by the many Superman fans who attended the event. She was gracious and patient with the numerous requests for autographs and photo ops.
>
> There was one instance when an older fan asked her what she thought about Noel Neill's dislike for her. This person was trying for a confrontation and had a portable tape recorder handy. Phyllis gave a diplomatic reply and said that she didn't understand it and certainly had no ill feelings toward Noel. She also said she felt Noel did a good job in the direction that the show took in the five seasons after she left. Later that evening, I had dinner with Phyllis and really enjoyed our conversation. She was a classy lady with a good sense of humor. After the Celebration we did stay in touch with the occasional phone call or lunch, and I remember her very fondly.
>
> The schedule of events was impressive:

June 10th

9 a.m.	*Adventures of Superboy* video, in the convention tent.
10 a.m.	Tommy Bond and **Phyllis Coates**, the actor and actress who portrayed Jimmy Olsen in the Superman serial and Lois Lane in the Superman television series, in the convention tent.
Noon	Lunch with the Superman celebrities and the Superman Trivia Contest in the convention tent.

1-3 p.m.	John Haymes Newton, TV's original Superboy, in the convention tent.
3-5 p.m.	Kirk Alyn, the first actor to portray Superman, in the convention tent.
5 p.m.	"The Life and Death of George Reeves," presented by author Chuck Harter.
5:45 p.m.	**Lois Lane Award**, sponsored by the *Metropolis Planet* presented by **Phyllis Coates**.
6 p.m.	Superman drama on stage.
6-8 p.m.	Ice Cream social on the courthouse lawn, sponsored by the Massac County Farm Bureau and Homemakers.
6:30 p.m.	Talent shows on the stage.
7 p.m.	Superman 4-mile road race and 2-mile super fun walk, Ft. Massac State Park.
7:30 p.m.	Country-Western line dancing.

June 11th

9 a.m.	*Adventures of Superboy* video in the convention tent.
9 a.m.	Pre-parade children's games on the stage.
9-6 p.m.	Collectibles exhibits Senior Citizens Center.
10 a.m.	Parade, from Washington Park to Riverboat Landing to Superman Square.
11-1 p.m.	Tommy Bond and Phyllis Coates in the convention tent.
Noon	Lunch with the Superman celebrities.
12:30	Superman drama on stage.
1 p.m.	John Haymes Newton, in the convention tent.
1 p.m.	Clark Kent-Lois Lane Pool Tournament, Trails Inn Billiards and Lounge.
1 p.m.	Fireman's Water Fight, Eighth and Market Streets.
1 p.m.	Super Dog Contest on the stage.
1-5 p.m.	Children's games on the courthouse lawn.
2-4 p.m.	Superman arm wrestling contest on the stage.
3 p.m.	Kirk Alyn, in the convention tent.
3 p.m.	Lois Lane Screams for ice cream. Enjoy ice cream with the Superman celebrities.

4 p.m.	Superman costume contest for children on stage.
5 p.m.	Jamie Murray-Myhr, Superman poster artist in the convention tent.
6 p.m.	Little Miss Supergirl and Superboy pageants on the stage.

June 12

8 a.m.	Antique and classic car show, in Fort Massac State Park.
9-11 a.m.	Tommy Bond and Phyllis Coates in the convention center.
9-6 p.m.	Collectible exhibits at the Senior Citizen's Center.
10-5 p.m.	200th anniversary of the American Ft. Massac, Ft. Massac State Park.
11-1 p.m.	John Haymes Newton, in the convention tent.
1 p.m.	Lunch with the Superman celebrities in the convention tent.
1-4 p.m.	Metropolis Garden Club Garden Walk.
2-4 p.m.	Tea in the Garden Walk.
3-5 p.m.	Kirk Alyn, in the convention tent.
5 p.m.	"Life and Death of George Reeves," in the convetion tent.
5 p.m.	Superman Screams for ice cream.

In 1996, Phyllis was cast in something called, *Hollywood: The Movie*. It was released on video only. This one hour and forty-two-minute abomination, exploitation video project never saw the light of day anywhere, but it is worth mentioning. According to the Internet Movie Database (IMDb) the plot tells of a "young over-anxious director trying to create the next great epic motion picture. In attempting to create a warm family film, he discovers that the only way he can get financing is by "showing Jessica Hahn's breasts."

The cast included Morton Downey, Jr., Imogene Coca, Julie Strain, and Jessica Hahn. Phyllis played "Old Dora" in which her character would magically transform into a young starlet. It was an ultra-low budget production of $50,000.

The shoot was in Kansas City, Missouri; Phyllis hated to fly as it was. Phyllis came back home and told me of the dreadful experience. She was especially shocked at Imogene Coca, whom she described as "really losing it."

1996 Hollywood Kryptonite book, Death of George Reeves

When the book *Hollywood Kryptonite* came out 1996, I read it and loaned it to Phyllis. It was an opportunity to discuss the George Reeves case with her. She hadn't been in touch with the rest of the cast for some time.

Phyllis and I had the occasion to finally compare some notes that were brought up by the "Kraptonite" book (how Jack Larson described it as). She was bewildered on much of what was written.

I never got any indication that Phyllis was ever romantically involved with George Reeves. Phyllis said that Toni (Mannix) always showed up during lunch (with a paper bag) that contained alcohol. Phyllis said that Toni liked her and often treated her to lunch and/or buy her clothing. She respected their relationship.

During that time of her life (1951) Phyllis was on her second marriage, and had a child who had a physical disability. Phyllis told me George insisted that Phyllis join him for a drink at 4 P.M. before continuing the day's work. This became a routine. Phyllis mentioned that she was starting to gain weight and realized this might not be good for her career. She said, "No one knew that what we were doing would even be looked at, much less cared about 50 years later." *Make that 73 years later, Phyllis!*

She had no problem walking away from the show. Over the years of the *Superman* run on television, Phyllis was in many other television shows and science fiction films. She was in one movie where she never got paid (*The Incredible Petrified World*). Phyllis was trusting to a fault.

1997 Edgar Kennedy Celebration in Monterey

The one and only Edgar Kennedy Celebration in Monterey was held during July 3-6, 1997. The International Laurel and Hardy Appreciation Society (better known as "The Sons of the Desert") held a mini-convention in recognition of film star and Monterey County native, Edgar Kennedy (born 1890). He died in 1948 but left a legacy of films, more than 500. An original Keystone Cop for Mack Sennett he also played foil to Charlie Chaplin, Laurel and Hardy, the Our Gang kids, the Marx Brothers, and supported John Wayne, Lucille Ball, and Doris Day in their films.

The event drew over 200 people from five different nations and Phyllis Coates volunteered to help out. Two of her very dear friends, Bart Williams and Lois Laurel Hawes, were coming up from Los Angeles to partake in the festivities. They included *The Perfect Day* picnic, the ice cream cone catching contest, a *Battle of the Century* softball game, public showing of films, participation in the City of Monterey July 4th parade, a Mid-nighty film event (where the conventioneers wore their exaggerated night clothes), and the launching of fireworks that night over the Pacific Ocean.

The celebration climaxed on July 5, 1997, for a "Policeman's Ball" night at the host hotel. The main feature was a radio reenactment of a radio show that Laurel and Hardy participated in during 1943, it was called *The Marriage of Stan Laurel*. The original broadcast featured Stan and Ollie, with Edgar Kennedy as the Justice of the Peace, and Patsy Moran. It was introduced by Lucille Ball.

In the radio reenactment, Stan Laurel was played by Jeffrey Weissman and Oliver Hardy was performed by Bevis Faversham. Phyllis played the Patsy Moran role and wore a bride's veil dotted with orange blossoms. Bart Williams was the director and sound effect engineer. Edgar Kennedy's grandson, Mark Kennedy, played his famous grandfather to the hilt. Unbeknownst to the rest of the cast and audience, right before the performance, Mark went to a barber and got his crown shaved. He topped it off with a nightcap as per the character. He already had a boisterous appearance in the play when he, in mocked frustration, pulled off his nightcap and threw it on the ground. The whole audience erupted in shock, screams, and laughter.

Phyllis played her part with softness; she and Jeffrey touched hearts with their performances. Bevis was a great Oliver Hardy and perfectly meshed together with his partner. Weissman and Faversham captured the magic of Laurel and Hardy as well they should, they were professional L&H performers for Universal Studios for many years.

Phyllis invited the cast over to her house afterwards for a wrap party. During the celebration weekend, she was all over the place making people feel at home. She signed anything put before her, even napkins. Everyone knew who she was, but as usual, she never thought of herself in an exalted way. Phyllis always preferred acting in front of an audience and the audience always showed their affection.

Jeffrey Weissman

Mr. Weissman is an accomplished actor on stage, screen and television. At the time of the Edgar Kennedy Celebration in Monterey (1997), he was teamed up with Bevis Faversham as performers at Universal Studios as Laurel and Hardy. For the skit, *The Marriage of Stan Laurel,* he and Bevis were introduced to Phyllis Coates for the first time, and they meshed completely for their roles. Jeffrey and Phyllis were terrific together as bride and groom. Jeffrey reminisced about participating in the skit and afterwards.

> Mark Kennedy threw everyone when he surprised both cast and audience by revealing during his slow burn tribute to his grandfather, having shaved his head, thus very much resembling Edgar. Phyllis enjoyed working with us, and she invited us to visit her at her home while in Monterey. We had a lovely time listening to Phyllis recount her days working with George Reeves. She was hospitable, relaxed and a delight. I recall seeing some Hurrell photos of a beautiful Phyllis in her prime. Years later I visited her in Sonoma where she once again was very hospitable, but had a rough period dealing with her son.[132]

Raymond Daum

There was an evening in the year 2000 when I invited Phyllis and Bart Williams (who came up from L.A.) over to the house to

---

132 Email interview from Jeffrey Weissman March 30, 2024

meet a friend of mine and have dinner. His name was Raymond Daum. He was a retired film professor at the University of Texas, but he was better known for a book he wrote: *Walking with Garbo*.[133]

Professor Daum was working at the United Nations building in New York in the 1960s and he had the opportunity to invite Ms. Garbo for a personal tour. She accepted and trusted him. They walked the streets of New York frequently and talked openly. After she died in 1990, Daum put together very personal remembrances about her in book form. When *Walking with Garbo* was published, it became a top ten *New York Times Best Seller* book.

Daum was very respectful and charmed both Bart and Phyllis, they liked him immediately. At some point, Raymond offered an observation but he prefaced his point by saying, "I'm not in the business, but…" Phyllis jumped right in, "You *are* in the business." That was a very nice thing to say.

After dinner, I thought I'd take advantage and showed my guests an episode from one of the Abbott and Costello television shows. This particular one (*Cheapskates*) featured Phyllis as a gangster's moll. Afterwards, I showed them a laserdisc version of *Superman and the Mole Men*."

We chuckled through the whole movie; Phyllis laughed the most. She said she had never seen it before. Near the end of the film, both she and Superman (George Reeves) were looking up into the sky where the director edited something poignant. Phyllis said, "So that's what we were supposed to be seeing."

---

133 Daum, Raymond. Walking with Garbo Harper Collins Publishers New York, New York 1991

Chapter Ten
Move to Sonoma

With Terri Hatcher "Lois and Clark-The New Adventures of Superman" (1994)

Visiting Phyllis at her home

BY 2005, PHYLLIS ANSWERED a call from her youngest daughter, Laura, to relocate north where she lived in Sonoma, California. Phyllis didn't have family close by in Monterey, so she bought herself a condo in wine country at 166 West Spain Street. Sonoma is named for Saint Francis Solanus and is the last mission built by the padres in northern California. It is now preserved as a state park and is within walking distance from Phyllis' home.

Laura was a special needs school teacher, and also volunteered to administer Phyllis' fan mail and communications. She set it up so that Phyllis could sign and sell her photos and autographs to her many fans. It was a good little hobby for Phyllis, and she really enjoyed this new arrangement. Phyllis gave wholehearted handwritten notes and letters with personalized autographs to those that sought them.

I had a new woman in my life at this point and I wanted Phyllis to meet her. It was a rainy day when Michelle and I went to see her. Phyllis was always a delight, and her distinct golden voice was reassuring. Her condo was filled with art in the form of paintings and antiques. It was all decorated with refined taste. Michelle was an art major in college and she was attracted to a series of framed original pen and ink sketches drawn by Lionel Barrymore that were personally autographed to Phyllis.

By 2005 I had written *Edgar Kennedy—Master of the Slowburn*, my first published book, and I wanted to give Phyllis a copy. I had the distinct pleasure of placing a copy in her hands. She was slightly astonished and said, "You're a *writer?*"

Then came time for dinner and Phyllis suggested one of the many restaurants around the mission. When we sat down, Phyllis noticed that it was very crowded and noisy. To make matters worse, she couldn't hear the waitress. Hearing was always a problem for Phyllis ever since she made *Panther Girl of the Kongo* when an accidental gun discharge occurred near one of her ears. Phyllis and I had that in common as I had the same problem when a deputy fired his gun accidently in a closed environment. My hearing was permanently impacted. Phyllis then suggested we meet at a quieter place; I welcomed it. We were entertained when Phyllis justified the move because of "those Minnie-Mouse voices" that the waitresses had.

When we got back to the apartment, we were all relaxed and enjoying each other's company. Michelle inquired if she could ask a question. Phyllis said, "Sure, I'll answer any question you'd like."

Q: "Did you ever kiss George Reeves?"

Without answering, Phyllis reached up with her right hand and in a stroking motion said, "He had the most beautiful face."

Phyllis then elaborated, "They never would let George and me look like we were 'playing around.'" She also remembered that the constant coat she wore was like a "horse's collar." She said, "We all wore the same clothes so it would match in editing. When we filmed, we'd shoot all the indoor scenes for all the scripts for the season. No one knew what was going on."

Q: Did you ever meet Noel Neill?

A: Once. George introduced us when I dropped by the set. Noel was furious. We could have had so much fun.

It was around this time that I also sent a copy of my book to Bart Williams in Los Angeles. I received a sparkling letter of appreciation from him. He was enthralled with the book and said he had talked to Phyllis about it. Bart said that Phyllis was looking for someone to help her put a book together about her life. He said they both agreed it should be me for several reasons.[134] I took the letter as a supreme compliment, but I was hesitant to accept. It might have been different if Phyllis was still living in Monterey; I could have started at the beginning of her recollections and captured them by tape recording. To take on such a subject matter, I would need to do my homework so I could prompt her with intelligent questions. At the time, there were no newspaper archives easily obtained on-line.

Bart both tempted and encouraged me further by saying, "Phyllis dated many leading men in Hollywood but would never discuss it.[135]"

I don't kiss and tell – Phyllis to Bart Williams

Despite Phyllis' classy attitude regarding her former beaus, this much we know: Phyllis was dating future director Jerry Warren when she was sixteen, and when she was in between husbands in

---

134 Bart Williams email to author June 13, 2006
135 *Ibid*

1953, she dated actor John Hart. All very natural stuff and hardly racy. There would have been concerns how forthright Phyllis would have been on this subject anyway.

Nevertheless, I started trying to build up Phyllis' family background for her genealogy. Some of the spellings were very unusual and I always had to call Bart to confirm. I still couldn't match up with the census with much of what I was told. All this became a strain on all three of us. I valued their friendship and I told Bart that he was better suited for writing a book about Phyllis, but he begged off saying that he was "Too close to Phyllis to do it." I was already committed to writing other books now that I was retired from the Sheriff's Department. Getting up to Sonoma was out of the question for sustained interviews. This was a project that was tabled, and I sensed that Phyllis was relieved by it.

Sept. 6, 2006 Hollywoodland

This film was an alleged biopic of George Reeves' life and death starring Ben Affleck as Superman. It certainly wasn't a documentary as it liberally used heavy doses of fiction to invent the facts. The title itself was misleading and the story dissolved into a mess.

Actress Lorry Ayres played the role as a slinky version of Phyllis for only a few minutes. There was a sequence where the actors were in Perry White's office pacing out a scene, when Affleck as Clark Kent, started dry-humping Lois Lane on the desk top. On the film, it played as an "outtake." Ayres, as Phyllis, laughed like a barroom hyena. It was dreadful.

Phyllis later told me she made it a point to see this film; it must be strange to see oneself as a character being played by someone else. Phyllis said to me, "I'm no square, but… I was a bit embarrassed." What modern moviegoers might not realize, is that there was a decorum of professionalism while making a movie or TV production back then. The movie didn't clear anything up pertaining to the cause of George Reeves' death, but offered plenty of doubtful scenarios. It should be noted that in 1959, Eddie Mannix was a very sick man with a debilitating heart condition. He championed George Reeves' ascent to director status. In the movie, Toni Mannix was a young, vibrant, sexy figure of a woman in 1959.

However, according to Phyllis, Toni had become "rather matronly." Some existing photos of her during that time period bear witness to that. *Hollywoodland* is one of the worst films I ever saw, and it bombed at the box office.

2007 David Tokar Dies

The years of being a heroin addict finally caught up with Phyllis' second born child. David Tokar Press died in the hospital in Salinas on August 26, 2007. By this time, he was 50 years old and died of natural causes. A doctor signed the death certificate, so no need for an autopsy. Phyllis was living in Sonoma and was estranged from her son by then. She had gone to bat for him numerous times but couldn't make an impact. There had been a previous time that David overdosed and the hospital staff reached Phyllis to tell her of his impending death. Naturally it shook her up, but her son recovered. This time it was final and there wasn't anything she could do. Phyllis always felt guilt about her son's demise, but the nature of the drug addiction meant there would be no happy ending. Interestingly, when Phyllis passed away, most of the obituaries mentioned that David died in 2011. It is erroneous and 2007 is the exact date as confirmed per Monterey County Coroner's records.

Saw Herself in Sara Palin

Sometime during the year 2007, my wife Michelle and I were shopping at Trader Joe's in Pacific Grove when we heard a familiar voice. It was Phyllis bending down in an aisle looking at the goods and was actually chortling to herself in good humor. I asked, "Phyllis is that you?" We didn't expect her to be in town since she lived so far away. She was happy to see us and explained that she had a court appearance regarding her ex-husband's property settlement. She was staying over at a girlfriend's house for the duration. We invited her over for dinner and were thrilled when she accepted.

Michelle and I picked her up later. My daughter Diana was invited as a guest as well. She remembered Phyllis from the time I had everyone over to watch *Superman and the Mole Men*. Phyllis was always polite and a down-to-earth person. Phyllis tried to encourage my daughter, "You can be an actress, too." Phyllis told us of the times when she lived on the Monterey Peninsula when she was invited to Seaside High School to teach students the basics of acting.

At the dinner table Phyllis started talking politics. Uh oh. It was really getting uncomfortable because she was talking about "communists taking over." This was during the time John McCain announced his candidacy for President of the United States and his running mate was Sara Palin. Phyllis was fascinated with the Vice-Presidential candidate; she didn't point it out, but there is a physical resemblance to Sara Palin and young Phyllis. We successfully avoided talking politics the rest of the pleasant evening.

New York City Collectors Show 2008

At the Manhattan Holiday Inn on May 24-25, Phyllis was a featured guest along with Larry Storch, Soupy Sales, and Beverly Washburn. The fans were in awe of her and very respectful. Phyllis' regular escort, Bart Williams, could not free himself nor was I available. A girlfriend also backed out but Bruce Dettman escorted Phyllis who was beginning to suffer vertigo symptoms. He did a great job guiding Phyllis to meet her fans. She posed for pictures, signed autographs, and answered all the questions put to her. As she was seated signing photos of herself, the people in line saw someone dressed in a Spiderman suit sneaking up on her from behind. All was quiet in anticipation when she was surprised with this superhero's presence. Of course, Phyllis shrieked, then good-naturedly they posed for pictures together.

Lone Pine 19th Annual Film Festival 2008

Phyllis was a special guest for this event. She reminisced to the audience that she was in the film *Cattle Empire* with Joel McCrea shot at Lone Pine. She also mentioned working in *The Lone Ranger*, *Gunsmoke*, and *The Cisco Kid* at this venue.

Sons of the Desert Convention

In June of 2010, Phyllis and Bart Williams surprised the conventioneers of the Laurel and Hardy Appreciation Society by attending a themed banquet night in Sacramento. She was not an announced guest, so no one knew she was coming. Bart clued me in; they came up for one special WWII dress-up theme with a live big band. Everyone wore various vintage costumes and hairstyles. Bart and Phyllis arrived and stopped the show; Bart was dressed as Franklin D. Roosevelt and Phyllis as his wife, Eleanor. I got close to her and she was talking in character as Eleanor Roosevelt the whole night. What a treat to hear. I hadn't heard that voice in a long time, but Phyllis nailed it. We had a nice little reunion. Most attendees were flabbergasted she was there and of course she signed autographs. Some of the attendees yanked their paper napkins off the table for her signature.

During the convention there was a German filmmaker, Andreas Baum, shooting a documentary on Laurel and Hardy. He lined up a few of the attendees to include Tyler St. Mark, Bart Williams, Lois Laurel Hawes, and Phyllis Coates to do on-camera interviews to augment his film. The result was released in 2011 as *Laurel and Hardy Their Lives and Magic.* In a very short interview, Phyllis was able to share what it was like working at the Hal Roach Studios in the 1950's. She was in quite a few TV shows there before the studio closed in 1963.

The convention also presented an opportunity for me to introduce Stan Taffel to Phyllis; Stan was a fan but had never had the opportunity to meet her. During this time, Stan was vice-president of the Cinecon in Los Angeles (he is now President). I introduced him to both Bart Williams and Phyllis, and Stan enthusiastically proposed that Phyllis be a special celebrity at the event. That happened in 2012.

Chapter Eleven
The Toasts of Cinecon

Cinecon (2012) with Richard Bare and Stan Taffel (2012).

Interview of Richard Bare and Phyllis Coates by Stan Taffel during the Cinecon September 2, 2012 at the Egyptian Theater, Hollywood #48

Film career achievements Society for Cinefiles

AS PART OF THE FESTIVITIES of the Cinecon weekend, the organizing committee invited both Phyllis and her first husband, Richard Bare, to address the audience. I had met up with her earlier in the day at the hotel and we shared a nice spontaneous picture together, taken by Chuck Harter. It was not posed and captured two old friends sharing a moment.

Phyllis was now eighty-five-years-old and at times needed a cane to help balance her walk. She walked arm-in-arm with Bart Williams to the front of the stage to an excited audience of film buffs, well aware of her film and TV credits.

There were two tall stools to climb on and Phyllis casually mentioned that she suffered from vertigo, then asked innocently, "Did you ever hear of such a thing?" To an audience of film appreciators, they sure did know of *Vertigo*, the Alfred Hitchcock film. Richard Bare now ninety-nine-years-old, and in great shape, walked up to Phyllis and touched her gently on the cheek, then climbed onto his chair to be interviewed by Stan Taffel.

Prior to introducing them to the crowd, a short film from the *Behind the Eight Ball* series was shown; it was *So You Want to Be Pretty*. It was directed by Richard Bare and featured Phyllis as the wife married to George O'Hanlon's Joe McDoakes.

The plot of the short had the married couple bored with each other, and even more imposing was the fact both had exaggerated over-bite teeth. Individually they decide to see a dentist unbeknownst to each other. The dentist was played by the terrifically eccentric Fritz Feld. Each procedure was a success so naturally, they wanted to meet other people. Alice McDoakes is now beautiful and George is dashingly handsome. They see each other in a bar, but don't recognize each other so they flirt and plan to run away together. That is until they realize the person that they are falling in love with is their spouse. They fall back in love and decide to reverse their teeth operation so that they can return to their normal life.

The combination of the comedy of the film short, and the fact that Phyllis and Richard were there made the evening magical. That film generated so much laughter, it was heartening for both of them to experience all those years ago. Phyllis basked in the glory at the audience reaction.

At the conclusion of the film Stan Taffel interviewed both Phyllis and Richard while sitting on bar stools in front of the audience.

Stan Taffel: Please tell us what memories come back after watching these comedies.

Richard Bare: Well, we made 63 shorts and *So You Want to Quit Smoking* was the first one [1942]. I shot it at USC because I was a young teacher in those days and they asked me if I would write and direct a short film that could give the students some actual experience. So I sat down and wrote *So You Want to Give Up Smoking*. I got hold of George O'Hanlon who was not more than an extra, he'd get one line here and there. We made the film, so I took it out to Warner Brothers and showed it to them and when the film was over, I was sitting next to a gent from New York and he says, "Well kid, how much do you want for it?" I said, twenty-five. He says, "You mean twenty-five thousand?" I said, "No, twenty-five hundred." He said, "Well that's different." They took me into the lawyer's office and said, "When this young man as soon as he brings out the negative, give him a check for twenty-five hundred, we're buying his short." So, I was elated and, on the way, back to the university, it occurred to me that I didn't own the damn thing. I went to the head of the department and told him that I sold the short. He asked, "What did you get for it?" I said, "Twenty-five hundred." He said, "Well, supposing you endowed the university with one thousand and we can forget the whole matter. That started the whole thing; it ran in the theaters and did really well, so they said, "Make another." So, I got George [O'Hanlon] again and put him under personal contract. He was to get $400.00. We had a suspicion there might be more. We made one called *So You Think You're Allergic*, and another one called, *So You Think You Need Glasses*.

Stan Taffel: OK, that was the beginning, so how did you get to cast Phyllis Coates as Joe [McDoakes] wife?

Richard Bare: (facing Phyllis) I'd like for you to tell how we met, if you can remember.

Phyllis Coates: I was under contract to Warners and they said, "We want you to meet Mr. Bare who does this series. And at that point and time in my career I said, I'd love to meet Mr. Bare and you took me on, right?

Richard Bare: Well, yes, fairly accurate. My version of meeting this charming young lady was at the Cock 'n Bull restaurant and she was introduced to me by a lady friend of mine who happened to be the secretary of your agent. So, we met that night and I was casting several other girls playing the part of Alice [McDoakes] and one by one, they dropped out, got married or they went on to bigger things. I had you [Phyllis] come out to the studio and read. I was enchanted and hired her. You were under contract to Richard Bare Productions; do you remember that? Anyway, somewhere down the line we fell in love.

Phyllis Coates: Oh yes.

Richard Bare: We went off to Vegas.

Phyllis Coates: It all comes back to me.

Richard Bare: I want to show Phyllis some pictures we took of our honeymoon.

Phyllis Coates(*Worried look*)

Stan Taffel: This is really a reunion for the both of them; they haven't seen each other for decades.

Richard Bare: And here we are on our honeymoon in Santa Barbara.

Stan Taffel: So, Phyllis, tell us how you got started. Was it with *Ken Murray's Blackouts*?

Phyllis Coates: Yes, and the Florentine Gardens, but I really cut my teeth on comedy, and Ken's Blackouts played at the El Capitan Theater. Ken said, "If you can put in the time, I'll put you in skits." I did a lot of skits with him and one thing led to another.

Stan Taffel: Now you worked at Republic, tell us what it was like working at Republic.

Phyllis Coates: It was tough but it was a lot of fun, I worked with western directors, you know, western people are different entirely from the Hollywood crowd; they are very down to earth. You get it and you shoot it and you hit your marks, and one time I didn't and I got knocked out. Lee Sholem was the director, he said, "Bring her back, we'll finish up the scene and she can go back." Boy those western guys, they knew how to set them up fast. It was a pleasure to work with them.

Stan Taffel: You got to work with him again on television, didn't you?

Phyllis Coates: Oh boy, did I.

Stan Taffel: There was a television show that most of us remember; do you remember working on a little something called *Superman*? The *original* Lois Lane on television! What was it like, because the character Lois Lane, which we have to talk about was really the first woman on television?

Phyllis Coates: I've been told that, yeah.

Stan Taffel: What was it like working on that show?

Phyllis Coates: Well, it was great, we worked six days a week and George [Reeves] had an open bar in his dressing room. We shot fast and George was great, a great man, just lovely. And his lady [Toni Mannix] liked me which made it easy, but oh boy we put a lot in the can in one day, from 6:30 [A.M.] till 6:30 or 7:00 at night and nobody batted an eye. You could touch somebody's props or their tools and nobody cared in those days. I had a little daughter who had a congenital hip and I was given a great apartment. The grips would come over and take her from one stage to another, you know, just friendly.

Stan Taffel: You did twenty-six episodes, which would be considered a season of *Superman* and then you didn't do anymore.

Phyllis Coates: I wanted to get out of *Superman* for personal reasons and I did a pilot for Jack Carson and Alan Jenkins. Didn't sell but at least I got loose from *Superman*.

Stan Taffel: Richard, for something like ten years you were doing the Joe McDoakes films on and off. So, tell me what was it like working with George O'Hanlon who most of us know as the voice of George Jetson, but these precious shorts, what was he like to work with?

Phyllis Coates: He was delightful; he was Dick's alter-ego.

Richard Bare: George and I discovered that we had the same sense of humor very early, thank God for that because that's what made the show a success. Strangely enough, when I was down at the university [U.S.C.] looking for somebody to play George, my wife at the time (turns to Phyllis), that was before you (laughter), she said, "Honey, I have just the boy that could play that kind of comedy." I said, "I don't know, he's your old boyfriend." I kept interviewing young men to do it and I couldn't find anybody that I thought was any good. She said, "Well, if you weren't so stubborn, I'll have him come out to see you." So, he came down to U.S.C. and I told him what we were going to do about a man that had the cigarette habit and he was trying all these different methods of humor, yet there was a seriousness of how you could really give up smoking. He pulled a cigarette out and started walking up and down doing it. I said, "You're the guy." He was just fantastic. The first short was not live dialogue, it was narrated.

Stan Taffel: So, you did a lot of directing and then of course you made the transition to television. Before we get to the one show that you're best remembered for, you worked for Rod Serling and you directed several episodes of *The Twilight Zone*.

Richard Bare: Oh yes I did, including my favorite episode.

Stan Taffel: This is the man who directed, *To Serve Man*. (applause). Rod Serling, what was he like?

Richard Bare: Well, the day I met Rod I had been hired by his production guy and Rod came in the room and I was expecting a long skinny guy, and he comes in and he looked like a quarterback from U.S.C. the way he put out his hand, "Good to see you." He was the antithesis of what you would think a writer of *The Twilight Zone was*.

Stan Taffel: What was the filming schedule like, how long did it take?

Richard Bare: We took three days(laughter).

Stan Taffel: Three days for a *Twilight Zone* episode? That's unbelievable. What everyone seems to know you best for is that you directed virtually every single episode of *Green Acres*. (applause) We have many fans in this room who grew up with *Green Acres* and who thank you from the bottom of their hearts for not just the five years it was on, but for the countless joy that the show continues to give.

Richard Bare: One month ago, I signed a contract to do *Green Acres* as a Broadway musical.

Phyllis Coates (clapping proudly)

Richard Bare: I've already written the book. Whether they're going to use it or not, I have no control over that, but I had acquired it a couple of years ago from the estate of J…who was one of the great comedy writers of all time, so we'll see how that works out. It'll probably take a year before it gets on the road to open up off-Broadway down here in Orange County.

Stan Taffel: And Arnold the Pig?

Richard Bare: Arnold is going to give us a problem when live; I'm not sure how they're going to handle it. Well, I won't be directing it, thank God.

Stan Taffel: So, Phyllis, you did a lot of other television as well; do you have any great memories of working on television aside from *Superman*? Because I know you did *The Cisco Kid*.

Phyllis Coates: I worked on a lot of shows. I worked with Joel McCrea, *Gunsmoke*. It's really hard for me to remember.

Stan Taffel: Now isn't it true that you made an appearance on a modern version of *Superman* called, *Lois and Clark*? Didn't you play Lois Lane's mother?

Phyllis Coates: I did play her mother; I came back to Hollywood. I lived in Carmel at the time and I didn't want to leave.

Stan Taffel: (to audience) Are there any more questions? Just raise your hand and speak really loudly.

Audience: What was your favorite Joe McDoakes?

Richard Bare: Well, I think my favorite was the one you just saw with the crazy people who couldn't kiss [*So You Want to be Pretty*].

Stan Taffel: Phyllis, do you have a favorite?

Phyllis Coates: George and I were dancing around imagining how beautiful we were. They were all fun.

Stan Taffel: Do you remember the pilot you did after *Superman*?

Phyllis Coates: We did *Superman and the Mole Men* and later it was divided into two episodes, but I saw it [the feature] in Scotland in its entirety and that's when the mole men came out of the ground with an Electrolux Vacuum Cleaner.

Audience: What was the one you did for Desilu, "Here Comes Alice, or There Goes Alice" [sic].

Phyllis Coates: I did a series called, *This is Alice* with a very talented little girl. Tommy Farrell, Lucien Littlefield, and I used David [Phyllis' son] as the baby.

Audience: That's the one you did with Beverly Washburn as the girl, right?

Stan Taffel: We're going back quite a few years here.

Audience: After your honeymoon, how long were you married?

Phyllis Coates: About seven months (laughter).

Richard Bare: It was a very interesting divorce because we were still in love and we continued to work together. I mean nothing had changed professionally

Audience: Have you seen the Charley Chase short, *Mighty Like a Moose*?

Richard Bare: Not that I recall. I think I read somewhere that there was a similar gag in there [*So You Want to be Pretty*], but I think that was George O'Hanlon's contribution.

Audience: This is a question for Mr. Bare. After becoming a successful comedy director, you changed course and did a couple of good crime melodramas. Why did you do that and go back to comedies?

Richard Bare: Oh, to make a living (laughter). I was on two contracts; one was the little independent company that I had where my profit was always the difference between how much, how cheaply I could make them. I'd get my son and I had George [O'Hanlon] under personal contract, then I married the other one [Phyllis] to kind of lock it all up (laughter).

Stan Taffel: Tell them about the later features you did.

Richard Bare: Jack Warner got to know me a little bit and vice versa. He said, "Give that kid a chance to direct a feature film. I did about six or seven low budget films for Warners and not one of them were in comedy. When television came along, they wanted somebody to produce their television. I said, "Well, what are they going to pay?" They said, "Five hundred dollars a week." "I said, hell, I make more than that directing." They said, "Well if you don't want to produce *Cheyenne* (which was their first show), who can you get?" I knew just the guy; I picked up the phone and I called Roy Hudgens over at Columbia and told him that he was just about ready to leave Columbia and to come over to my office. The next day he became my producer. I feel good about that.

Stan Taffel: You did some westerns like *The Dakotas?*

Richard Bare: And I did *77 Sunset Strip*. It was made as a feature. When it was done, they looked at it. They said, "Look, I think we have a series here. The feature was called *Girl on the Run* and it served as a pilot. So, they changed the name to *77 Sunset Strip*, and I directed a whole bunch of those.

Stan Taffel: So, Phyllis, I'm not saying this because you're here but you were always my favorite Lois Lane because when someone grabbed you, you'd be the one kicking and screaming. I felt bad for every actor that had to hold you down. What do you think about the more modern Lois Lane adaptations compared to yours?

Phyllis Coates: I wish you hadn't asked me that.

Stan Taffel: It's all right, we won't tell anyone.

Phyllis Coates: The whole mood changed, Noel and I were never able to become friends which I wanted to do. George [Reeves] brought me a script right when I was moving. He was in the Director's Guild; Eddie Mannix got him in. George had a script that was sci-fi. I told him, "Don't leave it with me, I'll lose it." He said, "Well, be in touch with me the minute you get moved." He died and I didn't expect it, nobody did.

Stan Taffel: Phyllis, did you have a favorite role that you played in your career; is there something that sticks out?

Phyllis Coates: Well, I worked with Ida Lupino [*The Untouchables* director, *A Fist of Five*]. What a thrill to be working with her, what a wonderful beautiful talent…tiny little moves. I've worked with some wonderful people, but it's been a long time since I've been in the business and in a way, I've kind of dropped it out of my mind. It's good to see Dick; it brings back a lot of good memories.

Stan Taffel: Well, you're going to see Dick this evening because we have a celebrity banquet at the hotel and we're honoring the two of you for your lifetime achievements. I do want to point out because I asked Phyllis two years ago when I was talking with her in Sacramento to please come to Cinecon. It took two years to do this and I asked Mr. Bare as well, and the only reason it totally happened is our friend Bart Williams who drove all the way to get her and they were in a car for seven hours.

Phyllis Coates: I never would have flown. Wendy loaned him a beautiful air-conditioned Cadillac, so I said, "O.K."

Stan Taffel: Well, this evening we will be having a wonderful dinner as our guests of honor. Thank you for being with us here and sharing your memories.

Afterwards, the couple took questions from the audience. At the conclusion of the event, it was adjourned across the street to the host hotel where a banquet was held for the two special guests. Many old Hollywood greats turned out: Barbara Hale whom Phyllis worked with on *Perry Mason*, Ann Jeffreys who also worked with Phyllis from the *Topper* series, as well as other dignitaries such as: Julie Newmar and Debbie Reynolds. As a surprise to Phyllis, Jack Larson came to the banquet. They hadn't seen each other since the first season of *Superman* when his role was that of Jimmy Olsen.

On behalf of the Cinecon, Jack Larson was the one to present Phyllis the prestigious Cinecon Career Achievement Award. Photos were taken of this honored event and captured Phyllis' beaming smile and crinkled nose.

This affair turned out to be the last public event for Phyllis. Richard Bare died three years later at the age of one-hundred-three-years-old. It was a memorable night for both of them to see others in the business saluting them along with the adoring attendees at the Egyptian theater. Jack Larson also died three years later. The Cinecon event was a memorable reunion for everyone involved.

Chapter Twelve
The Final Curtain

Phyllis Coates

THERE WERE TIMES over the years in Sonoma that Phyllis felt isolated from all her friends in Monterey. It certainly would have been easier for her and I to collaborate for a future book project. Telephone communications were out of the question between us because of our hearing limitations. Phyllis did not communicate by email; the computer was a foreign tool to her.

Moving to the Motion Picture and Television Home

In 2015 the inevitable time had come that Phyllis needed assisted living. Despite his terminal condition from cancer, Bart Williams and his friend, Tyler St. Mark, made all the necessary arrangements for Phyllis to be a patient at the place she wanted to be in her last days. It was the Motion Picture retirement facility for members of the movie and television industry in Woodland Hills, California. She certainly deserved the care. Bart Williams who was so helpful to Phyllis over the years succumbed to cancer that same year.

> *"I don't care about material things; I just want someone to take care of me."* – To author

Phyllis wiled the days away sitting in her wheelchair in front of the nurse's station to watch them work. They routinely gave her Coca-a-Cola that she finally got to enjoy; it was like nectar from the Gods to her. The onset of dementia made communicating to others impossible when, finally, the light dimmed out. Even Superman couldn't save her now.

Death
Phyllis Coates died on Oct. 11, 2023.

Upon news of Phyllis's natural death from the Motion Picture & Television Home, Phyllis' granddaughter, Olivia, drove from Oakland to Southern California to act as the family liaison. She made the final arrangements while her mother, Laura Press Olson (Phyllis' youngest child), was the one to announce her death to a multitude of media outlets. *The New York Times* covered her death as front-page news. It was proper respect for the journalist character of Lois Lane.

Phyllis' passing made headline news across the country. Obituaries mourned the end of her life in print, television and social media. She was 96 years old. Her fans and friends celebrated the person many only knew as "Lois Lane." Tributes came from sources around the world.

On one Facebook page dedicated to Superman, there was a photo image of George Reeves' as Superman sitting in a chair with his face in his hands, crying. We can all agree, though: Phyllis and her alter ego, Lois Lane, was still feisty after all those years. Her remains were cremated and are with the family. Little Gypsie Ann Stell is now at peace.

She lived a life.

Epilogue

Phyllis did not have a fairy-tale happy life, but you wouldn't be able to tell from her demeanor. At the age of sixteen, Phyllis was the main breadwinner of the family. When war broke out, she abdicated her high school education and went west with her mother and grandmother to drop anchor in Hollywood. From glamour girl to a freelance actress, her road ahead was not paved with yellow bricks or flowers. The odds were incredibly against her for sustained success and along the way she created an iconic characterization of "Lois Lane" for early television. Not satisfied as an actress with one identifying role, Phyllis broke the bonds of typecasting and enjoyed over 50 years in the business. She only wished that she could have been a better mother. As it is, she stands tall as a super woman on her own terms.

"You want me to be impressed by something I did in the past and let it define me? Hell no!" That was Phyllis Coates - Not Just Lois Lane.

Chapter Thirteen
What People Say About Phyllis Coates

Author's Top Ten Phyllis Coates Performances (Other than all the Lois Lane's)

1. **Panther Girl of the Congo** (1955)
   Phyllis stars as a jungle woman who swings on the vines with a short dress that would make the Abba chicks blush. What's not to like?

2. **I Was a Teenage Frankenstein** (1957)
   Getting killed by a monster while screaming as only Phyllis can do. Great fun.
3. (tie) **Behind the Eight Ball series** (a) *So You Want to Be Pretty* (b) *So You Want to Play the Piano* (1956)
   Phyllis as Mrs. McDoakes along with her husband go to extremes to fix their ridiculous overbite. Phyllis always preferred doing comedy, and this is one of the best. The second entry features Phyllis in an evening gown reacting to the neighbor's piano playing with great comedy timing.
4. **The Untouchables** – *Ain't We Got Fun* (1959)
   Phyllis as a cold gun moll in a gorgeous slinky black gown is worth the price of admission alone.
5. **Richard Diamond-** *Another Man's Poison* (1958)
   This is the sexist role in Phyllis' career. The way she toys with David Janssen is criminal.
6. **Gunsmoke** - *The Homecoming* (1964)
   Phyllis lies, cheats, and conspires in pitting the men folk to kill each other in delicious fashion, then plans to run away with her lover. "Women tend to hear things before men." One of her all-time best performances.
7. **Perry Mason-** *Case of the Black-eyed Blonde*
   Phyllis is a murderess and leads the cops in a car chase. She confesses on her death bed.
8. **The Lone Ranger-** *Woman in the White Mask* (1955)
   Phyllis is disguised in a wig and mask so she can rob people and speaks with a Mexican accent. She flirts with the Lone Ranger but it is all over the heads of kids watching.
9. **Terry and the Pirates** – *The Green God* (1953)
   This one was unexpected; Phyllis' character is a sweet southern belle bent on swiping the precious black necklace. She confronts Terry with a gun and dropped accent. She warns him that she can, "Sing, shoot, *and* fly a plane." Don't mess with her.
10. **Blues Busters** (1951)
    Phyllis is so young and pretty and tap dances her heart out in this Bowery Boys flick.

Phyllis' first daughter Zoe Christopher:

She loved animals. Please know that my "family dynamics" were opportunities, in the long run, and nothing to regret. I had 14 great years with my mother and I'll always love her, but to think that my strengths are traits I got from her would be a flawed oversimplification of a very complex mother/daughter relationship. What I did get from her is a deep and passionate love of the arts.

Zoe told me: "I never discussed her acting career with my mother, but she really enjoyed being the villain in her roles."[136]

Anthony Balducci-Phyllis Coates: Woman of Steel

Phyllis Coates played the long-suffering Alice McDoakes in Warner Bros' popular "Joe McDoakes" comedy short subject series from 1948 to 1956. Coates starred in many B-films, mostly westerns and jungle adventures. She memorably appeared as the fiancé of a mad scientist in *I Was a Teenage Frankenstein* (1957). She was regularly featured in popular television series, including *Death Valley Days*, *Gunsmoke*, *Rawhide*, *The Untouchables*, and *Perry Mason*. She stands out as a kindhearted barroom singer in a 1964 *Death Valley Days* episode called *The Left Hand Is Damned*. But Coates became a cultural icon for her no-nonsense, tough-as-nails portrayal of Lois Lane in the classic 1950s television series *Adventures of Superman*.

Coates *is* Lois Lane. The actress embodied all the qualities of the character originally established by Superman creators Jerry Siegel and Joe Shuster. Siegel said, "Our heroine was, of course, a working girl whose priority was grabbing scoops. What inspired me in the creation was Glenda Farrell, the movie star who portrayed Torchy Blane, a gutsy, beautiful headline-hunting reporter, in a series of exciting motion pictures." Lois broke away from the traditional damsel in distress archetype. Coates perfectly upheld that legacy. She portrayed Lois as an independent and strong-willed reporter who was not afraid to take risks in pursuit of a story. Paul G. Smart, a longtime *Superman* fan, wrote:

---

136 Phone conversation with author March 16, 2024

Coates' aggressive Lois played well against both Kent and Superman. Coates' Lois never hesitated to speak her mind... She would slap or step on the toes of a bad guy if he got in her way. On top of that, the actress had sex appeal. When Schuster first worked up the character designs for the *Superman* comic book, he focused on making Lois look like a woman who could attract an amazingly superior man. Coates had that same undeniable beauty and charm.

Coates only appeared in the first season of *Adventures of Superman* before being replaced by actress Noel Neil. Neil was kinder and gentler than Coates. She was well-liked by fans, but she lacked the toughness and independence that Coates had brought to Lois. She was more of a comic character and could at times be goofy. Coates set the standard for future interpretations of Lois and remains a fan favorite to this day. Her impact on the Superman franchise remains undeniable.

Rick Green-Phyllis Coates was the nicest celebrity I ever met.

Brad Farrell-As a longtime autograph collector, I have been lucky enough to have many opportunities to meet many of my childhood idols and favorite performers in my lifetime. As the number grows to about 2500 celebrities, there have been few that one could say were as nice and accommodating as Phyllis Coates. My first encounter with Phyllis came on July 18, 1992 at the Hal Roach Centennial Celebration on Catalina Island. She was kind enough to sign my program from the event and to take a photo with me. Unfortunately, this first encounter was somewhat jinxed as both the photo and the negative of our encounter were damaged beyond repair. I got another chance to get a photo with her in 1997 at the Edgar Kennedy Celebration in Monterey, California. But I didn't. This time I had her sign some photos for me, quite a few to be not very exact. These photos were ones I had found of her and Harpo Marx together, of which I had no idea of the source. She was kind enough to tell me that they were publicity stills, but that there was no filmed record of the meeting. She signed about ten of these great photos for me in vibrant red ink and I've held on to a few of them as prized possessions over the years, doling others out to fans.

When I next ran into Phyllis, it was on February 16, 2007, when she was doing an appearance and signing at the Hollywood Show in Burbank. Although she was there doing autographs, this time I just wanted to rectify the situation of not having a photo with her after our two previous encounters. She was as sweet as she was during our first two meetings, and kindly obliged by posing once again, this time for a digital camera where the image could never get battered by Kryptonite. But her kindness to me didn't end there. A few years later, I had my final meeting with her when she stopped by the Sons of the Desert Convention in Sacramento, California, on June 20, 2010. I had already exhausted her with signing autographs for me, so this time we just had a nice, pleasant chat at breakfast, and I once again asked for an updated photo of the two of us. Although her work is legendary onscreen, her true testament lies in how sweet she always behaved toward her fans.

The following comments pertaining mostly to Phyllis Coates are from the wonderful Facebook site: "Adventures of Superman Starring George Reeves." The members are passionate about the actors and characters of the show. Almost like *Gilligan's Island*, there are definite preferences to "Mary Ann" verses "Ginger." In this case, "Phyllis verses Noel." For the most part, both actresses are appreciated for what they gave to the "Lois" character.

Jay Brennan-Both Noel Neill and Phyllis Coates were great Lois Lanes. Neill was cute and fun, Coates was no-nonsense and quite a bit sexy.

J Patrick Kruger-Phyllis Coates, you are a National Treasure!

Cookie Curci-I THOUGHT she was the best Lois...she was beautiful... I could easily see Superman falling for her... I always felt the second Lois was more like Jimmy Olsen's sidekick.

Gary Gold-Gorgeous lady and talented. Great as Lois Lane; in serials; sometimes as a villainess as well as the Joe McDoakes shorts.

Kerry Manderbach-Well, I always though Phyllis did the perfect "early Lois" who was a bit hard-edged, a bit scornful of Clark, and unwilling to take a back seat to any man when it came to doing her job. Her version of the character perfectly mirrored the 30's-40s comic-book Lois. Noel Neill's version was the "accessible" Lois, who was more laid back and more sympathetic to Clark, while keeping the determined reporter's work ethic. Both Lois's were faithful to the comic's version, depending on the era.

Bob Coiro-The premise that a man could fly, thus becoming celebrity-famous, and then not be recognized by a close, daily associate because of a pair of eyeglasses was, of course, preposterous. To sell that notion to an audience of adults was the impossible job which sat squarely upon the shoulders of George Reeves and Phyllis Coates. Added to that was the idea that in a post-war world where job opportunities for women were limited to those of school teacher, nurses and secretaries, there could be such a thing as a "girl-reporter" (that's what the villains called her). The part required she be tough enough to stand up to hardened, violent criminals, toe-to-toe, yet in other cases, become terror-stricken to the point of fainting immediately following a scream worthy of Fay Wray.

Adventures of Superman could have very easily become as campy as Adam West's *Batman*, but it didn't—not as long as Phyllis Coates was on the set. Neither Coates nor Reeves over-acted or under-acted, but hit the nail on the head. They took what had already been established as a children Saturday afternoon matinee serial—something not taken seriously and completely changed it into a film noir entity worthy of grownups. That was an accomplishment. Though they didn't know it at the time, George Reeves and Phyllis Coates were creating a live-action legend that would live forever. And Reeves, a classically trained actor, recognized Coates' contributions to be as important as his own.

Jeff Collison-I first met Phyllis when she came into my office with Dean Witter Reynolds. She had this unmistakable voice I'd heard all my life and I just couldn't recall where until she told me her background as Lois Lane. We became great friends, going to lunch and talked frequently as she had wonderful stories of Hollywood.

Tyger Dacosta-What I like about her as an actress was, she refused to play stereotypical rules of women. Lois could have just played the ditzy "save me Superman role," but she took the role of Lois and made her a strong feminist who helped Superman on many occasions.

Anthony DiGiovanni-I was born in 1960, a year after the series ended. Growing up I was fascinated with Superman. All my toys were Superman. Growing up into adulthood, I was always magnetized to the *Mole Men* episode, and just loved the portrayal of Lois Lane by Phyllis Coates. She was so beautiful and had the most unique voice. I never had the opportunity to meet her; she will forever be the best Lois Lane.

Rowby Goren- She played a "hard-nosed" but likable and lovable Lois Lane. She played it with brains. Her suspicions about Superman's other identity were founded in "fact" and it was fun for me as a kid to observe tough reporter expressions when dealing with the Kent/Superman issue.

Jana Kaye Showecker-Awesome lady, I remember running home from school in time to watch her in *Superman*. She made me want to be a news reporter so I could interview Superman.

Bruce Dettman-Reporting from the New York City Collectors Show (2008) Phyllis captivated her audience and was the headliner for the show. Phyllis seemed to genuinely joy each and every fan expression. She signed autograph after autograph and it was obvious nearing the day's end, her writing hand was feeling the effects. But like a trouper, she didn't want to disappoint anyone. One highlight for the show was an unexpected visit by Spiderman; Phyllis was able to sneak a kiss from "Spidy." Most fans cheered it on, others were taken aback wondering what Superman might think.

Anthony Fusco-Phyllis played the role aggressively at a time when women weren't seen in that light on TV or movies. Phyllis was the definitive Lois Lane.

Russell Campbell-She played it tough as Lois. No one could scream and sometimes get physical with baddies like Phyllis. In one episode a bad guy henchman is sent into a room in which she was held captive to rough her up and he returns with scratches on his face looking sheepish. You
just knew Phyllis's Lois was not to be intimidated.

Gary M. Dymski-Rarely did she play "sexy" roles, but she was gorgeous. *Gunsmoke* episode in 1958, I think, was one role where she was allowed to vamp some.

Nowell Briscoe-I loved Phyllis when she was Lois Lane. She was more of a "go-getter" than Noel was who I thought was too soft for a reporter. I am so glad she is still with us and knows how much she is appreciated for the role she played in *Adventures of Superman*; I wish she had written a book about her experiences on the show as her fans would have loved it.

Jim Latimer-What a Superwoman!

Jim Yakov-She was the definitive "noir Lois" as befitted the early episodes. I remember one where she was trapped in a mine or something, and was wearing coveralls and had dirt on her face. Noel was the "light comedic Lois". I could never picture one hair of her (dark auburn or cheery redhead) out of place.

Rob Rose-Great actress and was a terrific Lois.

Monroe Jacobson-Happy Birthday, Phyllis. You are remembered as Lois Lane and other roles throughout your career such as the wife of Joe McDoakes in comedy shorts at WB, B westerns and serials and a *Gunsmoke* episode among other roles.

John Mitchell-I always thought she was the most beautiful woman.

Jay Boucher-An absolute living legend.

Michael Gold-Phyllis is one tough lady, she got clipped on the chin by accident from Frank Richard's in the episode *Night of Terror*.

Robby Stechman-Phyllis, I hope you have some idea how beloved you are by your fans

John Clark-A beautiful, serious and feisty Lois Lane. Thanks for my 70 years of enjoying *Superman*. (The best TV show ever!)

Jack Garrity-I wish she made the whole 6 seasons.

Angelo Rollo-Phyllis Coates, tougher and sexier!

Mark Giardina-Phyllis made the right decision to leave after season one. I agree that she would have never fit into the remaining run of the *Superman* series (1953-1958) acting like the damsel in distress.

Doug Yarbrough-She was the better Lois Lane and the first season in black and white is the best.

Douglas Prosch-When I was a kid, I was happy to see her in *I Was a Teenage Frankenstein*, but then horrified that Dr. F. fed her to an alligator(!)

Paul Macagliotta-Phyllis brought feistiness to Lois Lane that the character needed.
Too bad she wasn't available for the entire run.

Allen Tays-I enjoyed the first season of *Superman* when she played Lois Lane to the later ones. It had a film noir look to it, not so kidsy, the characters a little tougher, the criminals a little darker, thought she was an excellent Lois.

Peter Grabbe-When I was younger, Noel. As an adult, much prefer Phyllis.

Elizabeth Colette Melillo-Phyllis Coates. Noel could not help how the writers tailored the part to her, but her Lois seemed imprudent, getting into messes a reporter should know better than to attempt, and one always fawning over Superman and Clark. Phyllis' Lois is a highly competent, strong reporter, who has no patience with Clark's seeming timidity. (I really don't care how glamorous either one of them were in other roles — this is not a romance or 'look what you are missing' relationship with Superman. It is about crime-solving, and reporter's roles in the coverage.

John Lemons-Sorry Noel, but Phyllis is a better working girl Lois Lane. Where Noel came across as a better Den Mother.

David Yachaina-Hands down...Phyllis Coates. I loved her portrayal of a tough, sexy, no-nonsense reporter in season one.... plus, no one could scream like she did.

Patty Persons-When I was a kid, it had to be Noel or I was disappointed. But since I've grown up, now Phyllis is my special favorite. For that matter, the first season of *Superman* is also my favorite. Good plots, almost like noir at times

Allen Greggory-I have always considered Phyllis to be the Golden Age Lois and Noel the Silver Age version.

Dan Hayman-Phyllis Coates was def the better 'Lois'...she was the adult career girl that didn't take crap from anyone...Noel's character just seemed to wait around to eventually be saved by our super hero !...S1 was adult viewing...S2+ was for the kids !

James Irwin-Phyllis was the best, she was tough and would fight back She thought Clark was a coward. Season one was the best.

Ron Gilmore-Phyllis was movie star beautiful and brought a serious tone to the show that worked, Noel was very pretty and probably better suited for several of the more light-hearted scripts to come; simply put, I could never see Phyllis's Lois, not figuring out Clark was Superman, I could see NOEL's Lois Lane, not putting it together.

Robert Suttile-Phyllis Coates added the toughness of a woman working in a "man's world" and displayed that very well. Her Lois, though having a feminine side, was also very strong and exhibited all the traits we see in the modern liberated woman.

Eddie Patterson-Phyllis Coats is my pick; she loves to slap the bad guys in the face. She was a hard slapper, and a tuff female report.

Allen Winstead-Phyllis Coates was a strong and independent woman. The big difference is how they each responded to the bad guy of the episode. Lois was quite often captured by the bad guys and found herself in sketchy situations. When Noel Neil was caught by the bad guy, she always looked frightened and concerned — as if to say "Who will save me?" When Phyllis was taken prisoner by the bad guys, she always looked pissed off — as if to say "You're lucky I'm tied up or I'd kick your butt."

William Perez-Phyllis was a classic beauty. The kind you would see in high society. Noel was that pretty girl every guy wanted as a girlfriend.

Thomas Gay- Noel was great for the kiddie episodes that Kellogg's wanted...but Phyllis was the Lois of the comics...like she walked out of a comic book and on to the screen.

Joel Silverstein-I loved Noel. But Coates set a stronger, more thorny character appropriate for an adult show.

Dave Howser-Phyllis seemed more professional and less goofy. Better actress as well.

Wilhelm Figueroa-I was only 6 but even then, something told me that when I got older, Phyllis Coates was the one I would want to marry.

Michael Gagne- Hands down, Phyllis Coates. Stronger personality, less of a damsel in distress.

Jerry Lane-Phyllis was terrific, but she left us with abandonment issues.

Dave Fone-Phyllis was just lovely, even at age 26 for her first season as Lois Lane. Heart-shaped face; great jawline, classic profile. Too bad she had to wear her hair on *Superman* like she was 50.

Marty Morris-Phyllis was tough, smart, more like Lois Lane is.

Georg Plummer-I found Phyllis Coates to be more in the vein of Lois Lane, as competent and attractive, without being insouciant to Clark, as Noel Neill was. Nothing against Noel, I liked her, too. But, for having other commitments, Phyllis would have owned the part for the duration, like the rest.

Jim Trumbo-Love them both but Phyllis Coates seemed more edgy and smart.

Paul Smith–I felt the first Lois Lane was more of a real 50's career woman ...she didn't want to look like a "Dollie"...She wanted to be taken seriously in the newspaper game as an equal ... hence, the very plain business suits, and the shoulder bag she wore ...the second Lois Lane was more "Girlie".

John O Stevens-She was more like the Lois in the comic books. Professional woman, suspicious of and competitive with Clark. While I liked Noel Neil, I thought her Lois got a little silly towards the end of the series.

Joe Eckrich-As a reporter: Phyllis Coates. As most likable: Noel Neill.

Dennis Impallomeni-Phyllis Coates was tough and would smack a criminal and fight them, I loved that about her. Noel was the nicest Lois.

Frank Maimone-When you say pretty, you're thinking Noel. But when you say hot, you're thinking Phyllis!

Angelo Vetrano-Love Phyllis Coates. My favorite, tough as nails, reporter for the *Daily Planet*, Lois Lane. She made a big mistake leaving *Adventures of Superman* after the first season.

JT Thompson-Phyllis Coates was "Lois Lane." No nonsense and fiery reporter.

Craig Wichman-Noel was cute - Phyllis was the actor. For me, her missing is the only thing lacking in making the Second Season the very best.

John Reda-She was tough and didn't take crap from anyone. Watched an episode this morning and it was items hidden in porcelain statues. She took one and smashed it over the bad guy's head. Tough.

Jeff Moulton-Phyllis Coates was the best Lois ever. She played her as a hard, no-nonsense woman. Although Noel Neill was a looker, Phyllis Coates was a much better actress, and in my opinion much sexier.

Tim Gillespie-Phyllis Coates was my favorite Lois out of all of them.

Tom Tully-As a kid, I liked Noel better. As an adult, I prefer Phyllis - at least in part because I also like the older B&W episodes better. Plus, Phyllis had the best screams in the history of Hollywood.

Stephen Bazile-Phyllis Coates; after the 1st season the series went downhill for me.

Edward Patrick Fiore-Coates was a babe…she appeared on the Abbott and Costello show.

Jerry Reiner-I have long preferred Phyllis Coates' Lois Lane. She portrayed the character as confident and focused and tuff when she needed to be.

Tom Moore-I liked both. I do remember that Phyllis Coates had a blood-curdling scream.
Dave Banas-She was more "Lois Lane" than Noel Neill. Tough, fearless, aggressive. A single woman reporter had to be in those days.

Craig Hebert-Phyllis had the looks. Noel was bubbly.

Thomas Murphy-Phyllis played her part spectacularly!!! She screamed, slapped and shin-kicked…she is excellent.

Jay Holmes-Noel was cute and perky. Phyllis was hot!

James U Johnston-Phyllis played it perfect for the gritty first season….and she was physically attractive too.

Melody Holzman-Phyllis Coates…my favorite LL right after Teri Hatcher.

Michael Soto-Noel had more screen exposure as Lois; so, grew accustomed to her. But Phyllis played the part better.

Peter Bartolomeo-Phyllis Coats was a Hottie. All woman. The other chic was a bubblehead.

Jeff Moulton-I am surprised Phyllis didn't go on to be a major star. She was on a lot TV over the years and was excellent in everything. If you can, check out the *Untouchables* episode she's in. Very sexy. A very good actress.

Joe Febb-Phyllis Coates was hotter & had an attitude.

Ron Gray-Phyllis had spunk.

Joel Muniz-Phyllis was an old school actress. She can do everything. I wish she would've finished with the series.

Barbara Synnett Breitfeller-Loved her. Her character followed the themes of the first shows being more dramatic/ suspenseful. The tone lightened up in the later series.

Will Voelkel- [Phyllis]was stunningly gorgeous!

Paul Smith-She [Phyllis] would have beaten Professor Pepperwinkle and Mr. Zero to a pulp. Season one was the absolute best.

Dennis Radich-Phyllis was more desirable and mature for Superman while Noel was portrayed as more childish always hanging with Jimmy Olson.

Rick Bertoldo-I really love Phyllis Coates as Lois Lane. I think she's the G.O.A.T.

Her character is the type where, she would step on your foot or kick you in the groin before Superman got there, and maybe even afterward.

Michael Sachs-[Phyllis] played a reporter very authentically. Asking all the right questions to get to the truth.

Jeffrey C. Kirsch-Beautiful woman who was well-liked by all who knew her.

James U Johnston-I liked Noel....but as years past...I loved Phyllis. Her and the timeless grittiness of the season one episodes makes this 70yr man's day. Don't get no better than that.

Bill Chamberlain-I loved Phyllis in the role of Lois, she was a hard-nosed reporter unlike Noel, was a little more light-hearted, she was good very good, but for me Phyllis was a true Lois Lane.

Ronald J. Fields-Underappreciated, beautiful, and overly talented.

Chapter Fourteen
Film and Television Credits

Film Series

Joe McDoakes Series(29)1948-1956
1948
So You Want to Be in Politics
Joe wants to be elected into politics and campaigns to the stern, "Daughters of the War of 1812." In a gag ending, he is elected dog

catcher instead. This is Phyllis' first appearance in the series as Mrs. McDoakes.

So You Want to Be On the Radio
Joe is a quiz show contestant who gets the final $1,200 question wrong. Phyllis, as Joe's wife, nags him to bring home his conservative winnings, but Joe goes for it. One of his winnings is a blonde in a bikini. Mrs. McDoakes calmly remarks, "That thing will have to go back."

1949

So You Want to Be a Babysitter
Joe is forced by his wife (Phyllis) to babysit while she and her neighbors have a night on the town. Joe is abused by the mean little kid (Billy Gray) in abhorrent fashion. Phyllis and the neighbors come home to find Joe with a baseball bat after the kid. Phyllis wears a ridiculous ostrich outfit lined what looks like chicken feathers.

So You Want to Be Popular
Joe has to change his personality to be popular. Phyllis is an office girl here and shows up later in the skit as a French maiden to Joe's fantasy of himself as a dashing swordsman.

So You Want to Be a Muscle Man
Joe takes a body building course to keep up with his neighbor, a man with bulging muscles. As Joe's wife, Phyllis swoons over the neighbor's physique prompting skinny Joe to train in a Lester Apollo [Charles Atlas] home study course of records. Gilbert Waterman plays his personal trainer. Phyllis later worked with him in his TV role as *The Great Gildersleeve-Gildy Goes Diving* (1954).

So You're Having In-Law Problems
Both Joe's and Alice's eccentric relatives all arrive at the same time causing chaos. Gilbert Waterman is one of the relatives. All the nutty relatives with their bratty kid (Billy Gray again) cause upheaval and drive Mr. and Mrs. McDoakes batty. The best running gag stems from Joe's young frisky cousin who takes every opportunity to kiss Joe. Phyllis' reactions are priceless.

So You Want to Get Rich Quick

Joe is in line to inherit $100,000.00, but only if he has a male heir. He approaches a black marketer (Fred Clark) and fraudulently adopts a juvenile delinquent kid named, Stinky. When the inheritance check is made out in the kid's name, Joe tries to change his accordingly.

1950

So You Want to Throw a Party

Alice (Phyllis) gives Joe a list of friends to invite to their party. He gets the list mixed up with a list of his creditors instead. Someone suggests they play "Post Office" as a party game. Since Alice is the only female, everyone wants to play with her privately in the kitchen. Alice has to fend off everyone in single file.

So You Think You're Not Guilty

Joe gets a traffic ticket, and instead of paying a fine of two dollars, demands a jury trial. Joe professes his innocence and outrage at every stage and winds up in jail. Alice bakes him a cake with a planted file in it. Phyllis is extra lovely here with shorter hair and a pill box hat, one year before her Lois Lane role.

So You Want to Hold Your Husband

Joe has been taking his wife for granted, so Alice seeks marital advice from radio programs and, finally, a marriage counselor. The plan is to make Joe jealous by leaving him for another.

So You Want to Move

Outraged at the price demanded by furniture movers for the cost of $150.00, Joe decides to do it himself and ends up multiplying the cost. A very similar plot to some of those Edgar Kennedy shorts.

So You Want a Raise

Timid Joe is pressured by Alice to get a raise in salary from his bully boss (Willard Waterman).

1951

So You Want to Be a Cowboy

When Joe and Alice attend a western movie, Joe imagines himself as a cowboy: "Hop, Skip, and Jump-Along McDoakes" (a parody of Hopalong Cassidy) where he and Alice take on six henchmen and their boss.

So You Want to Be a Paperhanger
Alice makes Joe promise to have the room wallpapered before her bridge party arrives. He and his worthless neighbor, Marvin, fail at every turn.

So You Want to Buy a Used Car
Alice nags Joe into buying a used car. A used car salesman spots this pigeon and hard sells him an old lemon.

So You Want to Be a Bachelor
Joe and Alice have an argument. Joe goes to the basement and looks over old photos
from his bachelor days. Phyllis is extra cute here as Alice.

So You Want to Be a Plumber
Alice budgets $260.00 to hire a plumber to fix a leaky pipe. Of course, Joe would rather fix it himself, and with his goofy neighbor, floods the basement instead.

1952

So You Want to Get It Wholesale
Alice wants a new stove for her birthday. Joe searches for a deal and buys one that's "hot." He winds up in court for buying stolen merchandise. Comic Frank Nelson adds to the fun.

So You Want to Go to a Convention
Enroute to the annual Hoot Owls convention, Joe and his friend, "Good time Charlie," inadvertently board a plane to Palm Springs. They are interacting with girls when Alice shows up. Shades of Laurel and Hardy from *Sons of the Desert*.

So You Never Tell a Lie
Alice wants Joe to buy her a watch, but complications develop when Joe's boss has him buy a watch for the office contest winner.

So You Want to Wear the Pants
A hypnotist (Fritz Feld) transposes Joe and Alice along with their voices. Joe winds up at the National Guard with his wife's persona. Phyllis scores acting macho with O'Hanlon's dubbed voice.

1953

So You Want a Television Set

When the many neighbors come over to watch TV, they eat all the food and prompt Joe to the movies. He sits next to Doris Day and Gordon McCrea in a gag sequence. Shot during the making of the film: *By the Light of the Silvery Moon*.

So You Think You Can't Sleep

Joe suffers from chronic insomnia and seeks a cure from a specialist.

So You Want to Be an Heir

Alice wakes up Joe to read him a telegram that he will inherit his grandmother's estate if he gets to her bedside before she dies. Joe stands to inherit a million dollars if he can reach his grandmother before she passes. Joe discovers that all his relatives (all played by O'Hanlon) want to dispose of him.

So You Love Your Dog

Joe loves his dog, Dusty, so much he sleeps with him in bed instead of his Alice. Dusty does everything wrong by helping burglars get into the house.

1954

So You're Having Neighbor Trouble

Joe decides to tape-record his neighbor's loud party as evidence of peace disturbance violations. He forgets to turn off the machine while he loudly complains to Alice that "all the cops and judges are crooked." Joe and his neighbor wind up in court.

1956

So You Want to Be Pretty

Joe and Alice go on separate vacations to have plastic surgery done on their extreme overbite. They meet at a bar and don't recognize each other, but soon enjoy flirting with each other. The gag with the teeth was borrowed from the Charley Chase short: *Mighty Like a Moose*. (1926)

So You Want to Play the Piano

When Alice is enraptured by the neighbor's piano playing, George takes lessons to also play.

Alice is unimpressed, telling Joe, "Some people have it and some people don't."(Last film appearance of Charlie Hall in a bit role as a piano mover).

So Your Wife Wants to Work
Alice is bored and wants a job outside the home. Joe reluctantly arranges this through his boss expecting her to fail and return home. Alice performs admirably above and beyond Joe's capabilities at the office. It is she that gets promoted instead.

Phyllis in Western Genre Television
(4) Cisco Kid *Outlaws of Texas*
(7) *Death Valley Days*
(1) *The Range Rider*
(3) *The Lone Ranger*
(1) *The Adventures of Kit Carson*
(1) *Frontier*
(3) *Gunsmoke*
(2) *Tales of Wells Fargo*
(1) *The Sheriff of Cochise*
(2) *Rawhide*
(1) *Black Saddle*
(1) *The Virginian*
(2) *Gunslinger*

Phyllis in Western Genre Films
Stage to Blue River
Canyon Raiders
The Longhorn
Man from Sonora
Oklahoma Justice
Nevada Badmen
The Gunman
Fargo
Canyon Ambush
Wyoming Roundup
The Maverick
Scorching Fury
Marshal of Cedar Rock
El Paso Stampede
Gunfighters of the Northwest
Blood Arrow
Cattle Empire

TV Series
Adventures of Superman (1952-1953 television season)

Episode #1   *Superman on Earth* (Sept. 19th)
This is the first episode of the first season; it explains how the super baby rocketed to earth and was raised by a kindly couple. It introduces the main cast at the end and a dynamic exploit by Superman.

Lois Moments: Already suspicious of Clark Kent she never lets her gaze off of him.

Episode #2   *The Haunted Lighthouse* (Sept. 26th)
Lois wasn't in this one at all; all the action takes place with just Jimmy Olsen and Clark/Superman along with a supporting cast of characters.

Episode #3   *The Case of the Talkative Dummy* (Oct. 3rd)
Clark, Lois, and Jimmy attend a ventriloquist act that goes wrong when the dummy appears to talk by itself. Upon further investigation, they link what the dummy appears to have said to a series of armored car hijackings. Lois is dressed in her evening gown.

Episode #4   *Mystery of the Broken Statues* (Oct. 10th)
A crook and his dopey thugs are going to all the antique shops in town, buying cheap figurines, and smashing them to find a hidden key. Lois gets kidnapped and fights back, smashing a porcelain statue over a bad guy's head.
Lois Moments: Lois says to her kidnapper: "Enough with the sweet talk, get to the point."

Episode #5   *The Monkey Mystery* (Oct. 17th)
The daughter of an Eastern European scientist flees to the United States to give a secret formula to the president before the communists who killed her father can get to it.
Lois Moments: Lois receives information on the girl's whereabouts from an organ grinder and his monkey.

Episode #6   *Night of Terror* (Oct. 24th)
While on vacation, Lois stumbles upon a ring of criminals who are smuggling fugitives into Canada. She and the innkeeper's wife are captured, and it is up to Jimmy and Superman to save them. This is the one where Lois confronts a bad guy and is knocked out with a punch. Phyllis really was knocked out and admitted she was "standing in the wrong spot." After a brief break, she got up to complete the shoot.
Lois Moments: The script didn't call for Phyllis to get that close to the bad guy and she is inadvertently punched unconscious.

Episode #7   *The Birthday Letter* (Oct. 31st)

A crippled young girl writes Superman a letter asking him to take her to the fair for her birthday, but before he arrives, she is kidnapped by a group of counterfeiters who need information that she has been given by mistake. Lois happens on the scene of the little girl's room and is discovered by the kidnappers. Phyllis' own young daughter was in a leg cast, but this little girl wore braces. The ending scene where Superman takes her flying is the most charming in the series. It's no wonder everyone loves George Reeves.

Lois Moments: Lois shows awkwardness when caught in the same room as the kidnappers and tries to outsmart them.

Episode #8   *The Mind Machine* (Nov. 7th)

A mobster kidnaps a scientist and takes possession of his invention. The crook uses the device to damage the minds of people testifying before an investigative committee. The victims die a short time later. Superman races to find the mobster before Lois Lane testifies before the committee. Superman rides on an airplane to find the hide-out, then decides the best course of action is to slug/knock-out the pilot, put the plane on auto-pilot, then change into his costume and fly out the rear door. This is the one when a bad guy throws his empty gun at Superman and he ducks. Apparently, the Superman double in this scene doesn't know that if bullets can't hurt the big guy, then neither can a thrown handgun.

Lois Moments: Lois is in great danger by the mobsters as she is about to testify in court.

Episode #9   *Rescue* (Nov. 14th)

While Lois is in Carbide, Pennsylvania, gathering information for a story about the town's mining system, an old prospector is trapped in a cave-in. Lois attempts to rescue him, but when she is trapped in the mine with him it is up to Superman to save them both.

Lois Moments: Lois is typically headstrong and stubbornly puts herself at peril to get to the old minor who is trapped in the mining shaft. Superman saves them at the last moment of course and disappears just when Clark Kent shows up to ask, "What happened?" Lois beams and triumphantly tells him, "I finally got Superman to take me out."

Episode #10   *The Secret of Superman* (Nov. 17th)
Dr. H.L. Ort is using an advanced version of a truth serum to hypnotize employees of the Daily Planet in an attempt to discover Superman's secret identity. Watching the main cast members acting hypnotized and talking in a robotic voice is a hoot.

Lois Moments: The dialogue she exchanges with the lead bad guy: "Save your bedside manner and double talk. Get to the point."

Episode #11   *No Holds Barred* (Nov. 28th)
Bad Luck Brannigan, a wrestler working for a crooked promoter, uses "the paralyzer" to cripple opponents. Clark Kent discovers the promoter has imprisoned an immigrant dubbed "the swami," who has extensive knowledge of the body's pressure points. In his Superman identity, Clark sees the immigrant. "The swami" instructs Superman in his techniques. As Clark, he then teaches a college wrestler — who has publicly challenged Brannigan — how to counter "the paralyzer."

Lois Moments: Not many in this episode unless watching the wrestling matches with Perry White on his console TV count.

Episode #12   *The Deserted Village* (Dec. 5th)
When Lois has trouble getting her nurse on the telephone, she and Clark drive to the small town of Cliffton to see what the problem is. After arriving, they find that the town is mostly deserted. The three remaining townspeople have hit on a natural ingredient for making explosives.

Lois Moments: Clark wants to separately investigate something (as Superman) and tells Lois not to drink the tea. When she asks why, Clark doesn't explain, he just tells her to be "a good girl" till he comes back. Lois has none of that, she thinks Clark is going to out scoop her, so she goes into a cave and gets into trouble.

Episode #13   *The Stolen Costume* (Dec. 12th)

This is a very unusual episode. First of all, Lois is not in this. A burglar climbs a rope to Clark Kent's apartment, finds a hidden closet and steals Clark's Superman costume. A cop opens fire on him as he's running away, but the burglar makes it to the apartment to give the costume to his boss and gun moll. Kent wouldn't be Superman without his duds, so he finds the two crooks who want to bargain with him, and they know his secret identity. No deal. Superman whisks them up and flies them to an alleged cabin on top of the world somewhere. He dutifully tells them not to try to escape and that he will bring them food. They don't listen and attempt to climb down the snowy mountain until both fall to their death. That's one way to solve the problem.

Lois Moments: None. If Lois was there, she might have been more compassionate. This episode is a good example of how the first season was certainly not geared just to kiddies; it was a crime drama with noir overtones.

Episode #14   *Treasure of the Incas* (Dec. 19th)

While Lois is on her way to an auction featuring South American items, a man asks her to purchase an Inca tapestry for him. Soon after, the man is killed and the tapestry is stolen from Lois, so she, Jimmy, and Clark follow the murderer to Lima to find the tapestry and catch the criminals behind the murder.

Lois Moments: Lois's journal instincts kick in regarding a mysterious Incan fabric. She is approached by a dangerous Peruvian poacher who wants the tapestry. Lois's life is in danger as he approaches her and she lets out a patented scream before she is knocked unconscious.

Episode #15   *Double Trouble* (Dec. 26th)

A man aboard a ship to Metropolis is smuggling something valuable into the country, but when one of his partner's henchmen shows up to help him get the item through customs, the passenger kills the other man. The passenger then dresses up as a woman, and, in an attempt to give his partner the slip, he gives Jimmy, who is at the dock to interview an actress, an empty box and tells him to give it to the men who are waiting for him. When Jimmy is kidnapped by the men, Superman must save him—but in order to do that, he first must figure out why Jimmy was kidnapped, solve the murder, track down the passenger, find out what is being smuggled, and find the passenger's partner.

Lois Moments: Nothing worth mentioning. She is in one shot only, and that is as a witness to Jimmy being kidnapped. There was no follow through on her part because she was assigned to interview a movie star.

Episode #16   *Mystery in Wax* (Jan. 2nd)

Madame Selena (Mira McKinney) and her husband own a wax museum in Metropolis. She claims to have visions that prominent people will die within six months. And indeed, the people do appear to commit suicide. Madame's latest vision: Perry White will die. McKinney's over-the-top performance is second to the great Gloria Swanson's act of madness in *Sunset Blvd.* filmed the year before.

Lois Moments: The epitome of a snoopy and inquisitive reporter with an attitude. Lois embodies a female role model in this; Madame Selena is worried of her, and for good reason. Lois breaks the case wide open, and saves the Chief from incarceration in a cage. It is all in a day's work. Superman helped too.

Episode #17   *The Runaway Robot* (Jan. 9th)

The inventor of a mechanical man is kidnapped by burglars. They have evil plans for the eccentric inventor (Lucien Littlefield), who they coerce to use his robot to break into a bank and clean out the vault. They didn't realize that Lois Lane was peeking through the keyhole and a witness to their scheme; they yank her in as well.

Lois Moments: This episode might have the most epic Lois moments of all. The bad guys tell her to "shut up," to which she screams, "I won't shut-up." Then, like a wildcat, she claws at her captures with slaps and kicks. She jumps up and down screaming until contained.

Episode #18   *Drums of Death*(Jan. 16th)
No Lois in this one. When Jimmy and Perry White's sister go missing in Haiti while filming voodoo practitioners, Perry and Clark go looking for them.

Episode #19   *The Evil Three*(Jan. 23rd)
No Lois Lane again. Perry White and Jimmy Olsen, while on a fishing trip, end up staying at a rundown hotel. It has only three occupants — two men who are trying to kill each other and a wheelchair-bound old woman who laughs like a maniac. Superman races to help his friends before they fall victim to the "evil three." (Not to be confused with Lon Chaney's *The Unholy Three*).

Episode #20   *The Riddle of the Chinese Jade*(Jan. 30th)
Harry Wong, manager of Lu Song's antique store, decides to help thief John Greer steal a priceless jade statue from Song. Although no one is supposed to get hurt, the plan changes when Song's niece Lily witnesses the robbery and is kidnapped by Greer. Superman, who, as Clark Kent, is interviewing Song for the scoop on his donating the statue to a museum, must solve the crime.
Lois Moments: When confronted with a gun, Lois is just about to let him have it with her purse.

Episode #21   *The Human Bomb*(Feb. 6th)
"Bet A Million" Butler, who will "bet on anything," wages $100,000 he can keep Superman under his control for 30 minutes. He shows up at the Daily Planet and abducts Lois Lane, forcing her onto the ledge of the newspaper's office building. Butler, calling himself only the "human bomb," has strapped dynamite to himself. After Superman arrives, the "human bomb" says he'll detonate the explosive unless Superman agrees to stay put for 30 minutes while a robbery takes place. Superman agrees but has no intention of allowing the robbery to take place.
Lois Moments: Lois Lane is forced to stand on the edge of a skyscraper with a lunatic for most of this episode. When the bomber is subdued and brought back, Lois confronts him and slaps him across the face.

Episode # 22   *Czar of the Underworld the Human Bomb* (Feb. 13th)

Lois Lane is not in this one. A movie is being filmed about mobster Luigi Dinelli (brilliantly played by Anthony Caruso). The film is based on a series of articles that Clark Kent wrote for the Daily Planet. Dinelli is more than displeased; he orders a hit on Clark.

Episode # 23   *Ghost Wolf* (Feb. 20th)

The Lone Pine Timber Company, which is owned by the Daily Planet and supplies it with the pulp wood to make its paper, is in danger of shutting down after a series of mishaps. When the last of its employees is scared off due to evidence of a werewolf on the premises, Perry White sends Clark, Jimmy, and Lois to investigate. Lois and the team are clothed in outdoor garb in the outdoor environment. The "Werewolf" everyone is concerned about looks like someone's pet dog.

Lois Moments: Lois screams as the wolf jumps through her window. Later when she is freshening up at the stream, she encounters the wolf again, then screams and faint.

Episode # 24   *Crime Wave* (Feb. 27th)

As a massive crime wave unfolds, Superman vows to put top mobsters behind bars. His ultimate target is the mysterious "No. 1 man." The top criminal devises a trap for the Man of Steel. Superman rounds up all the "Most Wanted" crooks in Metropolis to clean up the town. This episode must serve as the "Poster Child" for the ACLU, Superman runs amok.

Lois Moments: Lois is present through all the developments, but mostly as a concerned employee in Perry White's office. Nothing to confront.

Episode # 25   *The Unknown People* (part 1) ** (Aug. 10th)

Clark Kent and Lois Lane travel to Silsby, site of the deepest well ever drilled. But when they arrive, the well is being shut down and the oil company manager present isn't saying why. Meanwhile, two short beings with large heads and furry hands come up from the well to explore. Luke Benson leads a mob of townspeople wanting to kill the "unknown people." Despite Superman's efforts to calm things down, the mob has tracked the two creatures to the top of a dam, trying to kill them. What the mob doesn't know is the creatures cause things they touch to glow in the dark—and may be radioactive.

Episode # 26   *The Unknown People* (part 2) ** (Aug. 17th)
One of the "unknown people" is shot while atop a dam near Silsby, Texas. Superman catches him before he falls into the water and takes him to the Silsby hospital. Superman, in his Clark Kent identity, assists a doctor who operates on the creature. The doctor discovers his patient has all the organs and internal body structure as humans. Meanwhile, the Luke Benson-led mob tries to kill the other visitor from the center of the Earth. That creature escapes, later bringing up more of his people along with a weapon. Superman races to defuse an explosive situation.

The *Unknown People* was actually edited from *Superman and the Mole Men* for TV.

This is Alice

Phyllis played the mother in this television series aired October 1958-August 1959; it was an American situation comedy starring nine-year-old Patty Ann Gerrity. All episodes were directed by Sydney Salkow.

Episode titles:
The Princess
A single mother runs a dress business that so far has been unsuccessful. Alice is worried that the woman and her daughter will move away so the little girl works to drum up customers for her friend's mom.

Alice Goes to Washington
Chet has a business trip to Washington DC and Alice asks to go along. Her dad agrees as long as Alice behaves and she's allowed to bring her friend Soapie. The two kids naturally find all kinds of mischief to be involved in.

Alice Plays Detective
Alice learns a friend's parents are planning on getting a divorce. Alice takes it upon herself to find out what the problem is and fix it so the couple will stay together.

Big Louie Comes Through
Town bookie Big Louie has a bad reputation but Alice knows he's a softie at heart. Alice convinces Louie to use his demeanor to assist a family down on their luck.

American Beauty
Alice becomes chummy with the contestants at a beauty pageant. When Alice learns one woman has broken her engagement to focus on her career, the girl tries to help the brokenhearted fiancé.

Quiz Show
Alice is thrilled when she gets an opportunity to be on a game show. But the Holliday family is in a quandary when they find out Alice's competition is Chet's boss.

Mrs. U.S.A.
Alice finds out her parents would like a second honeymoon. Alice learns the grand prize to a pageant is a Niagara Falls trip. Alice enters her mother; confident Mrs. Holliday will win.

Problem Child
Alice neglects her school work because of a space club she is interested in. When her parents learn she is failing her classes it leads to a major argument.

One in a Million
A wealthy man has been confined to his bed by his doctors but leaves just the same. Alice mistakes him for a homeless man and invites the older gentleman to her house for a home cookedmeal.

House Beautiful
A beautiful blonde upsets the Holliday household with her decorating ideas.

Pie in the Sky
Alice desperately wants to win the school cooking contest. Alice decides to bring in a ringer, the local owner of a bakery, to help her achieve victory.

When the Bow Breaks
Alice meets a yacht captain who is in love with a lovely heiress. Problem is the lady is about to marry another man. Alice learns the fiancé is only getting wed for the woman's money so Alice develops a plan to break them up.

No Place Like Home
Alice and her parents embark on a family vacation that should be full of adventure. Chet and Clarissa find out that having the curious Alice along can create unexpected situations.

Rock 'n' Roll
Alice's friend has a huge crush on a popstar and has sent him several fan letters. But when he fails to respond the little girl becomes unhappy so Alice takes matters into her own hands.

Dandy Donovan
Alice accompanies a friend of her father to an equine auction. Due to a mix-up the dad accidentally buys a horse. Alice is convinced that the animal has a future on the race track.

Two Yanks in Georgia(No description)

Pig in a Poke
Alice buys a pig from a tramp and finds herself in trouble with her parents when they question how she got the animal.

Trial Balloon
Alice gets one of her wild ideas and enlists her friend Soapie's assistance. The kids inflate a child's pool and when it ascends the two take a ride. But they have no control and soon the town folk are panicked with Coast Guard called.

Fortune Teller
Alice gets caught up in the excitement of putting on a local carnival. Alice agrees to be the fortune teller but forgets she's just playing a role.

Callahan
A young Irish man wants to bring his girlfriend to America so they can wed but has no money. Alice thinks the lad could win a local boxing match to get the cash. But the arrival of the fiancé causes complications as she's against fighting.

Mail Order
Alice encounters a scientist who's developed a formula for a new furniture polish. Alice thinks she knows a way to market the product and make a little money for herself.

Song for Sale
Alice's Sunday School teacher is in trouble for singing songs of her own composition. Alice likes them and figures out a way to make everyone happy.

The Weight Lifter
A family member comes for a visit and puts the entire Holliday family on an unneeded strict diet. Alice rebels and encourages her parents to do the same.

The Prophet
A man who tells fortunes has charmed many of the ladies in town but Alice is suspicious. A well-to-do woman is about to sign over part of her wealth when Alice exposes an event from the man's past.

Christmas Story
Alice gets a job selling Christmas trees to do a good deed. Alice has learned that a kindly older lady is poor and not expecting any gifts so the little girl decides a surprise is in order.

Hypnotist
Alice learns about hypnotism and wants to try it out. Father Chet agrees to be the subject and Alice with a pocket watch attempts to put her dad under her spell. The results turn out different than the little girl anticipated.

Rags to Riches
Alice once again is in need of funds and decides she needs to a long-term solution. Alice turns to a local millionaire for advice.

Class Reunion
Alice joins her father Chet when he attends his class reunion. There Alice meets a young couple in love but unhappy. Alice works to fix the obstacles.

Circus Time
The circus is in town with Alice and her pals looking forward to going. But a runaway meets Alice and he's running away from the circus where his parents work. He wants a normal life and Alice tries to help.

Man's Best Friend (No description)

Rodeo
Alice has a Brahma bull in her backyard and convinces her father Chet that a rodeo is in their future so they should keep the bovine. A series of misadventures result in Alice riding the bull through the town square.

Alice Plays Cupid
Alice's favorite teacher is retiring and has little to look forward to. Alice notices a spark between the instructor and the school's janitor so the girl decides to help the romance along.

Guest in the House
A sophisticated lecturer arrives in town but has a superior attitude concerning the townspeople. Forced to stay longer than anticipated, the unhappy man is taken in hand by Alice who shows him all her community has to offer.

Help Wanted
The Holliday's employ a part-time housekeeper whom Alice befriends. Find an eligible wealthy bachelor in town and Alice thinks the two adults would be perfect as a couple.

Paper Drive
Alice and her pals enter an old mansion in search of additional stuff for a paper drive. The friends find a message scrap that could change drastically the fortunes of a local man.

The Elephant
The Holliday parents are perplexed when daughter Alice brings home an elephant as a pet. What to do with the wild animal becomes the focus of the family.

Freedom of the Press
Alice and her soap box derby car go off course, creating chaos at an outdoor tea party. The socialite hostess wants Alice and her family to pay for the damages.

Too Many Fathers
Alice gets the mistaken notion she is adopted and that a famous comedian is her actual father. When Alice learns the comic is performing in Philadelphia, she runs away to meet her real dad.

The Letter

A couple is excited about their golden wedding anniversary and seeing their son, coming to celebrate. But he informs them he can't visit because of work so Alice takes charge of the party to make the day memorable.

Movie Serials
1953

Jungle Drums of Africa (Edited into a feature: U-238 and the Witch Doctor)

Chapter One: *Jungle Ambush*
Chapter Two: *Savage Strategy*
Chapter Three: *The Beast Fiend*
Chapter Four: *Voodoo Vengeance*
Chapter Five: *The Lion Pit*
Chapter Six: *Underground Tornado*
Chapter Seven: *Cavern of Doom*
Chapter Eight: *The Water Trap*
Chapter Nine: *Trail to Destruction*
Chapter Ten: *The Flaming Ring*
Chapter Eleven: *Bridge of Death*
Chapter Twelve: *The Avenging River*

1954

Gunfighters of the Northwest
Chapter One: *A Trap for the Mounties*
Chapter Two: *Indian War Drums*
Chapter Three: *Between Two Fires*
Chapter Four: *Midnight Raiders*
Chapter Five: *Running the Gauntlet*
Chapter Six: *Mounties at Bay*
Chapter Seven: *Plunge of Peril*
Chapter Eight: *Killer at Large*
Chapter Nine: *The Fighting Mounties*
Chapter Ten: *The Sergeant Gets His Man*
Chapter Eleven: *The Fugitive Escapes*
Chapter Twelve: *Stolen Gold*

Chapter Thirteen: *Perils of the Royal Mounted*
Chapter Fourteen: *Surprise Attack*
Chapter Fifteen: *Trails End*

1955

***Panther Girl of the Kongo*- (Chapter Synopses from the Pressbook)**
Chapter One: *The Claw Monster*

Jean Evans, in Africa to take moving pictures of wild animals, wins her name *The Panther Girl*, by shooting down a man-killing panther. The grateful natives agree to help her with her picture taking but are stampeded when charged by a grotesque monster with a shell-covered body and immense claws. Jean gets a few pictures of the monster then sends to town for Larry Sanders, famous guide and big game hunter. In his isolated jungle bungalow, Dr. Morgan, once a famous chemist, has developed a hormone compound which causes ordinary crawfish to grow into monsters. With the help of his henchmen, Cass and Rand, he is using his monsters to terrorize the natives so that he can exploit an illegal diamond mine. Cass and Rand enlist the aid of a renegade tribe of Returi to drive one of the monsters to the village. Two of the Returis attack Larry while Jean continues along on the trail of the claw monster. The beast reaches over the top of a boulder, clamps onto her shoulder, and begins slowly squeezing her to death.

Chapter Two: *Jungle Ambush*

Larry breaks away from the natives in time to drive off the claw monster with rifle fire, and he rescues Jean. Morgan orders his two henchmen to return to the village and try to learn what Larry's plans are. Though suspicious, Larry lets them see the film Jean has taken of the monsters. Morgan's men realize that if these pictures are shown to the authorities the jungle will be thoroughly searched. With some of the Returi natives, they attack Larry on his way to town with the film. Gunfire and arrows force him to take shelter a short distance down the road. He holds off Rand and the natives until knocked unconscious by a club. As he lies in the road, Cass drives a jeep over his body.

Chapter Three: *The Killer Beast*

Larry revives and saves himself by turning lengthwise so that he is between the wheels of the speeding vehicle as it passes over him. Morgan and his men destroy the film, leaving them temporally safe from official investigation, but they must still drive the natives out of the district so they released another claw monster. Jean and Larry set out to hunt down the monster, and Jean is attacked by two Returi natives. She is forced to drive from a high cliff and swim across a lake, only to be immediately captured. The natives leave her tied to a tree in the jungle and pound out a drum rhythm which starts an angry gorilla on the prowl. His roaring attracts Larry, who arrives just as the gorilla is about to crush Jean. Larry attempts to shoot the animal but is knocked out, and the gorilla moves in to crush Jean in his mighty arms.

Chapter Four: *Sands of Doom*

Larry revives in time to shoot the gorilla and save Jean. Larry, concerned about the hostility of the Returi natives, decides to warn other white men in the district, and goes to visit Morgan in his bungalow. Larry tells him that he has sent for a constable to come out and investigate the native trouble. Morgan passes this information on to Cass and Rand, who organize their Returi natives to ambush Jean and Larry when they start out with the constable (Harris) to explore the jungle. The natives retreat across a quicksand river bed, then move the markers designating the safe ford. Larry is trapped in the quicksand and exposed to native arrow fire. As Jean and Harris attempt to rescue him. Larry gradually sinks out of sight.

Chapter Five: *Test of Terror*

Harris wounds one of the attacking natives, the others retreat and Jean rescues Larry from the quicksand. Larry and Harris capture the wounded Returi and take him to town. When Larry and Jean again set out on the trail of the claw monster, they discover that Cass and Rand are attempting to herd the monster closer to the village. They trail the outlaws to the old abandoned mine where Morgan has discovered the diamond-bearing gravel. Jean and Larry attempt to capture them, but in the ensuing fight are cornered at the dead end of a small tunnel. Unable to drive them out, Cass and Rand throw dynamite into the tunnel, bringing down the roof and apparently entombing Larry and Jean.

Chapter Six: *High Peril*

The explosion breaks an opening through the roof of the tunnel, allowing Jean and Larry to escape. They return to the village, secure rifles and start again for the mine with Jean riding her trained elephant. The Returi natives rig a vine trap which sweeps Jean off the elephant, and leaves her lying unconscious in the path of an advancing claw monster. The elephant locates Larry and brings him back in time to rescue her. Jean and Larry now mount the elephant and take off after Cass and Rand, who reach their jeep and get away. Larry locates them that night in a saloon, but they put up a fight which leads onto the roof of the building. As the battle continues, Larry is knocked against the railing which gives way and sends him toppling over the edge.

Chapter Seven: *Timber Trap*

Larry catches onto a flagpole a short distance below the window, and makes his way safely into the building. Cass and Rand then send a native to the village to report he has seen claw monsters in a certain canyon. Larry and Jean immediately set out to hunt the monster at the point where Cass and Rand are waiting for them. With bundles of dynamite. However, Larry comes upon Cass and Rand from an unexpected direction, and in the ensuing gun battle, the heavies attempt to blast Larry out of position with a charge of dynamite. Jean arrives in time to upset their plans, and the dynamite with the burning fuse is dropped at the base of a large tree. In attempting to escape, Cass is seized by Larry and they are struggling together when the dynamite goes off, bringing the tree toppling down upon them.

Chapter Eight: *Crater of Flame*

Larry and Cass roll aside in time to miss the falling tree, and Cass escapes. Larry and Jean set out by canoe on another attempt to investigate the mine. They are fired upon by Cass and Rand, and

Jean is forced to go ashore in an attempt to circle around the heavies. Larry continues up the river but Rand spots him, the canoe is upset and Larry knocked unconscious. He floats down and a crocodile is about to attack him when Jean dives in and kills the crocodile with her knife. Jean and Larry reach the mine and Cass and Rand start throwing in burning branches to smoke them out. Larry shovels the burning branches into an open pit, but Cass and Rand charge in and Larry is knocked into the flaming pit.

Chapter Nine: *River of Death*
Larry falls onto a ledge beside the flames where he is rescued when Jean secures a gun and drives out Cass and Rand. Jean and Larry now trap one of the claw monsters in a pit but Cass and Rand allow the monster to escape. Jean has the camera ready and gets some pictures of it. However, realizing that Cass and Rand may attempt to get the film, Larry hides it in Jean's bungalow. While he is gone, Cass and Rand attack the village, drive off the natives, and capture Jean. When Larry returns, they try to ambush him on the dock. He breaks away and is overcome in the ensuing fight when Jean is knocked backwards into the water.

Chapter Ten: *Blasted Evidence*
Larry dives in to rescue Jean and the outlaw's escape. Knowing the film must still be in Jean's bungalow, Cass and Rand secure a homemade bomb from Morgan and prepare to blow up the bungalow that night. In the meantime, the District Commissioner has arrived on Larry's invitation to look at the film which Jean has now developed. The pictures of the claw monster convince him of the necessity of sending out government aid, and Larry and Jean tell him the complete story, recalling several of their experiences with the monsters and with Cass and Rand. As they are concluding their talk, Cass and Rand sneak up to the building and toss in the bomb. The ensuing explosion blasts the doors and windows from their structures.

Chapter Eleven: *Double Danger*

When the bomb lands on the floor, Larry throws a heavy table over it so that the force of the explosion is diverted. Cass and Rand are driven off and the Commissioner promises to send out constables immediately. In the meantime, Jean and Larry start into the jungle to look for the villagers who were driven off by Cass and Rand. Larry is attacked by two of the Returi natives and knocked off a cliff into a lake. Jean swings through the trees and dives in to rescue him, and they continue into the jungle until they find the trail of the natives who attacked him. He captures one of them just as Cass and Rand approach. Seeing Larry outlined against the sky on top of cliff, they open fire. Apparently hit, Larry topples off the cliff.

Chapter Twelve: *House of Doom*

The bullet which topples Larry ricochets off his revolver and he falls only a short distance into some brush, unhurt. When Jean and Larry set out with the two constables to search the mine, they find the trail blocked by several natives. After a short fight they capture the entire band. The constables start back with their prisoners, while Jean and Larry continue to the mine where they find Cass and Rand busy sifting out diamonds. Driven back into tunnel, Cass lights the fuse on a stick of dynamite to throw out at Larry, but a bullet drops him and the dynamite explodes, bringing down the roof of the tunnel and burying both outlaws. A bottle of chemical found in the mine cues Jean and Larry to investigate Morgan, and when they reach his bungalow, they find one of the claw monsters in a crate. Morgan pretends to be friendly, then threatens them with a flask of poison gas. Larry tackles him and, in the ensuing, fight the flask of gas is shattered. Morgan is trapped in the deadly fumes, but Larry batters an opening in the rear wall through which he and Jean escape.

Phyllis Coates Television Roles
1949
Your Show Time
-The Mummy's Foot
w/Herbert Anderson

1950
The Cisco Kid
-Wedding Blackmail...Marge Lacey

1951
Stars Over Hollywood
-Nor Gloom of Night
w/Buddy Ebsen
A murder is reported by a mail carrier who becomes a suspect

The Cisco Kid
-Haven for Heavies...JoAnn Doran
-Phony Sheriff...Miss Lacey
-Uncle Disinherits Niece...Marge Lacey

The Sun Was Setting...Rene
Directed by Ed Wood

1952
Death Valley Days
-How Death Valley Got its Name...Virginia Arcane

Craig Kennedy, Criminologist
-Fugitive Money ... Natalie Larkin
w/Donald Woods

Scorching Fury...Mrs. Penn
w/ Richard Devon

The Files of Jeffrey Jones
-The Healthy Corpse
-No Weeds for the Widow
w/ Don Haggerty/Gloria Henry

The Range Rider
- Trail of the Lawless ... Doris Burton
- Pale Horse ... Jane Tracy

w/ Jock Mahoney

Hollywood Opening Night
- Nor Gloom of Night (repeat of Stars over Hollywood)

Schlitz Playhouse
- A String of Beads

w/Joan Caufield, Tom Drake

Racket Squad
-One for the Books

w/ Reed Hadley

Adventures of Superman
w/ George Reeves

-Superman on Earth/The Case of the Talkative Dummy/Mystery of the Stolen Statues/The Monkey Mystery/Night of Terror/The Birthday Letter/The Mind Machine/Rescue/The Secret of Superman/No Holds Barred/The Deserted Village/The Stolen Costume/Treasure of the Incas/Double Trouble.

1953

Adventures of Superman
-Mystery in Wax/The Runaway Robot/The Riddle of the Chinese Jade/The Human Bomb/Czar of the Underworld/Ghost Wolf/Crime Wave

The Lone Ranger
- The Perfect Crime (1953) ... Naomi Courtwright
- Stage to Estacado (1953) ... Ann Wyman

w/ John Hart, Jay Silverheels

Terry and the Pirates
-The Green God ... Georgia Pettigrew

w/ John Baer
Gorgeous doll (Phyllis) wields a pistol to try and obtain the Black Pearls. She is overcome and subdued by Terry.

The Abbott and Costello Show
- Cheapskates ... Millie Montrose

Your Jeweler's Showcase
-The Bean Farm
w/Otto Waldis, Robert Hutton
Over the objections of his children, an aged bean farmer on who's land oil is thought to have been discovered, cleverly exposes his intentions of his daughter's (Phyllis) fiancée.
- Cell 14 ... Betty Tucker
w/ Steve Brodie
The happy homelife of an ex-convict is disrupted by a former cellmate.

The Red Skelton Hour
- McPugg's Last Fight ... Supporting Sketch Player

I'm the Law
- The Button Story
w/George Raft

Summer Theatre
-Myrt and Marge...Marge Minter

Ramar of the Jungle
- The Doomed Safari ... Donna Sharp
w/ Jon Hall

Death Valley Days
-Soloman in All His Glory...Margie McMahon

My Hero
-The Catering Story
w/ Robert Cummings

The Green God…Georgia Pettigrew

Mike Roy's Kitchen
Phyllis Coates turns chef to show Mike Roy how to make a seafood casserole on the barbecue.

Crown Theater
-Dry with Three Olives
w/ Hans Conried
Introduced by Gloria Swanson

1954
General Electric Theater
-Here Comes Calvin…Connie
w/ Jack Carson, Allen Jenkins

Public Defender
- Moonshine … Amberlee Tolliver
w/ Mort R. Lewis

The Duke - … Gloria/girlfriend
w/ Paul Gilbert, Allen Jenkins
13 Episodes-series regular

The Adventures of Kit Carson
- Riders of the Hooded League
- The Hermit of Indian Ridge … Jane Sanders
w/ Bill Williams

Crown Theatre with Gloria Swanson
- Dry with Three Olives (1954)

Death Valley Days
-The Light on the Mountain…Annie Stewart

It's a Great Life
-Denny's Big Night…Ann

1955
Mike Roy Kitchen
Actress Phyllis Coates turns chef to show Mike Roy how to make a seafood casserole on the barbecue

Frontier
- King of the Dakotas: Part 1&2 … Medora De More
A greedy French nobleman migrates to the Dakotas. In his lust for power, he ruthlessly misappropriates land from the settlers.
w/Tom Tryon/Alan Hale Jr.

The Great Gildersleeve
- Gildy Goes Diving … Sally Fuller
w/ Willard Waterman

Lassie
- The School … Miss Vernon
w/ Jan Clayton, Tommy Retting

Science Fiction Theatre
- Barrier of Silence… Karen Sheldon
w/ Adolph Menjou
A scientist uses unusual methods to cure an amnesia victim.

Stage 7
- Debt to a Stranger … Alice
w/Gene Barry, Lyle Talbot
A border patrol sheriff receives a call from a rancher to pick up an illegal alien. He must then investigate the illegal's charge that he had been cheated by a rancher.
-Appointment in Highbridge … Kay Murray

An unusual story of a romance of between a British Army captain and an American Army nurse (Phyllis)/*Quinn Martin*, future producer of **The Fugitive** and **The Invaders** wrote this one.

Willy
- Willy and El Flamenco... Betty Estrada
w/June Havoc

The Lone Ranger
- The Woman in the White Mask (1955) ... Jane Johnson
w/Clayton Moore

The Millionaire
- The Jack Martin Story ... Alice Sands
w/Paul Langton
An innocent man who finds himself in the death cell of the state penitentiary as a result of maneuvers by a crafty and unethical lawyer, has only hours to prove his case after an anonymous benefactor presents him with a check for a million dollars. Phyllis plays his fiancé.

Topper
- King Cosmo the First
w/ Leo G. Carroll

Professional Father
w/Steve Dunne/Barbara Billingsley

Western Union...Nancy Carnes
(TV movie)
w/Richard Anderson

TV Movie Guide
- "I'll Pick More Daisy's" ...Don Wilkerson's mother!
A time element tale that would have fit nicely in a future **Twilight Zone** episode. Phyllis plays Denning's mother.
w/Richard Denning

1956

The Magical World of Disney
- Along the Oregon Trail ... Mrs. Martin

Crossroads
- God in the Streets
w/ Jeff Morrow, Frank Sully

Chevron Hall of Stars
- Debt to a Stranger
- Harrigan's Ghost ... Mary

It's a Great Life
- Private Eyes (1956) ... Lola Denton

Four Star Playhouse
- Once to Every Woman ... Marsha

Navy Log
- The Web Feet ... Marge...Husband is forced to leave his bride-to-be on the eve of their wedding for a military mission that he can't tell his bride about.

TV Reader's Digest
-The Man Who Beat Death...Nancy...Tennis star Bill Talbert played himself and his lifelong battle against diabetes. Phyllis plays the wife.

This is the Life
- I Killed Lieutenant Hartwell ... Betty

Cavalcade Theater
-The Gift of Dr. Minot...Barbara Leland
w/ Walter Coy who stars as Dr. Minot, a Boston physician who won the 1934 Nobel Prize

1957
Leave It to Beaver
- New Neighbors ... Betty Donaldson
Beaver's brother Wally and his friend, Eddie Haskell, warn Beaver about becoming involved with a married woman. (Eddie's first appearance in the series).
w/Jerry Mathers

1958
This Is Alice
- When the Bough Breaks/Weight Lifter/Two Yanks in Georgia/Trial Balloon/Too Many Fathers/The Prophet/The Princess/The Letter/The Elephant/Song for Sale/Rodeo/Rock and Roll/Rags to Riches/Quiz Show/Problem Child/Pig in a Poke/Pie in the Sky/Paper Drive/ One in a Million/No Place Like Home/Mrs. U.S.A./Man's Best Friend/Mail Order/Hypnotist/House Beautiful/ Help Wanted/Guest in the House/Freedom of the Press/Fortune Teller/Class Reunion/Circus Time/Christmas Story/Callahan/American Beauty/Alice Plays Detective/Alice Plays Cupid/Alice Goes to Washington/Dandy Donovan/Big Louie Comes Through
w/Patty Ann Gerrity, Tommy Farrell
*(Phyllis plays the mom (Clarissa Holliday) the whole series.

Richard Diamond, Private Detective
- Another Man's Poison ... Monica Freeborn
A bullet meant for Diamond kills a passerby.
w/David Janssen

Gunsmoke
-Wild West...Hattie Kelly
w/James Arness/Murray Hamilton
Marshall Dillon believes a little boy who tells him his pa had been kidnapped by a couple of hombres and then he goes into action. Phyllis Coates was cast as "Hattie," the boy's step-mother.

Perry Mason Inez Fremont
-Case of the Black Eyed Blond
Phyllis Coates' character was the killer on this Perry Mason episode.
w/ Raymond Burr

General Electric Theater
- The Last Town Car, Part 1& 2 (1958) ... Heather

The Sheriff of Cochise
- Woman Escapes ... Vera Watson
- I'll Pick More Daisies (1955) ... Mother
w/John Broomfield

Tales of Wells Fargo
-Alias Jim Hardie...Pat Denton

1959

Rawhide...Nora Sage
-Incident of the Judas Trap
Men driving cattle are attacked by wolves and a cunning killer. Phyllis is killed off-camera.
w/Eric Fleming, Clint Eastwood

Hennesey
- Hennesey and the Lady Doctor ... Dr. Patricia Granger
w/Jackie Cooper

Lux Playhouse
- The Case of the Two Sisters ... Ellen Packer

Black Saddle
- Client: Dawes... Maggie
w/Peter Breck/Russell Johnson
Pretty Phyllis is a murderess.

Westinghouse Desilu Playhouse
-Trial at Devil's Canyon…Belle

Death Valley Days
-One in a Hundred…Mary
Phyllis' character is a recently widowed pioneer and attracts the attention of a cavalry man who is escorting a wagon train through "injun" territory.

The Untouchables
- Ain't We Got Fun (1959) … Renee Sullivan
w/Robert Stack

1960
The DuPont Show with June Allyson
- The Trench Coat … Penny
w/ David Niven
Tale of a salesman dejected by the constant chiding of his boss; the salesman puts on a strange coat and his life changes.

The Best of the Post
- The Murderer … Mollie
The husband wants to stay on the farm, the wife wants to escape her drab life, and it all ends in murder.
w/Stephen McNally

Hawaiian Eye
- With This Ring … Laura Seldon
w/Anthony Eisley, Connie Stevens

The Untouchables
- The Frank Nitti Story (1960) … Ellie Morley
Eliot Ness breaks up Nitti's extortion racket with the help of Phyllis Coates as Ellie Morley. Phyllis' character gets mowed down by a machine gun as she is in a public telephone booth reporting to Ness.

1961
Gunslinger
- Johnny Sergeant … Teresa Perez
w/ Tony Young

Tales of Wells Fargo
-Bitter Vengeance…Ruby Martin

Perry Mason
-Case of the Cowardly Lion…Frieda Crawson

Rawhide
- The Little Fishes (1961) … Elizabeth Gwynn

Tales of Wells Fargo
- Bitter Vengeance (1961) … Ruby Martin

1962

Gunsmoke
- Phoebe Strunk … Rose Kinney

The Untouchables
- A Fist of Five … Angela Lamberto

1963
Death Valley Days
-A Gun is Not a Gentleman …Lois Bouquette

1964
Perry Mason
-Case of the Ice-Cold Hands
Perry defends woman accused of murdering a man from whom she allegedly stole money. Phyllis played the wife of the deceased.

Death Valley Days
-The Lucky Cow…Edna Wiley
w/Steve Brodie

A "scheming" Indian chief sells cows to unsuspecting settlers, steals them, only to sell them back to the same settlers.
-The Left Hand is Damned…Dora Hand
w/ Peter Haskell, Pat Priest
A young gunslinger's right hand is crippled after a gun fight.

The Patty Duke Show(pilot)
- The Cousins … Secretary

Slattery's People
- Question: Which One Has the Privilege? … Helen Mayfield

The Virginian
- Smile of a Dragon …Mrs.Marden
w/James Drury

Gunsmoke
-Homecoming…Edna

1965
Moment of Fear
-The Case of the Two sisters
w/Michael Wilding, Fred Clark
A newsman enlists the aid of an eccentric bachelor to solve a murder.

1966
Summer Fun
- Thompson's Ghost … Milly Thompson
w/Bert Lahr

1988
Whisper Kill (TV Movie)
w/Loni Anderson
Loni is an outspoken small town newspaper editor involved with threats and murder.

1989
Kiss Shot (TV Movie) ...Ruby Tibbs
w/ Whoopie Goldberg

Goodnight Sweet Marilyn (TV Movie) ...Gladys Baker
w/Paula Lane

1991
Mrs. Lambert Remembers Love (TV Movie) ...Katherine
w/ Ellen Burstyn

Midnight Caller...Meredith Gaynor
- The Added Starter
w/ Gary Cole

1994
Dr. Quinn, Medicine Woman
- The Washington Affair: Part 1&2 (1994) ... Mrs. Howard
w/Jane Seymour
Assassins target President Grant.

Lois & Clark: The New Adventures of Superman
- The House of Luthor ... Ellen Lane
w/Teri Hatcher

Phyllis Coates Films:
1948
So You Want to Be in Politics Oct 2 1948
Smart Girls Don't Talk Oct. 9, 1948
Cigarette Girl (uncredited)
w/Virginia Mayo
Directed by Richard Bare

1949
The House Across the Stree Sept. 10
Camera girl (uncredited)
w/Wayne Morris/Janis Paige
Directed by Richard Bare

Look for the Silver Lining
Rosie (uncredited)
w/June Haver/Ray Bolger

A Kiss in the Dark
Mrs. Hale (uncredited)
w/David Niven/Jane Wyman

My Foolish Heart
College Girl on Phone (uncredited)
w/Dana Andrews/Susan Hayward

So You Want to Be a Baby Sitter (Short) Jan 8
Alice McDoakes

So You're Having In-Law Trouble (Short) Aug 27,
Alice McDoakes

So You Want to Be a Muscle Man (Short) July 2, 1949
Alice McDoakes

So You Want to Get Rich Quick (Short) Oct 28
Alice McDoakes

1950
So You Want to Move (Short)
Alice McDoakes

So You Want to Hold Your Husband (Short)
Alice McDoakes /

So You Think You're Not Guilty (Short)
Alice McDoakes

So You Want a Raise (Short)
Alice McDoakes

So You Want to Throw a Party (Short)
Alice McDoakes

Outlaws of Texas
Annie Moore
w/Whip Wilson/Andy Clyde
Directed by Thomas Carr

Blues Busters
Sally Dolan
w/Leo Gorcey/Huntz Hall

My Blue Heaven
Party Girl (uncredited)
w/Betty Grable/Dan Dailey

1951
Stage to Blue River
Joyce Westbrook
w/Whip Wilson/John Hart/Fuzzy Knight

Canyon Raiders
Alice Long
w/Whip Wilson/Fuzzy Knight

Valentino
Universal Studios Casting Clerk (uncredited)

The Longhorn
Gail Robinson
w/Bill Elliot/Myron Healey

Superman and the MoleMen
Lois Lane

So You Want to Be a Plumber (Short)
Alice McDoakes (uncredited)

So You Want to Be a Bachelor (Short)

So You Want to Be a Cowboy (Short)
Alice McDoakes / Cindy Lou (uncredited)

Man from Sonora
Cinthy Allison
Johnny Mack Brown/Lyle Talbot

Oklahoma Justice
Goldie Vaughn
w/Johnny Mack Brown

So You Want to Buy a Used Car (Short)
Alice McDoakes

So You Want to Be a Paper Hanger (Short)
Alice McDoakes

Nevada Badmen
Carol Bannon
w/Whip Wilson/Fuzzy Knight
Phyllis plays the niece in this one.

1952
The Gunman
Anita Forester
w/Whip Wilson/Fuzzy Knight/Rand Brooks

Fargo
Kathy McKenzie
w/Bill Elliot/Myron Healey/Fuzzy Knight

Canyon Ambush
Marion Gaylord
w/ Johnny Mack Brown

Flat Top
Dorothy Collier
w/Sterling Hayden/Richard Carlson

Wyoming Roundup
Terry Howard
w/Whip Wilson

Invasion U.S.A.
Mrs. Mulfory
w/Gerald Mohr/Tom Kennedy/Peggie Castle

The Maverick
Della Watson
w/Bill Elliot/Myron Healey/Rand Brooks
Directed by Thomas Carr

Scorching Fury
The mayor's wife
w/Richard Devon

Valentino
Phyllis is cast as a Universal casting clerk in the 1920's who swoons to a new actor on the lot by the name of Valentino. She is uncredited and has no speaking lines.

So You Want to Get It Wholesale
Alice McDoakes

So You Want to Go to A Convention
Alice McDoakes

So You Never Tell a Lie
Alice McDoakes

So You Wear the Pants
Alice McDoakes

1953
Here Come the Girls
Phyllis
w/Bob Hope/Rosemary Clooney

Jungle Drums of Africa-Serial
Carol Bryant
w/Clayton Moore

Marshal of Cedar Rock
Martha Clark
w/Allan Lane/Robert Shayne and John Hamilton

Perils of the Jungle
Jo Carter
w/ Clyde Beatty

Topeka
Marian Harrison
w/Bill Elliot
Directed by Thomas Carr

El Paso Stampede
Alice Clark
w/Allan Lane

So You Want a Television Set
Alice McDoakes

So You Think You Can't Sleep
Alice McDoakes

So You Want to Be an Heir
Alice McDoakes

So You Love Your Dog
Alice McDoakes

1954
Gunfighters of the Northwest
Rita Carville
w/Jock Mahoney/Clayton Moore

1955
Panther Girl of the Kongo
Jean Evans
w/Myron Healey

So You're Having Neighbor Trouble

1956
Girls in Prison
Dorothy
w/Richard Denning/Adele Jergens

God is in the Streets (Short film)
Unknown Role
w/ Russell Johnson

So You Want to Be Pretty
Alice McDoakes

So You Want to Play the Piano
Alice McDoakes

So Your Wife Wants to Work
Alice McDoakes

1957
Chicago Confidential
Helen Fremont
w/Brian Keith/Beverly Garland

I Was a Teenage Frankenstein
Margaret
w/Whit Bissell

1958
Blood Arrow
Bess Johnson
w/Scott Brady/Paul Richards/Don Haggerty

Cattle Empire
Janice Hamilton
w/Joel McCrea/Don Haggerty/Gloria Talbott

1959
The Incredible Petrified World
Dale Marshall
w/John Carradine

1970
The Baby Maker
Trish's mother
w/Barbara Hershey

1988
Whisper Kill (TV Movie-unavailable for viewing)
w/ Loni Anderson/June Lockhart
A San Francisco reporter and the editor of a local newspaper follow a slasher's trail in Watsonville.

1989
Kiss Shot (TV Movie)
Rudy the waitress
w/Whoopi Goldberg/Dennis Frantz

Goodnight, Sweet Marilyn (Video release only)
Gladys Baker (Marilyn's mother)
"The Tom Cats are after you, that's how it is, baby"

1991
Mrs. Lambert Remembers (TV Movie)
Katherine
w/Walter Matthau/Ellen Burstyn

1996
Hollywood: The Movie (Video release only)
Old Dora
w/Julie Strain/Imogene Coca

Phyllis Coates Theatrical Performances

Ken Murray's Blackouts–El Capitan Theater (1943)
Earl Carroll Vanities Tour– (1945)
Anything Goes U.S.O. Tour– (1946)
Girl Crazy—U.S.O. Tour–(1947)
Blaze of Glory–Laguna Summer Theater (1954)
Circle of Wheels– El Capitan Theater (1959)
Send Me No Flowers– Gallery Stage (1961)
Never Too Late– Center Theater Palm Springs (1978)
Love Letters– Monterey Conference Center (1993)
The Wedding of Stan Laurel(skit) Edgar Kennedy Celebration in Monterey (1987)

Phyllis Coates as Self in Documentaries

The Screen Director Short (w/ Richard Bare) staged archive footage 1951
E! Mysteries & Scandals TV Series 1998
Added Attractions: The Hollywood Shorts Story TV movie 2002
The Last First Comic 2010
Laurel & Hardy: Their Lives and Magic TV 2011

Bibliography

Bare, Richard. 2001 Confessions of a Hollywood Director. Scarecrow Press, Inc. Lanham, Maryland, and London

Blottner, Gene 2011 Wild Bill Elliot: A Complete Filmography. McFarland & and Company, Inc. Publishers Jefferson, North Carolina, and London

Cassara, Bill. 2020 Hollywood in Monterey-Chronicles of a Cop. BearManor Media 4700 Millenia Blvd suite 175 PMB 90497 Orlando, fl. 32839

Fitzgerald, Michael G. Magers, Boyd. 2002 Ladies of the Western: Interviews with fifty-one more actresses from the silent era to the television westerns of the 1950s and 1960s McFarland & and Company, Inc. Publishers Jefferson, North Carolina, and London

Freese, Gene. 2013 The Life and Films of a Hollywood Stuntman. McFarland& and Company, Inc. Publishers Jefferson, North Carolina, and London

Goldrup, Jim. 2012 The Encyclopedia of Feature Players of Hollywood, Vol. 1
BearManor Media 4700 Millenia Blvd suite 175 PMB 90497 Orlando, Fl.

Grossman, Gary. 1976 Superman Serial to Cereal. Big Apple Film Series Popular Library Publishers 600 Third Ave. New York, N.Y.

Hayde, Michael J. Flights of Fancy. 2009 BearManor Media 1317 Edgewater Dr. #110 Orlando, Florida

Kashner, Sam and Schoenberger, Nancy. 1996 Hollywood Kryptonite St. Martin's Press Publishing Company, New York

Maltin, Leonard. 1972 The Great Movie Shorts. Da Capo Press, Inc. A Subsidiary of Pienum Publishing Corporation 233 Spring Street, New York, N.Y.

McGee, Mark Thomas. 2014 Talk's Cheap, Action's Expensive-The Films of Robert L. Lippert. BearManor Media P.O. Box 71426 Albany, Georgia

Moore, Clayton Thompson, Frank. 1998 I Was That Masked Man Taylor Trade Publishing Lanham, New York, Dallas, Boulder, Toronto, Oxford

Weaver, Tom. 1991 Science Fiction Stars and Horror Heroes McFarland & and Company, Inc. Publishers Jefferson, North Carolina, and London

Magazines:

Life June 14, 1948

Variety April 1, 1959

Hollywood Reporter May 5, 1959 Vol. 154 issue # 46 "Circle of Wheels"

Hollywood Reporter May 22, 1961 Vol. 164 issue # 27 "Send Me No Flowers"

Hollywood Reporter Jan. 15, 1960 Vol 158 issue 23 "The Trench Coat" –The DuPont Show

Hollywood Reporter Vol 135 issue 22 Nov. 6, 1952 "Rebound" w/ Hans Conried

TV Guide 1994

People Magazine May 1994 "Fast Paced Lois"

Classic Images #483 September 2015

Phyllis Coates Artist contract – "*Craig Kennedy Criminologist*" July 21, 1952

Film Fan Monthly July-August 1974 "So You Want to Know About George O'Hanlon"

Adventures of Superman Facebook Page: https://www.facebook.com/groups

George Reeves as Superman Facebook Page: https://www.facebook.com/groups

Pressbook. *Outlaws of Texas* (1951)

Press Book. *Panther Girl of the Kongo* 1955

Final Divorce Decree. Gypsie Ann Stell aka Phyllis Coates vs Richard Bare   Jan. 11, 1949

Final Divorce Decree. Gypsie Ann Stell aka Phyllis Coates vs Robert Nelms Oct. 11, 1953

Final Divorce Decree. Gypsie Ann Stell aka Phyllis Coates vs Norman Tokar Apr. 27, 1960

Final Divorce Decree. Gypsie Ann Stell aka Phyllis Coates vs Howard Press Dec. 22, 1988

Newspaper Mentions:

Times Record News
(Wichita Falls, Tx)
Nov. 1, 1925
Feb. 27, 1926
Nov. 6, 1928

Bryan Daily Eagle
Nov. 20, 1928

Amarillo Globe Times
Nov. 20, 1928

Brownsville Herald
June 28, 1934

Pampa Daily News
Sept. 8, 1934
Sept. 16, 1934

Abilene Reporter
Oct. 29, 1939
July 3, 1948

San Angelo Morning Times
May 26, 1939
April 21, 1941
Dec. 12, 1941

The Odessa American
Nov. 22, 1942
Feb. 19, 1943
Dec. 20, 1943
Jan. 11, 1944
Sept. 30, 1945
July 14, 1944
May 23, 1946
Sept. 15, 1946
Feb. 2, 1947
Sept. 14, 1947
Mar. 19, 1961

Austin American
Oct. 6, 1944

Crystal Lake Herald
Nov. 8, 1945

Fort Worth Star Telegram
May 24, 1942
May 30, 1943
April 22, 1943
Jan. 11, 1949

Los Angeles Daily News
July 6, 1945
July 6, 1945
April 13, 1946
July 6, 1947

Los Angeles Citizen News
May 2, 1945
July 28, 1948
Mar. 23, 1951

Daily Item Sunbury Penn
June 22, 1947

New York Daily News
July 6, 1947

Arizona Republic
Sept. 16, 1947

Lubbock Evening Journal
April 2, 1948
Omaha World News
Nov. 11, 1949
Press Democrat
Nov. 16, 1948

Dallas Morning News
June 10, 1948

Showman's Trade Review
Mar. 20, 1948

Valley Times
Mar. 13, 1948
May 28, 1948
Dec. 2, 1949
May 23, 1951

Los Angeles Times
Feb. 28, 1945
Aug. 19, 1945
Sept. 14, 1947
Oct. 26, 1947
Mar. 11, 1948
April 2, 1948
Mar. 28, 1948
July 5, 1948
July 6, 1948
Oct. 13, 1948
Dec. 2, 1948
Jan. 15, 1950
Feb. 6, 1951
July 6, 1950
Mar. 9, 1951
July 27, 1951
Sept. 20, 1951

Oct. 19, 1951
Nov. 29, 1951
May 22, 1952
Nov. 3, 1952
Nov. 7, 1952
Jan. 10, 1953
Oct. 2, 1953
Mar. 29, 1953
Sept 30, 1955
Oct 18, 1955
July 30, 1954
May 22, 1959
Jan. 13, 1994
April 5, 1994
Oct. 27, 1996
Aug. 27, 2012

Los Angeles Mirror
Oct. 1, 1953

Appendix

June 13, 2006
Very dear Bill,

Just wanted to say…congratulations to you and Michelle. I had a good long talk with Phyllis yesterday, and she is very happy for both of you.

Last year you and I talked a bit about Phyllis possibly writing a book about her life. Over the years Phyllis and I talked about it and she has always been pretty reluctant. Well, I have finally brought her around to understanding that the process of sorting of a lifetime, and putting it into book-form would be very liberating and therapeutic. Believe me, she knows the difference of telling the truth in order for the whole thing to be any good to anyone. I pointed out that at the age of 16, she slugged a nun in the chops for insisting she would never amount to anything. And that was her exit from high school. She rounded up her crazy (I am not kidding) mother, Jackie (who always insisted she be introduced as her sister) and her alcoholic grandmother in tow. Got them on a bus and left the tiny oil-town in Texas behind for the lights of Hollywood

There was a chance meeting with Producer Ken Murray of "Blackouts" fame that began her work learning to talk like a lady. Along the way, she was married to some pretty heavy-hitters in the film industry and had some very titillating affairs with attractive film stars along the way.

I know she feels a failure as a mother herself (son David's drug addiction) but she understands that all these things are just the fabric of a life pretty well lived. She was raised a Catholic with all the built in guilt-trips, but has spent her life gaining spiritual knowledge.

Why am I telling you all this? The time has come, the Walrus said, to speak of many things. I think she is ready to open up and work on her autobiography. I am too close to her to be the co-author with her. I know I can be of help, but it seems to that you are the one to put it in book form. I KNOW she realizes that this is the time to jump into an important project, and that it would be good for her.

This is something I want you to think about. I will wait to hear from you before I talk to our "Gypsie" about it. If you have a moment let me know what you think about this. Once again, I wish you and Michelle all the best in life together. You both deserve it.

With love and admiration, Bart Williams

Index

Abbott and Costello 72, 161
Abbott, Bud 72
Adams, Edie xiii
Affleck, Ben 165
Albertson, Mabel 67
Allard, Dave viii
Allbritton, Louise 33-34
Allison, June 95
Al Seamon Agency 17, 34
Alyn, Kirk 155-157
Anderson, Herbert xix, 37
Anderson, Judith xiii
Anderson, Loni xix
Ames, Walter 55-56
Arden, Eve 52
Arness, James xix
Asner, Ed 53
Ayres, Lorry 165
Baer, John 70
Bailey, Raymond 75
Bainter, Nancy viii
Balducci, Anthony xiii
Ball, Lucille 81, 90, 159
Bare, Richard L. vi, 3, 23-27, 29-31, 33-35, 37-30, 56, 81-82, 103, 169-178, 235-236, 243-244, 169
Barron, Flo 21
Barrymore, John 26
Barrymore, Lionel 163
Bart, Lynn 73
Baum, Andreas
Beardsley, Lloyd viii
Beatty, Clyde 71
Belafonte, Harry xiii
Benton, Kimm viii
Berkeley, Busby 17
Billingsley, Barbara 74, 87
Bing Crosby Productions 101
Binyon, Claude 66
Bissell, Whit 4, 82-83, *139*
Blakeney, Olive 73
Bliss-Hayden School of Acting 21

Bliss, Lela 21
Bob Hope Show 91
Bolling, Major General A.R. 18
Bond, Tommy 113-114, 155-157, *245*
Boylan, Buddy 21
Bowery Boys 43
Brady, Scott 62, 86 *131*
Brandon, Henry 112, 118, 120
Bressler, David viii
Brophy, Sallie 87
Brooke, Hillary 62
Brooks, Geraldine 29, 32
Brooks, Rand 22, 63
Brown, Johnny Mack 44, 48
Bruni, Frank 16
Buckles, Tori Chesebrough viii, 104
Burr, Raymon xix
Byrnes, Edd "Kookie"
Caan, James 96
Carillo, Leo xix, 43
Carlson, Richard 62
Carr, J.D. Mrs. 33
Carr, Thomas 49, 58, 63
Carradine, John 26, 93
Carroll, Earl 17, 34
Carroll, Leo G. xix, 76
Carson, Jack xix, 58, 67-68
Carter, Rosalynn xiii
Caruso, Anthony "Tony" 118-120
Cassara, Douglas viii
Cassara, Michelle Benton ix, 126
Castle, Peggie 62
Chaplin, Charlie 57, 159
Chase, Charley 118-119, 176
Christopher, Zoe [aka Crinker Nelms], viii, xv, xx, 41, 57, 69, 80-82, 93, 97, 102-103, 117
Clark, Dane 29, 32
Clark, Fred 66, 101
Clarke, Betty 36
Clarke, Robert
Clooney, Rosemary 65-66

Coates, Paul V. 26
Coates, Phyllis [*aka Gypsie Ann Stell,* Nelms, Press] iv, v, x, xii, xiii, xiv, xviii, xx, 1-5, 7-25, 27-46, 48-246, 248-250, *145-146*
Coca, Imogene xix, 157-158
Cohen, Gary viii, 120
Collura, Bill
Como, Perry 43
Costello, Lou 72-73
Cook, Sheriff 3
Cooper, Jackie xix
Corey, Jeff 51
Cruz, Brandon 153
Curtis, Billy 51
Curtis, William 121-122
Dahl, Arlene 66
Darwell, Jane 81
Daum, Raymond 160-161
Davis, Anna 10
Davis, Joan 81
Day, Doris 4, 95, 110, 128, 159
DeBorba, Dorothy *145*
De Kova, Frank 96-97
Dettman, Bruce viii, 167
DiCarlo, John viii
Dillane, Bill viii
Disney, Walt xvii
Dohnert, Diana viii
Downey, Morton Jr. 157
Downs, Johnny 66
Drew, Martha 21
Duke, Patty xix
Dunn, Steve 73
Duryea, Dan 62
Dylan, Bob 102
Eastwood, Clint vii, 110, 113, 128
Eastwood, Maggie 113, 127
Ebsen, Buddy xix, 44
Eckels, Lew 21
Edgar Kennedy Celebration in Monterey 158,
Edmonds, Andy viii
Elliott, Wild Bill 45, 61-62, 67
Evans, Edith x

Falconer, Don
Falk, Peter xiii
Farrell, Glenda 4
Farrell, Tommy 86, 176
Faversham, Bevis viii, 159, 145-146, 152
Feld, Fritz 170
Field, John viii, 40, 118
Fields, Ronald J. viii
Fine, Larry 14
Finegan, Richard viii
Fisher, Pat 11
Fitzgerald, Michael G. 85
Flynn, Errol 26
Fontaine, Joan 4
Fort Roach 24
Frampton, Jessie 27
Franz, Dennis 123
Freese, Gene 69
Garbo, Greta- Walking with Garbo 161
Garland, Beverly 82
Gerrity, Patty Ann 86
Gershwin, George 20-21
Gielgud, John x
Gifford, Frances 79
Gilmore, Art 25
Gilpin, Joe C. 32
Goldberg, Whoopi xix, 123-124
Gould, Dave 16
Gorcey, Leo iv, 43
Grey, Virginia 62
Grant, Carey 26
Greene, Rick viii
Griffith, James 66
Grossman, Gary viii, 49, 54, 58. 80, 93
Guinness, Alec x
Gurney, A.R. 127
Haggerty, Don 61, 86
Hahn, Jessica 157
Hahn. S.S. 65
Hale, Allan Jr. 75
Hale, Barbara
Hall, Charlie 203

Hall, Huntz 42
Hall, Jon 17
Hal Roach Studios 50, 72, 76, 113, 168
Hamilton, John xviii, 52, 67
Hamilton, Murray 87
Harden, Dan 21
Hardy, Oliver 127
Harker, Jane 30, 38
Hart, John 45, 68-69, 73, 165
Harter, Chuck viii, 155-156, 170
Hascall, Gary viii
Haskell, Eddie 75
Hatcher, Terri xix, 153-154, 162
Havoc, June 76
Havel, Arthur 21
Havel, Morton 21
Haver, June 15, 34
Hawes, Lois Laurel 3, 111-113, 118, 259
Hawes, Tony 111-113, 118-119, 127
Hayden, Harry 21
Hayden, Sterling 62
Hayworth, Rita 103
Healey, Myron 45, 62
Healy, Ted 14
Hershey, Barbara 98, 102
Hickok, Wild Bill 99
Hitchcock, Alfred 170
Hilton, Colin viii
Hodiak, John 66
Hope, Bob 65-66
Howard, Moe 14
Howard, Shemp 14
Hurt, John xix
Hutchinson, Paul 88
Hyde, Herman 16
Janssen, David xix, 84
Jeffreys, Ann 178
Jenkins, Allen xix, 58, 67
Jergens, Adele 81
Jones, Dickie xiii, 61
Jones, LaJuana 11
Jones, Paul 66

Kane, Becky viii
Keaton, Eleanor
Keith, Brian 82
Kennedy, Edgar 25, 63, 159-160
Kennedy, Glenn viii
Kennedy, Mark viii, 160, 145, 152
Kimball, Judy 95
King, Muriel 21
Knight, Fuzzy 44, 62, 67
Korman, Harvey xiii
Kratzer, Emile 105
Lahr, Bert xix, 101
Lake, Florence 63
Lane, Lola 4
Lane, Allen "Rocky" 67
Langdon, Harry xviii
Larson, Jack xviii, 52, 91, 158, 178
Laurel and Hardy 50, 112, 118-120, 158-159, *See: Sons of the Desert* 168
Laurel, Lois 21-22, *146*
Laurel, Stan 21
Leigh, Janet xiii
Lemmon, Leonore 93
Leslie, Nan 87
Lewis, Joe Mrs. 33
Littlefield, Lucien 176, 208, 138
Lockhart, June 87
Loftus, Enid 35
Lollobrigida, Gina xiii
Lombardo, Guy 96
Loring, Lisa 153
Luber, Bernard 48-49
Lupino, Ida 96-97, 177
Lynch, Allen T. 65
MacMurray, Fred 15, 34
MacRae, Gordon 129
Magers, Boyd 85
Mahoney, Jock xix, 61, 69, 73
Maltin, Leonard viii
Maley, Jim viii
Manderbach, Kerry viii
Mannix, Eddie 92, 165, 177

Mannix, Toni 91-92, 158, 165-166, 173
Manly, William 60
Maren, Jerry 51
Marks, Gertrude 91
Marriage of Stan Laurel, The 159
Martin, Tony 66
Marvin, Lee 96
Marx, Harpo 23, 32
Marx Brothers 159
Mary Tyler Moore Show
Mathers, Jerry xix
Maxwell, Robert 48-49, 76
May, Westley
Mayo. Virginia 30, 66
McCain, John 167
McCrea, Frances 85
McCrea, Joel 85, 167, 175
Meece, Ted viii
Melcher, Terry 4, 128
McMillan, Jane 116
Milland, Ray 92
Mitchell, Cameron 96
Mitchell, Millard 66
Mitchum, Bob [Robert] 57
Mills Brothers 16
Monroe, Marilyn, 22, 111, 126
Montana, Montie 153
Montgomery, George 153
Moreno, Rita 62
Moore, Clayton xiii, xix, *60*, 68-70, 73, 68, 70, 73, 77, 120
Moran, Patsy 159
Morris, Ken 62
Murray, Ken 2, 7, 13-15, 34, 81, 91, 111, 125
Myhr, Jamie Murray 157
Neibaur, Jim viii
Neill, Noel xviii, xx, 49, 61, 93, 155, 164
Nelms, Robert 40-41, 58, 63-65, 69
Newmar, Julie 178
Newton, John 95, 155-156
Nicole, Alex 73
Niven, David 36, 95

Noonan, Tommy 91
Norcross, Aline 11
Northrup, Patricia 32
Novak, Kim 27
O'Brien, Virginia 113-114
O'Conner, Carroll 99
O'Hanlon, George 3, 24-25, 28-29, 31, 40, 42, 61, 66, 81-82, 128, 170-171, 173, 176-177, 141
Ohmart, Ben viii
Olivier, Laurence x
Olson, Laura P. viii, 19
Opal, Marcia viii, xiv
Our Gang Kids 159
Owens, Ronn 125
Page, Patty xiii
Palin, Sara 166
Pangborn, Franklin 72
Parker, Kit [kit Parker Fims] viii, 59, 128
Payton, Barbara xiii
Peterson, Paul 153
Petkovich, Anthony ix
Pierce, Jack 50, 83
Pierson, David B. viii
Piscopo, Joe 119
Poitier, Sidney xiii
Polson, Dorotha
Porter, Cole 18
Pratt, L.A. Mrs.
Press, Howard Dr. 98-99, 104, 107-108, 111, 245
Press, Laura [Laura Press Olson]vi, 74, 99, 103-104, 107, 123, 162-163, 180
Ray Corrigan Ranch 62
Ray Courts Show 152
Redgrave, Michael x
Reed, Donna 62
Reed, Walter 126, 147
Reeves, George vi, xvii, xviii, 1, 5, 48-52, 54-55, 58, 91-93, 109, 114-115, 121, *138*, 156-158, 160-161, 164-165, 181, 186-187, 205, 224, 245, *138*

Renaldo, Duncan xix, 43
Reynolds, Debbie 178
Rich, Allen 90-91
Richards, Paul 86
Richardson, Ralph x
Roach, Hal 127
Ross, Annie 120
Roth, Jack viii
Rydzewski, Steve viii
Sadewater, Randy viii, 57
Sales, Soupy 167
Sanborn, Fred 14
Sarecky, Barney 49
Satterfield, Bob viii
Scott, George C. xiii
Scott, Gordon 153
Scully, Vin xiii
Sennett, Mack 159
Serling, Rod 174
Seymour, Jane xix
Shakespeare, William x
Shallert, Edwin 72
Sharpe, Karen 62
Shayne, Robert 52, 67, 105, 118, 127, 144
Shayne, Stephanie 106, 118
Sheri, Jean 21
Sholem, Lee 49, 53-54, 172
Shuster, Joe 5, 48
Siegel, Jerry 5, 48
Simon, Neil xiii
Skretvedt, Randy viii, 112
Sokolov, Herold
Smith, Pete 24-25
Smart, Paul G. viii
Smith, Hal 153
Smood, Patty 11
Stack, Robert xix, 96
Stanley, Helene 62
Stanwyck, Barbara 57
Steffen, Virginia 87
Stell, Jackie 2, 8- 9, 13-15 [Aka Jackie Lorraine "Luzzie" Teel] 8
Stell, William Robert "Rush" 2, 7-9, 33, 35

Stell, Melvina 35
St. Mark, Tyler vi, viii, xii, 168, 146,
Storch, Larry 167
Storm, Gale 62
Strain, Julie 157
Strauss, Robert 66
Switzer, Carl "Alfalfa" xiii, 43, 120
Taffel, Stan viii, 25, 168-178, *169*
Talbert, Bill 80
Teel, Jackie Lorraine [Rappee] 8, 116
Temple, Shirley 9
This is Alice
Thomas, Harry 50
Todd, Thelma 114-115
Tokar, David [Press] vi, vii, 78, 81, 87-88, 99, 103, 111-112, 121-123, 166
Tokar, Norman vi, 74-75, 87
Tong, Sammee 87
Townsley, Marcy 11
Toxton, Candy 17
Tryon, Tom 75
Vail, Myrtle 71
Valesquez, Irene viii
Van Zandt, Phil 76
Verdugo, Elena 62
Vilencia, Jeff viii, 39
Wadworth, Jane 27
Wallace, Stone viii
Warner, Jack 176
Warren, Jerry 15, 93-94, 164
Warren, Jim 54
Washburn, Beverly 176
Wayne, John 56, 120, 159
Weaver, Tom viii, 53, 114
Webb, Jack 26
Weissman, Jeffrey viii, 159, *145, 152*
Welles, Orson 26, 103
Westcott, Helen 62
Williams, Andy xiii
Williams, Bart vii, 5, 12, 105-106, 112, 127, 129, 152, 159, 160, 164, 167-168, 170, 178, 180, 249, *141, 146,* 150
Wilson, Marie 14

Wilson, Whip 41-44, 46, 61, 66
Winchell, Walter 96
Wood, Ed Jr. 44
Woods, Donald xix
Wray, Fay 57
Wyman, Jane 4, 36
Young, Alan 127-128
Zane, Nan viii
Zeroun, Duon viii
Zeroun, Bob viii, 118-119

L-R: Kirk "Superman" Alyn, Chuck Harter, Phyllis, Tommy "Jimmy Olsen" Bond. 1994 at the Superman Festival in Metropolis, Il. (Photo courtesy of Chuck Harter)

About the Author

After Bill Cassara graduated from San Jose State University, his career path took him to the San Jose Police Department Records Division, a Deputy Sheriff for the Santa Clara County Sheriffs Office, a Police Officer for the City of Seaside. and ultimately, hired as a Deputy Sheriff in 1981, stationed on the Monterey Peninsula. He was very involved with the community. Bill retired in 2007 and was a friend of Phyllis Coates for over 20 years. He is a lifetime movie buff and a Hollywood biographer. He has authored five other books for BearManor Media:

Edgar Kennedy-Master of the Slowburn (2005)
Vernon Dent-Stooge Heavy (2010)
Ted Healy-Nobody's Stooge (2014)
Henry Brandon-King of the Bogeymen (co-written) (2018)
Hollywood in Monterey-Chronicles of a Cop (2020).

Bill and his wife, Michelle, live in Rancho Cucamonga, California.

Made in United States
North Haven, CT
10 November 2024